CU00736103

CHARLIE WALKER is an adventurer, writer, and public speaker. He has travelled over 50,000 miles by human power. Between adventures he lives in London, where he rides a bicycle daily.

ON ROADS
THAT ECHO

A bicycle journey through
Asia & Africa

by

CHARLIE
WALKER

Copyright © 2019 Charlie Walker

The right of Charlie Walker to be identified as the author of this work has been asserted by him in accordance with sections 77 and 78 of the Copyright, Designs and Patents Act, 1988.

All rights reserved. No part of this publication may be reproduced or transmitted, in any form or by any means, electronic, mechanical, photocopying, recording or otherwise, without the prior permission of the author.

ISBN: 978-1-9999349-2-7
ISBN: 978-1-9999349-3-4 (eBook)

Cover design and photography by Charlie Walker.

To my mother

MAPS

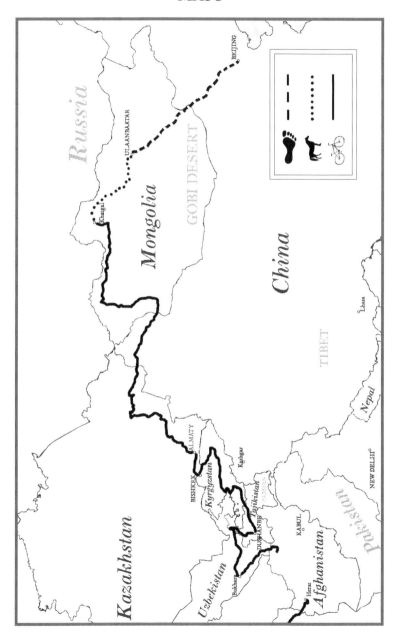

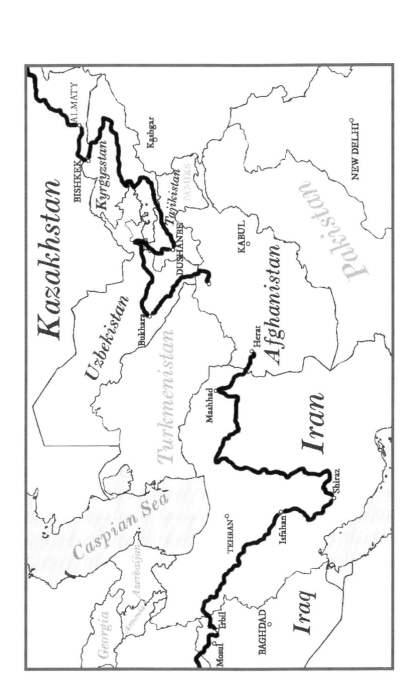

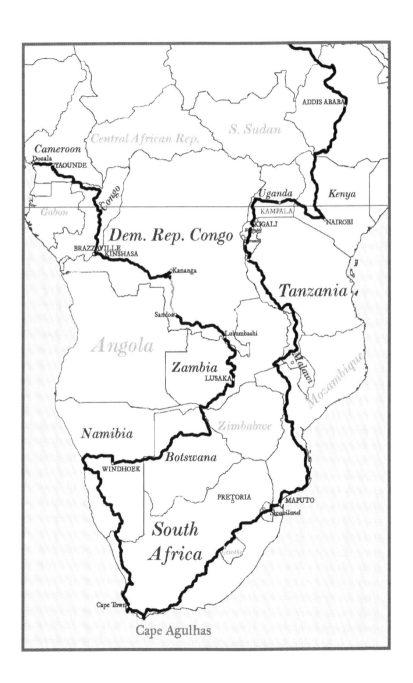

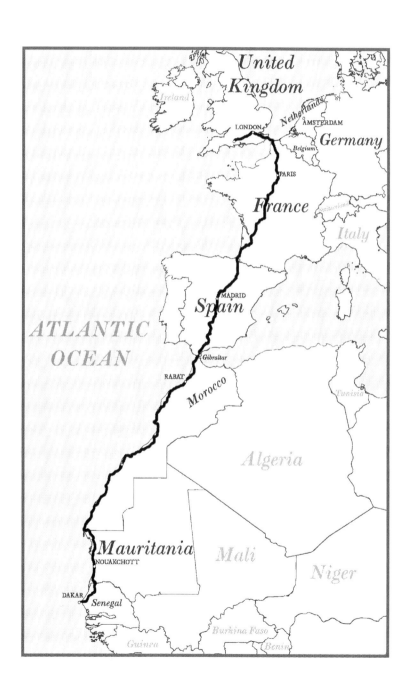

PART I: ASIA

*What is history? An echo of the past in the future; a reflex
from the future on the past.*
- Victor Hugo

PROLOGUE

If you go with a map all you'll ever come back with is a more detailed version of the same map.
- Benedict Allen, *The Proving Grounds*

I looked ahead in panic. We were in trouble. We never had the chance to stop and scout ahead on land. For the last hour we had fought our way through a narrow, overgrown channel, often jumping overboard to hack through branches. The quick, clear water ran through tangled Congolese forest of the darkest green. When I forced my rusted machete through the last blocking vines, our lumbering pirogue, a hollowed-out tree trunk, surged suddenly into the piercing daylight.

We were midstream and speeding helplessly towards a churning field of rapids. Boulders littered the wide, broiling waterway, each one threatening to undo us. Both banks of the narrowing river taunted us with a scrolling succession of unreachable landing places. The tang of adrenal fear registered on my tongue. Already exhausted, we braced for battle. I gripped my part-broken paddle of crudely carved wood with whitening knuckles. Our heavy wooden canoe was unwieldy and steering was a physical fight against the coursing current. It was imperative to remain facing forwards so as not to be capsized. Archie shouted something from behind me, directions perhaps, but it was lost to the rapids' clashing roar.

It was only our fourth day on the remote river and we had alerted nobody to our plan. Nobody knew where we were. We were utterly unprepared and I was afraid.

We slalomed the first few jutting rocks in a fearful panic of adrenalin. Spuming water danced and sprayed all around us. The side of our canoe was only a hand's breadth above the water and inundation seemed certain. A submerged rock nudged our tail, spinning us into an unplanned pirouette over the surface of a whirlpool. I grabbed the side of the canoe to avoid being flung out. Yet, somehow, we spun on around and came out facing forwards.

We pitched relentlessly on, and for the first time I dared to believe we might pass through intact. But then the water became faster – too fast – and the rocks too many. We sped into a cloud of spray and hit another hidden boulder. We spun again and this time tilted. Water gushed over the side and, in a desperate attempt to avoid the pirogue sinking or smashing, we leapt overboard.

The fierce, uncaring river dragged us indifferently onwards. A current forced me under the surface and I felt the skin on my back break as it scraped over something jagged. A second later I heard a yelp as Archie thwacked his ankle on a rock. I tried to keep at the surface and avoid being shoved under again. Thrashing my arms, I struggled in vain towards the listing pirogue. Our bags were being carried away in different directions, bouncing off the rocks as they went.

Finally we were spat out and it was over. The river widened and the water calmed, but the flow was still fast. The pirogue's nose was underwater and the rear was only held near the surface by the empty water containers we used as buoyancy aids. We hurriedly swam back and forth in the still-speeding water, shepherding errant bags to the moving 'base' of our sinking canoe. All the while, with a bend in the river ahead, we were fearful of being plunged down another field of rapids.

At length, we hauled everything to the thickly wooded west bank. The sun was setting, its warmth dropping with it. Our pirogue's nose caught in underwater tree roots and took several dives to extricate. I had been wet for the last two hours and began to shiver uncontrollably. We needed to make a fire quickly.

We had survived the rapids but lost our map in the process. From here on it would be exploration into the unknown.

ONE

WAKING UP

What we do now echoes in eternity.
- Marcus Aurelius, *Meditations*

The winter was long and indulgent, a time of excess and sloth and submission to the many temptations Beijing had to offer. I gained weight. My flesh sat soft, pale and plentiful about my bones. I maintained a cyclist's limitless appetite but stopped cycling. McDonalds offered home delivery in Beijing – the perfectly hideous antidote to hangovers born of cheap, low-quality alcohol in bars that never closed.

The hard, granular leg muscles that had powered me thousands of miles across Asia slackened and shrunk. For five months I passed forty hours a week slouched before a computer screen on the twenty-fifth floor of a glass-and-steel tower. The floor-to-ceiling windows rarely revealed more than the faint outlines of similar structures wrapped in a smog-pressed, colour-leaching blur.

An unnamed dumpling restaurant was my daily lunchtime sanctuary. The pork and chive *jiaozi* were steamed in a bamboo box and came in servings of eight to be dipped in dark vinegar with sesame oil and chilli flakes stirred though it. I ate until full and then always ordered one final helping. I was greedy and revelled in being so. Beijing's easy living turned me from dancing flame to dying ember. But every ember is a fire in waiting.

I arrived in Beijing after eighteen months and 18,000 miles of cycling across tundra and jungle: through sand and snow. I set out from home as a naive, tremulous twenty-two-year-old boy, but after loneliness and frostbite and heartbreak I shed boyhood. I also needed rest. The goal I had set myself, to reach the furthest capes in Europe, Asia and Africa, would require another two or three years to complete. At times exhaustion had numbed my senses and I shuttered myself, ignoring the beautiful, subtle nuances of places and people, and the intriguing hints of history that resonated through the worlds I was exploring. I had reached the top of Europe and the bottom of Asia, but returning home via the bottom of Africa would involve the breadth of Asia again, and twice the length of Africa, on my long-suffering secondhand bicycle, Old Geoff.

Beijing's winter weather hovered for months at a dry -5°C. Not pleasant, but I knew it was much worse to the north. For a long time my heart had been fixated on Mongolia. However, I wanted to visit the rolling green steppe grasslands under a sky of edgeless blue, rather than a wintry wasteland of white and grey that frequently dipped to -40°C. Memories of a perilous struggle through Tibet the previous winter were still too freshly scattered across my subconscious. And so I waited. I made friends, I rented a room, and I went through the motions of office work. The pulses of my peripatetic past echoed softer with every passing week. I tasted near-normality for a time, but it was all just an inhalation. I was a spring recoiling, readying to rush forth again. The echoes were soft and seldom, but they still lived, and I knew they would once again boom off lofty valley walls and across the deserts that haunted my dreams.

Winter finally mellowed and colour returned to the world. It was time to wake up.

*   *   *

I eyeballed the portrait of Chairman Mao. He stared back at me, a rounded face and benevolent half-smile over a tunic collar buttoned tight around a fat neck. The man himself lay embalmed a hundred metres away, with a long queue waiting to pay homage. The sky was a calming blue washed with soft pinks. The night's slight chill was melting away and a perfect early spring day was dawning on Beijing.

Thirty minutes earlier, at 5.22 a.m. precisely, I had watched a crisply uniformed phalanx of People's Liberation Army soldiers perform their daily flag-raising ceremony. A couple of thousand domestic tourists gathered to watch the performance, their cameras flashing every second or so. Forty soldiers paraded smartly out of Tiananmen Tower while a marching band played the national anthem. The flag of China – five gold stars on bold communist red – was clipped to the flagpole and hoisted over exactly two minutes and seven seconds – the amount of time it takes for the sun to fully rise above the horizon. The soldiers returned to the tower, the tourists headed off on their various sightseeing itineraries, and the flag hung lifelessly in the still morning air.

I procrastinated for a few minutes. I knew that once I started, I could only truly rest once I reached Ulaanbaatar, Mongolia's capital, almost 1,000 miles away. Old Geoff had stood on the exact same spot with me three years earlier at the start of my first long ride. We had travelled northwest together for a fortnight, crossing the eastern Gobi Desert. Now, faced with the same journey a second time, I opted to allow Geoff a longer hibernation. He would stay put in a friend's cupboard and I would walk to Mongolia. I hadn't trained, but then I'd never trained for anything in my life.

I considered my ill-preparedness: the £8 pair of fake 'Timberland' shoes that I'd neglected to wear even once since purchase; the £5 fake 'North Face' rucksack bought in a Nepalese mountain village years earlier; my general state of flabbiness after a stationary winter. Pushing these thoughts aside, I put one foot in front of the other; the first of well over a million steps.

The city dragged itself out of bed as the sun rose and I plodded steadily north. After an hour, I stepped into a Beijing dumpling restaurant for the final time. It was more of a stall than a restaurant, smaller and dirtier than my local haunt, but the pork and chive dumplings were just as tasty.

During the morning, I crossed the city's first five ring roads. These tarmac belts had encompassed my life for five months. I hadn't seen nature and open green spaces since pedalling across the southern sections of these same roads back in November. My life's focus had contracted to the city of 20 million people, to the new friends I made, and to the numbing marketing job I'd chanced my way into.

As I progressed through the afternoon, low, forested hills became visible in the distance, materialising out of the smog haze. They grew closer at an irritatingly slow pace as the parade of identikit thirty-story apartment blocks reached ever onwards.

I crossed the sixth ring road late in the afternoon but the urban sprawl stretched beyond it. In vain, I began looking for somewhere to camp. After months of paying rent and guiltily enjoying the extravagance of a comfortable bed, it seemed a point of principle that first night that I sleep for free, outside and on the ground.

I was limping by the time I reached the hills. The sun had long since set and I stumbled through the half-light until I found a bare patch of earth. I dropped my backpack and slumped heavily down beside it. Everything ached: feet, ankles, shoulders, hips, knees, neck, and back. At twenty-eight miles, I'd walked more than a marathon. More, in fact, than I'd ever covered on foot in a day.

Banking on dry weather, I had left my tent with the bike. Instead, I opted for an army surplus bivvy bag, which I spread over a thin foam roll mat. I'd foregone many things in favour of travelling light, and my rucksack weighed about 12 kg without food or water. To further save weight, a *National Geographic* would provide both reading material and loo paper; each page repeatedly scrunched and unscrunched to achieve a more fibrous, absorbent state.

I was too tired to care about the uneven ground or to tend to my burning feet. A slim crescent moon appeared in the east and Beijing's innumerable orange lights blanketed the south. I lay back and a dead, dreamless sleep came quickly.

Waking under the paling sky, I felt like I'd been in a boxing match. It hurt to move, and when I rolled slightly to one side a whole new system of muscles erupted in complaint. I lay on my back staring into space for a long time, trying to muster the courage to sit up. The inevitable seeds of weakness scattered themselves across my consciousness. *You could be back in the city centre and on a friend's sofa in under two hours,* I thought. *Why not hop on a bus, take a few days rest, and get Old Geoff out? You'd still get to Mongolia quicker than by this silly walking.*

I indulged my whingeing weaker nature for long enough to prepare and eat some porridge, telling myself I would turn back. But I knew deep down that I would be walking all the way to Mongolia. I could feel the gradual re-awakening of the same primal drive that pushed me from Britain to Beijing. It had lain dormant through the winter but its eyelids were flickering and soon it would be wide awake.

The first few steps on the tender soles of my feet were torturous as my cheap shoes offered no support at all. I set off stiffly with a pitiful limp but soon realised walking that way didn't alleviate the discomfort, so I forced myself to tread normally. I tried to accept and even embrace the pain until it slipped from my mind.

The road was narrow and wound uphill all day. I passed through patches of forest and areas of rocky hills with shoots of tender green grass between the brown bristle. There was a freshness in the air, the scentless cold giving way to new life and the earthy whiff of freshly turned fields. Occasional mattress-sized slabs of ice lay stubbornly on the ground, sheltered from the sun in the crooks of streams. When I finally reached the pass, my hips and feet were the loudest complainants. There was a ten-metre-long section of crumbling Great Wall on a hill at the top. It looked very ancient and primitive; it was little more than a head-high mound of toppling stones with earth packed between them and bushes now growing from its flank. It must have been an offshoot from one of the earlier incarnations of the wall, likely built by the Northern Wei dynasty in the fifth or sixth century. Some silhouetted snatches of a grander stretch of wall were visible, crenellating the spine of a distant hill.

I laid out my sleeping mat under a nearby walnut tree and set about lancing my first blister, a deep one that I couldn't see on the surface but could feel. The needle was from a hotel sewing kit and I vaguely sterilised it with a lighter. It flexed as I drove it deep through the pad of my foot, deeper than felt sensible. Just when I started to doubt that the blister was actually there, something gave way and the fluid shot out. I squeezed around the area until no more fluid oozed, and then smeared a dab of antiseptic cream over it.

The first miles the next morning offered no respite. I had anticipated the downhill as an easy start. When cycling, the climbs are the toils and the descents are the spoils. However, on foot the downhill is simply punishing on different parts of the body. My knees soon started to throb, my lower back ached with the new angle, and I felt a similarly deep blister welling up in the pad of my other foot. I checked my speed against the kilometre markers and was irritated to find I went the same speed downhill as uphill. My steady march was three miles per hour. I would need to walk almost nine hours to fulfil my goal of a daily marathon.

I began to understand what I'd let myself in for. Cycling is five times faster than walking, and perhaps half as punishing on the body. My rough calculations therefore found walking to be ten times harder than cycling. I began to persuade myself of how effortless the eighteen months of pedalling Old Geoff had been. This made me sullen and I plodded onwards in a grump, stopping every two hours to dunk my burning feet in icy streams. I knew I wasn't angry at walking as such, or even at the tough task I'd set myself. I was pissed off with myself for slipping into such a state of unfitness. I was embarrassed at my habits in Beijing and annoyed by the proportion of my income that I'd frittered on alcohol. Each unnecessary late-night drink in Beijing could have bought me a whole meal in a simple café later in my journey.

On the third day, my road and its parallel river plunged into a gorge and cut through a gap in the main body of the Great

Wall that I'd glimpsed the night before. Neatly laid stones banked away almost vertically either side of me, up the gorge and onto the hilltops. This section was part of the Ming dynasty effort in the fifteenth and sixteenth centuries, built a full thousand years after the forlorn pile of stones I'd camped by the previous night. The world-famous wall was probably the most impressive time-, money-, and labour-wasting monument to paranoia ever built. It was also ultimately futile as the raiding Mongols repeatedly made it through and took what they wanted as plunder. Genghis Khan's army successfully invaded numerous times in the early thirteenth century. Some of his successors even casually swam with their horses around the wall's end where it plunged into the Pacific.

Later that day I stopped for a late lunch in a small village called Si Hai. Trees blooming in a pretty spring pink lined the track through the houses. The only restaurant consisted of a few string chairs ranged around a dusty front yard attended by a beaming old woman with no teeth. She pointed me to a sagging seat and in two minutes had fried a plateful of vegetables and peanuts.

The table before me was incongruous: a huge circular stone perched on a pile of bricks. It was one metre across and thirty centimetres thick, with a square hole bored through its centre and rudimentary patterns carved around its edge; I realised it was an old millstone. I asked the woman how old it was and she was pensive for a moment before saying 'two thousand'. It seemed unimportant to her and the answer was clearly a guess. But she could well have been right. In China, people grow up knowing their lives are just another minuscule fraction tacked onto the end of a staggeringly long timeline. Most of the Chinese people I met seemed impressively ignorant of their history, and what little they did know was from the Communist Party's approved script. However, the echoes of 5,000 years of civilisation inevitably reverberated through the lives of the unwitting modern Chinese. The millennia-old millstone had become a makeshift table that would likely be discarded if the woman could afford a new, mass-produced replacement. It might then be rediscovered and reused in another thousand years as the tokens of the past continue to resonate through the present.

For a few days I continued along the peaceful roads, wiggling through basic brick villages garnished with fresh blossoms. The weather continued to smile on me and, slowly, I relaxed into my new way of life. The simplicity of my days began to charm me. I refined my evening routine of picking a patch of earth for a bed, cooking a simple dinner, and lancing new blisters. Lying in the open, gazing at the infinitely speckled night sky was a privileged way to drift off. After ten hours' sleep, waking to a blood-red east was always an invigorating start to the new day.

The people I met were hard-working, friendly, and photogenic. The villages were the preserve of the elderly, and their dark, lined faces cracked into broad smiles at the sight of my camera. Their children and grandchildren had mostly joined the mad dash to China's swelling cities. Every year 35 million more Chinese move to urban areas. I found myself wondering what will happen when the current crop of agrarian grandparents have entered the soil themselves. They are possibly the last true Chinese peasants in a once-timeless tradition. Future farmers will be fully grown city kids with unfulfilled dreams.

On a Saturday morning a family of weekending Beijingers invited me in for lunch. They sat in a neglected courtyard around which ran a prettily dilapidated bungalow that smelled of rotting wood. Stray playing cards littered the ground and empty *baijo* (rice liquor) bottles were heaped in piles. There were no children, and a shrinking granny sat, toothless and grinning, in a wheelchair outside the circle of increasingly drunk men and women. One man had nine fingers and another nine toes. They were all equally asymmetrical and affable.

The land grew drier and more brown as I progressed north. Stooped men ploughed arid land with patient donkeys, and stocky sows rooted through piles of rubbish beside the road. The little village shops all sold the same scant range of goods. In one shop a dog vomited casually in the corner while two women argued happily, apparently about the price of an egg.

I turned onto farm tracks for a couple of days. The villagers that spotted me there, away from roads, had wide-eyed, open-mouthed stares of astonishment that took several seconds to break into the usual brown-toothed smiles. In one village a man saw me and stopped in his tracks, rooted to the spot, until I had passed. Out of the corner of my eye I then saw him dart sideways and disappear behind a wall. A muffled shout followed and when I looked over my shoulder five heads popped up behind the wall, one by one, in a line.

The brown rocky hills gradually became yellow grasslands and I crossed from Hebei province to Inner Mongolia. Darker, wider faces began to appear among the majority Han Chinese, and small, hardy horses replaced the donkeys. The odd shepherd drifted slowly behind flocks of shaggy brown sheep, and chubby marmots darted in and out of their burrows. I overheard occasional snatches of the guttural Mongolian tongue and road signs bore both Chinese characters and the intricate traditional Mongolian script, now replaced in Outer Mongolia by Russian Cyrillic. Mongolians are a minority in the province of Inner Mongolia, comprising less than a fifth of the population, but they still outnumber the Mongolians living in the nation of Mongolia by two to one.

Inner Mongolia is vast – the same size as Scandinavia – yet it's still only China's third largest province. It has more than a quarter of the world's coal reserves and has become a vital economic asset. For many centuries, control of the area bounced back and forth between the Chinese and the various nomadic tribes that roamed the steppe. However, when the Mongols broke out and raced across Asia in the thirteenth century, Genghis Khan's grandson, Kublai, completed the conquest of China. He set up his capital, Shangdu (or Xanadu), in Inner Mongolia, about one hundred miles east of my route. A sprawling empire was administered from this short-lived city for twenty-two years, until the capital was moved to Beijing. Mongol rule, known as the Yuan dynasty, is a sour chapter of history for the Chinese. They saw the steppe-dwelling Mongols as uncouth, ugly, and uncivilised. To be ruled by these barbarians for almost a century was a tough pill to swallow, but in the mid-fourteenth century the Mongols were defeated and fled to their ancestral lands. Little wonder then that the succeeding Ming dynasty worked so hard to wall them out, with the most extensive additions to the Great Wall project that had already been running for almost two millennia.

The start of Inner Mongolia was also the beginning of the headwinds that I knew would be against me all the way to Ulaanbaatar. I remembered this quarrelsome wind from cycling the route. It had exasperated me back then and I had often lost my temper with it. However, I had covered 400 miles in two weeks and had now found my feet. With the punishing, repetitive routine I had quickly lost weight and gained strength. I was beginning to pace rather than plod, and I no longer winced as I lanced my blisters.

The days morphed from pleasantly warm to hot and the land gave way to desert. Feeling in need of a shower and a night in a bed, I walked into Sonid Youqi and checked into a £3-a-night hotel.

TWO

WELCOME TO MONGOLIA

When Mongolians party the rest of Asia locks its doors.
- Chinese proverb

The first task in town was to search for new shoes. The soles of my cheap, fake pair were wearing worryingly thin and my big toes were starting to poke through the tops. Unsurprisingly, no shoes in Sonid Youqi fitted me. I had struggled to get big enough shoes in Beijing in the first place. However, I met a shopkeeper with some English who introduced herself as Amanda. In her mid-thirties, Amanda was strangely tactile considering how bad I must have looked and smelled. She found someone to glue layers of rubber onto the soles of my shoes. I guessed it wouldn't last two days but it was better than nothing.

Afterwards, Amanda invited me to dinner in a Sichuanese hot pot restaurant with her and her husband. Mr Amanda was a squat, bull-like creature who rarely smiled and didn't seem particularly pleased to have me around. The three of us sat in a private room draped with tinsel and faux silk. As we set about the vast quantities of spicy, piping hot food, beer and *baijo* started to flow. Sipping was apparently taboo. Every glassful was downed after a toast. Both Amanda and her husband were significantly smaller than me and became drunk very quickly.

Before long Amanda was stroking my inner thigh under the table. I tried to stop her but she was persistent, and in my increasingly fuzzy state I worried that obvious resistance might alert her husband. My protestations weakened and I sat awkwardly, making polite, slurred conversation with the unsuspecting man. Suddenly we were in their car, swerving all over the road on our way to a KTV (karaoke) parlour. The couple sat close either side of me in a private booth and we took turns at tuneless crooning. Amanda took every opportunity to touch me when her husband wasn't looking.

Their friends, a younger couple, joined us and Mr Amanda stood up to sing a love song. He was mid-flow when Amanda leaned over and clamped her lips onto my neck, sucking at it like a rabid teen. Her husband looked around and we locked eyes in mutual confusion. There was an excruciating pause before the shouting started. In seconds we are all outside.

The husband yelled at Amanda. She screeched back at him. I was ignored. He seized her by the hair, pulling her downwards while she clawed at his face with long, red nails. She suddenly went limp and fell to the pavement. I tried to help her up but her friend rushed forward and slapped me. Amanda jumped up and slapped her husband hard. He slapped her back and I stepped between Mr and Mrs Amanda. I saw his punch coming but was too booze-clumsied to dodge. His fist glanced off the side of my head and everyone suddenly fell silent. Amanda chastised her husband in a low voice and he sat down in the road and started crying. Things seemed to have cooled down so I gratefully made my exit.

A 7 a.m. knock brought me to my door. Amanda stood next to her husband, whose head was bowed penitently; both wore the same clothes as the night before. We all apologised and then ate breakfast together in awkward silence.

Carrying three days of food and wearing my poorly modified shoes, I walked out of town for the eighty-mile stretch of barren nothingness to the Mongolian border where the headwind had the sand biting at my exposed calves. By evening, the wind had matured to a mild sandstorm and I slept in an abandoned hut by a railway running parallel to the road. Rats scampered through the detritus heaped around me and occasionally dropped from the rafters.

The wind blew on in the morning and it started to rain – a cold, biting downpour that cut into me as I struggled forward. The weather was sweeping south out of still-frozen Siberia and for two or three hours the rain turned to wet, heavy snow that stung my face. There was nowhere to shelter, but the novelty of desert snow pleased me. Despite its scorching summers, the Gobi is the largest 'cold desert' outside of Antarctica. To keep warm I walked briskly and distracted myself with half-remembered fragments of stage monologues. It was strangely liberating forcing myself into the weather bellowing King Lear's glorious provocation:

> *Blow, winds, and crack your cheeks! Rage! Blow!*
> *You cataracts and hurricanoes. Spout*
> *Till you have drench'd our steeples …*

Close to Erlian, the border town, I walked under a vast statue of two sauropods. They stood on either side of the road, with their twenty-metre-long necks stretching towards each other and meeting in the middle in an odd kiss. The surrounding area, known as the Erlian Basin, started yielding dinosaur fossil finds in the 1920s and has since become one of the world's most prolific paleontological sites. Fifty or so smaller dinosaur sculptures, similar to velociraptors, dotted the landscape. I had read that if I wandered a mile or so away from the road I would be in with a good chance of finding a fossilised dinosaur egg simply lying on the ground. However, I was tired and hungry and the extra rubber soles had started to flap off my shoes, which was annoying me. I walked into the town, ate some greasy food, and again searched in vain for new shoes. Towards sunset, as another windstorm was whipping up, I walked to the outskirts and made my home on the concrete floor of one of many unfinished apartment blocks. Wind whistled past the glassless window, carrying litter out into the desert, and the sinking sun was swallowed by dancing clouds of dust.

In the morning I tore off the futile repairs to my shoes and walked to the border. It took fifteen minutes to convince the Chinese immigration official that I was indeed the man in my passport photo. He asked to see other photos of me. Clearly the well-fed, clean-shaven individual in the passport looked nothing like the drawn, bearded man stood before him. Just three weeks and 500 miles had returned me to the scruffy vagrant who cycled into Beijing at the onset of winter.

I left China and crossed into Mongolia, the thirtieth country of my journey. Zamyn-Uud is a border town with a dangerous, uneasy feel to it. Paul Theroux describes it as 'the perfection of a frontier: sandy desert, blowing dust, nothing growing, a desolate wreck of a town looking absolutely on the edge.'

A few thousand people called it home but there were few actual buildings. Instead, there was an extended suburb of circular felt yurts, or *gers* as they are known locally. The people seemed a transient bunch. Nomads usually do. They survived either from their herds of two-humped Bactrian camels kept in the desert, or from the passing trade between China and Mongolia. Manufactured goods went north and unrefined natural resources went south.

In the square by the railway station, I got talking to a young man called Ganshagai who offered to help me find a cheap room. A drunk, egg-shaped man standing nearby said he had one and we drove there in Ganshagai's Toyota. The room was in a half-finished building and had three chairs pushed together for a bed. I asked how much and he replied simply: 'beer!'

I fetched some cans from a shop and the three of us sat down to drink. A sneering, weasely man wandered in. He was evidently unwanted by my companions, but he started talking ingratiatingly from his perch on the floor, begging for beer. The egg-shaped man stood up and kicked the weasel hard in the face three or four times. This done, the weasel was given a can and swigged contentedly, beer and blood trickling together from his swollen lip.

I noticed on my previous visit that Mongolia has a rough, macho culture. Men often seemed to eye me as if sizing me up for a fight. The lifestyle is rugged and physical. Wrestling is the national sport and a diet of little other than meat, dairy, bread, and potatoes ensures a thickset populace.

Ganshagai said he was uneasy about me sleeping in the room. There was no door and he feared I would be attacked in the night. He suggested we could stay with his friends on the outskirts of town. On route to their *ger*, we picked up frozen mutton dumplings and two bottles of Chinggis Khan vodka. In the five-metre-wide tent was a family of nine comprising three generations. I was presented with the first glass of vodka and, remembering the custom, dipped my middle finger in. I flicked a little liquid upwards as an offering to Tengger, the sky god. Then I flicked a little downwards, an offering to the Earth, before tipping the remainder down my throat.

Ganshagai, the family's father, and I laboriously finished both bottles of vodka and a third that appeared from under a blanket. I desperately wanted to sleep but politeness dictated I stick it out until either I keeled over or they called it a night. The excited children watched and giggled as the unwashed foreigner was slowly tortured with eighty-proof hospitality. The night became a wretched blur of the colourful tent interior and the paint-stripping alcohol.

Drunk and deliriously tired, I was finally allowed to stretch out on the crowded floor. It seemed fitting to spend my first night across the border sleeping in a *ger* having partaken in the national pastime: alcoholism.

After a breakfast of dumplings served in a bowl of salty milk tea, I thanked my hosts and Ganshagai dropped me off by the train station. I was fretting over the trouble I might have carrying sufficient water for the journey ahead. The daytime temperatures would be high and places to resupply would be few and far between.

I bought a week's supply of food in the supermarket, where there were only two aisles: food and beer in one, vodka in the other. As I stood contemplating two different brands of instant noodles, a fistfight broke out in the vodka aisle. Two shirtless men swung and tore at each other as best they could in their drunken state. One fell into the shelving, smashing about twenty bottles, and the other launched himself at his adversary. They grappled, rolling around in a mess of vodka, broken glass and blood, until a policeman arrived and beat them repeatedly with a stick. When I left the shop, they were stood penitently, side by side, heads bowed and swaying slightly, while the policeman shouted at them. It was 10.30 a.m.

I filled bottles with eight litres of water and walked to the northern edge of town. A hundred yards beyond the last building, where the paved road ended abruptly, I stopped. A tangle of criss-crossing tyre tracks twisted away in all directions. The dusty, desolate expanse of dry emptiness reached from my feet to the horizon. There were 130 miles to Sainshand, the next place where I could be certain of resupply. Squinting into the dusty headwind, I stooped under the weight of my pack. A bulging plastic bag of food that wouldn't fit in my backpack hung from one hand. Once the water ran out, I would have to rely on finding nomadic families or hope that one of the rare vehicles driving the route might pass near me. I consulted my compass, faced northwest, and started walking.

THREE

GOBI

In the end, no-one can cope alone. In Mongolia it's a group effort. You rely on each other. As long as everyone plays their part and offers hospitality, you are never at a loss, except in the Gobi.
- Benedict Allen, *Edge of Blue Heaven*

After an hour I reached an *ovoo*. These cairns are common across Mongolia and are worship points for Shamanism. This one consisted of a wooden post about five metres tall decked with thousands of blue and yellow cotton rags that passing travellers had added for luck. Tradition dictates that passing travellers should circle an *ovoo* three times clockwise and make an offering of some sort for safe passage. The post was surrounded by the offerings of rocks, vodka bottles and broken car parts. As symbols of religion and superstition, *ovoos* were outlawed during the communist era. Mongolia was never officially part of the USSR but the 'Mongolian People's Republic' was a Moscow-controlled satellite state for seventy years until it gained full independence in 1992.

While I was photographing the cairn a jeep arrived and ran three rings around me before stopping. Each passenger poured a splash of vodka on the *ovoo* and then took a healthy swig. They wished me good luck in Russian and departed in a cloud of dust. I checked my compass and walked on.

The next week was hard, hot, and lonely. The Gobi was a wasteland of dust and rock with the odd ridge of wind-sculpted sand. Animal skeletons, mostly camels, punctuated my progress, bleached a brilliant white and sometimes with an intact hoof or some fur still clinging to them.

Every couple of days I spied a *ger*, usually several miles in the wrong direction. Most had camels loitering nearby, and the inhabitants always welcomed me in, fed me, and seemed to require no explanation of why I was walking across the desert. By one *ger* I sat for an hour, watching a shepherd tirelessly draw bucket after bucket of water from a twenty-metre-deep well and pouring them into a wooden trough for two hundred eager goats.

I was always short of water. Rarely creeping above 35°C the heat was bearable, but it was extremely dry. My dark orange urine hinted at how dehydrated I was and I regularly had odd cramping spasms in my hands, feet, and back. The headwind had me perpetually parched and my swollen tongue sticking to the roof of my mouth. One day, an old man on horseback appeared and rode quietly alongside me. I explained with sign language that my mouth was dry. He scooped a small pebble off the ground, wiped it on his trousers and told me to keep it in my mouth. The pebble made me salivate, preventing my mouth from drying. It also forced me to breath through my nose so as not to lose precious moisture from evaporation off my tongue.

The days were trying. My feet continued to suffer and I felt physically ruined by evening. But I loved the nights. The wind was calmer and sleeping outdoors in the desert was a magical experience. Camels sometimes wandered past as I lay reading in the twilight, their tough mouths picking at the sparse tufts of spiny grass. The stars were brighter and sharper than anywhere else, the Milky Way arched from one horizon to the other, and the loneliness of the day melted into a contented solitude.

The day before I reached Sainshand was the windiest I had experienced. I leaned heavily into the gale, wearing a handkerchief over my nose and mouth to keep sand out. It continued to strengthen, and by the end of the afternoon it was getting hard to move but I could find nowhere to shelter. The sand bit at any exposed skin and I battled on until it was simply too painful to fight anymore. When I unstrapped the bivvy bag from my backpack it violently unfurled into a two-metre-long windsock, and I nearly lost it. With difficulty I got my pack inside the bivvy and bundled in after it. With the opening tied shut beyond my feet, I lay in the darkness while the roaring wind wrapped the bag tightly around me. I slept little during the following twelve hours of fury.

The wind died suddenly at 5.30 a.m., so I shouldered my pack and trudged the final twenty miles to Sainshand. A wild-looking dog joined me for the last two hours, trotting a yard ahead of me, guiding me, but disappeared as soon as we reached the outskirts. I found the same cheap hotel I'd stayed in three years earlier. It was in a disintegrating concrete building with a relief of Lenin set into its side. I washed, ate, and read for a day – nothing else. It was my first day off since leaving Beijing a month earlier. Sand kept falling from my hair and dust came out when I blew my nose. The mirror revealed an odd reflection: stretched, burned and old.

The week-long walk to the town of Choir (pronounced *choy-ear*) was less gruelling but relatively boring. The northerly wind blew less insistently and it wasn't as hot. There were two villages along the route so I travelled lighter. Infrequent lorries trundled by, each giving me a dust bath. My feet continued to ache and blister. I heard myself whimpering with my first steps of each day. The soles had worn through on both shoes and I swapped out improvised cardboard inner soles twice daily.

One night I accidentally slept on a beetle nest and woke to find several hundred small, oil-black insects crawling over me and inside my sleeping bag. Small lizards, disturbed by my footfall, scampered away every twenty metres or so. They liked to bask on flat rocks and, on a couple of occasions, sleep in my shoes.

The tarmac road started at Choir where the desert gave way to grassland. Small herds of feral horses roamed the landscape, and if I got too close they fled, hoping to evade capture. All horses in Mongolia are owned and have markings on their flanks, but most are turned loose to fend for themselves throughout the brutal winter. Survivors are rounded up again in spring or summer, as and when they are needed for food or labour. I saw boys of no more than four hauling themselves up the reins to the giddy height of their horse's back before thundering away in a cloud of dust. I daydreamed of sitting astride my own noble steed and drifting across the steppe; my mount doing the hard work and my feet taking a well-earned rest.

While walking early one morning, a Mongolian man suddenly appeared beside me carrying a flaming torch. He wore a tracksuit and cap which both read 'World Harmony Run'. I jogged with him for a mile while we tried to communicate, until a support van drew alongside carrying five other runners from Russia and Mongolia. The torch was on a 40,000-mile journey through one hundred countries, carried by runners all the way. I put my pack in the van and ran with the torch for five miles. It felt great to move faster and step lightly without weight on my back.

When the runners handed back my pack they left me with hugs and warm smiles. I was suddenly alone again, exhausted, adrenalin-drained, and struggling to walk on throbbing feet. The pain grew over the next two hours, and I was shivering and borderline delirious by the time I approached a cluster of small huts beside the railway.

I was taken in by Ganbold, his wife Obi, and their six young children. They lit the stove in an old log hut next to their home and helped me onto a wooden cot. I was brought a bowl of potato and mutton soup which set me sweating. The whole family happily sat in a circle around me while I slurped it down. I don't remember them leaving me, but after sixteen hours of unconsciousness I woke feeling weak but fresher. As I struggled to thank them, Obi and Ganbold smiled and nodded knowingly, eyes twinkling.

I gathered momentum as I neared Ulaanbaatar. The roadside kilometre markers told me my pace had increased. The grasslands were entrancing, and the enormity of the landscape dwarfed the scattered *gers* and amplified their remoteness. It grew colder, freezing at night and often raining in the day. Heavy clouds threatened one evening as I approached a lone *ger*. I had learned the custom that it is rude to knock before entering as it suggests the visitor doubts the hospitality of the inhabitants. I pulled open the door and stooped under the chest high lintel, not knowing that I was walking into another bizarre night of drunken hospitality.

An old woman inside gave me some barley flour gruel and invited me to stay. Two grandsons of eleven and five played with goat bones on the bare earth floor. Looking around me, I noticed there were no electric appliances. In fact, there was little of anything. It was the poorest home I had visited in Mongolia. The only light came from a couple of tallow candles on an ancient wooden cabinet.

The dark sky began to deliver just as the mother and father arrived on horseback in the fading light. Both were impressively drunk. The husband fell from his saddle and crawled into the tent where he squatted on his haunches and fell asleep. He hadn't noticed the foreign stranger in his home. His wife wobbled in and cupped my face in her hands. Her breath was heavy with stale alcohol and droplets of rain glistened in fine hairs on her upper lip. She soon started trying to stroke my leg in the dim candlelight. I moved away repeatedly, but she persisted and I began pushing her away.

Every time she made an advance her sons and her mother shouted and dragged her back. Eventually, catching me unaware, she thrust her hand down my shorts. Her eldest son launched himself forward and began beating her, the granny seized a cushion and started smothering her, and the distraught five year old started manically thumping his grandmother's back.

All this proved too much for me. Losing self-restraint, I swept the smaller boy off the floor and bellowed at the rest of them as loud as I could. Four surprised faces turned to me, looking a little frightened. The father had keeled over during the fracas, but still slept, and the mood was tense. I didn't know what to do, so I put the younger boy down and sat on a stool by the cabinet. Unfortunately, I leaned back too far and my hair strayed into the candle's flame. Weeks of accumulated filth and grease was set alight and it took a few seconds of beating from granny with her cushion to put it out. They all laughed and I laughed with them, the tension evaporating.

We laid out mats on the floor to sleep and the little boy curled up next to me, a convenient buffer against further advances from his mother. I was awake when cracks of dawn light became visible through the tent, so I pulled on my shoes, picked up my rucksack, and crept silently out the door.

It rained incessantly on the day I entered Ulaanbaatar: a mixture of *ger* townships and brutalist Soviet buildings with one or two sleek glass skyscrapers in the centre. The traffic thickened and I was repeatedly soaked by passing vehicles crashing through puddles. I found my way to Sukhbaatar Square at the heart of the city, where a comically fat statue of Genghis Khan sits outside the State History Museum. Six weeks and almost 1,000 miles of walking ended in a sombre sense of anti-climax. The rain and the cold had sapped my sense of achievement and there was nobody to greet me; nobody even knew I was there. I checked into a hostel, lingered in a hot shower, and threw away the ragged remains of my shoes.

FOUR

HORSE TRADERS

In Mongolia I wondered if it was possible to be happier. When the
horses were good, and the weather fine, I felt I was in paradise.
- Stanley Stewart, *In The Empire of Genghis Khan*

The monotonous landscape scrolled past in a hazy blur during the fifteen-hour train ride back to Zamyn-Uud. From the border it was a twelve-hour bus journey to Beijing, where I needed to collect Old Geoff and renew my Mongolian visa.

During my time in the city I set my heart on the idea of buying a horse when I returned to Ulaanbaatar. It seemed a fitting way to travel across the steppe. The Mongol hordes had, after all, conquered most of Asia due largely to their incredible prowess on horseback. I fantasised about cruising across the landscape with my own noble steed. I mentioned this plan to a small, hirsute Spanish man called Sancho whom I met in the Mongolian embassy. He got wrapped up in the idea too so we exchanged email addresses.

With my bicycle and a fresh two-month visa, I made the return journey and started following up contacts in search of a horse for sale.

A cousin of mine travelled through Mongolia in the 1990s and met a man called Moggy in a post office. He ended up spending a winter living in a *ger* on the steppe with Moggy's family. I emailed Moggy to ask if he could help. He replied that he was working on a zoological project in France but that I should call his nephew, Dashkar. I did so and was promptly invited for dinner.

Both Dashkar and his wife were diminutive with warm, mischievous smiles. He had a nice habit, a tick almost, of winking his left eye and snorting whenever he smiled. Their giggling three-year-old daughter tugged at my hair while we talked horses. He gave me some pointers for what to look out for.

'Long teeth, too old. Short teeth, too young. You want energetic but not crazy, Calm but not lazy. Winter was recent. Most horses will be skinny and won't want to be ridden. You want a fat one that can afford to loose weight. Make sure the back is strong and has no lumps or wounds. Also, check the bottom of the hooves. Make sure there are no cracks or mushrooms…'

'Mushrooms?' I asked.

'Like a mushroom. I can't remember how to say it.'

'Fungus?'

'Yes, check the hooves for fungus.'

I was too embarrassed to admit that I had only sat on a horse once or twice in my life and could use tips simply on how to ride one. Dashkar put me in touch with a man in a village outside the city who could find me a horse. I was told to ask around for Puujee once I reached the village.

I cycled the forty-five miles to Bayanchandmani the next afternoon and was quickly directed to Puujee, who had been expecting me. He was a big-bellied man with eagle-patterned cowboy boots and a snuff habit. His teenage daughter acted as translator.

'First, drink vodka. Next, look horse,' was his first statement.

I was subjected to half a bottle of paint-stripping vodka and a few bowlfuls of *airag*, Mongolia's gag-inducing national drink of fermented mare's milk. Seven of us then bundled into an Ulyanovsk Soviet minivan and clattered for twenty miles along vague grassland tracks. Puujee and I did our best to talk in pidgin Russian during the journey as his daughter was somewhere at the back buried under three or four of her younger siblings. The sun was nearly setting when we piled out next to a couple of isolated *gers* in an idyllic valley all of their own. I was introduced to a herder called Khunbish whose name (I learned later) translates as 'not a human'.

Khunbish was already stumbling drunk. He slung an arm across my shoulder and pointed to a couple of horses on short tethers, one bay and one brown. I propped Khunbish up as we walked to the horses. They were both mares and, I was told, seven years old. Just the age I wanted. They were also both a little smaller than I had hoped. Their backs reached to about my chest but they looked able to bear me and a small amount of kit. With a small crowd looking on I hesitantly checked the horses over, trying to appear relaxed and knowledgeable.

Grabbing the lighter bay's head first, I lifted her upper lip. The grass-flecked teeth looked long to me, but maybe that was a normal length for a horse. How long are a horse's teeth? Not sure what to think, I gave a knowing grunt after checking each mouth. They both looked a bit skinny, but maybe that was normal too. How fat is a horse supposed to be? I slapped at their flanks three times each, nodded, and grunted once more.

Next I ran my hand down each of their spines. They both felt lumpy. There were spines after all. How lumpy is a horse's spine meant to be? There were a couple of small scabs but nothing terrible. I gave an audible sigh of disapproval.

With difficulty I checked the underside of the brown's front hooves. They looked more or less as I imagined the underside of a Mongol horse's hooves to look: unshod and with no shiitake sprouting from them. When I went to lift a rear hoof, Puujee ran forward shouting '*nyet, nyet, NYET!*'

I jumped back, feeling foolish. In all my efforts to act the seasoned equine trader, I had forgotten that horses have a habit of kicking fairly hard with their hind legs.

Laughing, Khunbish shouted something. I looked to Puujee's daughter.

'Now you must ride them. That is the only way to know them,' she said.

Khunbish placed a high wooden saddle on the darker horse. It suddenly occurred to me that the last time I mounted a horse had not been a success. A few years earlier I had made it through to dawn at a New Year's Eve party on the Dorset coast. With two others, I drunkenly stripped down to underwear and headed for the beach to kick off the year with an icy swim. On our way through a field we spotted a huge, handsome gelding grazing peacefully. He looked so sleek, dark and beautiful. I scratched his nose softly and he seemed to like it. Emboldened, and drunk, I stepped around his side, barefoot and dressed only in pants, and pulled myself gently onto his bare back. For a charmed few seconds, he stayed calm as I sat there. Feeling more confident, I grasped his mane and gave a gentle squeeze with my heels. He sprung into action, darting and bucking this way and that, suddenly desperate to be rid of me. I clung on for only a few seconds before being thrown to the frozen earth. I was not a horseman.

Khunbish stepped back. I nervously placed my left foot in the stirrup, gripped the saddle, and threw my right leg over. The mare took a couple of sidesteps but otherwise remained still. I took up the reins and squeezed her belly with my heels. Nothing happened. I gave a gentle kick. Still nothing. Khunbish laughed, slapped the horse's bum, and shouted '*cho!*' Suddenly we were trotting joltingly forwards. Someone else bellowed '*cho*' and she broke into the smooth rhythm of a canter. My hips soon found the right motion, and it felt good. I wheeled her round a couple of times, passing the crowd and yelling the magic command. '*Cho, cho, cho!*'

I brought her to a halt and hopped off. When I tried the bay she seemed more stable and responsive and faster in the canter. She was slightly fatter too. I dismounted and, fixing my face with a disinterested expression, I asked how much. The daughter translated.

'It is good you are happy with horse. Father says you talk money tomorrow.'

Khunbish was beaming as he shook my hand. We climbed into the minivan and returned to Bayanchandmani, stopping at a couple of homes along the way to drink more vodka. I slept in Puujee's *ger* and we bargained in the morning. He opened with 800,000 tögrög (about £400) and we batted numbers back and forth for a while before settling on 400,000 tögrög. He said the horse would be in Bayanchandmani in two days so I would return then with the money. I cycled back to Ulaanbaatar feeling satisfied that I hadn't been ripped off.

Two days was enough to gather the things I needed from the market: saddle, bridle, stirrups, saddlebags, lockable hobbles, a ten-metre tether, a metal stake, and a hatchet – the blade for chopping firewood and the back of the head for hammering the tethering stake into the earth. I also got hold of some topographical maps made by the Soviets in the 1950s that would take me as far as Lake Khövsgöl, about 400 miles northwest of Ulaanbaatar as the crow flies.

I stashed Old Geoff and my tent at Dashkar's and took a bus back to Bayanchandmani. But Puujee was nowhere to be seen, and neither was his daughter. I waited through the afternoon watching some old men showing off their prized goats to each other. By evening there was still no sign of Puujee. His wife gave me dinner and I fell asleep. I woke briefly at 3 a.m. when Puujee staggered in singing softly as he zigzagged his way to bed.

In the morning I stood staring at the horse tethered outside the *ger*. It wasn't my mare. The size was the first clue: its back was only up to my navel. The penis was a pretty clear giveaway too. Puujee stepped outside, topless and with water trickling from his face onto his belly. Probably by design, his English-speaking daughter was still nowhere to be seen. I tried my Russian.

'This different horse,' I said.

'You…horse!' he replied, pointing first at me and then the pony.

'This very small horse. Boy horse. Where is *my* horse? Girl horse?'

'Good horse! Very good horse! Can go far.' He smiled and patted his belly.

I placed my saddle on the horse and took a test ride. Surprisingly he seemed as strong and stable as the mare I had bargained for. I handed Puujee the money and consoled myself with the fact that at least the horse's balls were absent. I had planed on naming my mare Nicki, but seeing the size of the pony I now owned I settled on Little Nicky. I didn't know that Mongolians never named their horses. It's not nice to name something that you will eventually eat.

I loaded my saddlebags with four days' supplies and mounted Little Nicky. Puujee's wife performed a safe passage ritual, flicking a few drops of fresh mare's milk on my shoes and the horse's hooves. I shook their hands and set off at a walk. The village was soon out of sight behind me and Mongolia's vast green interior swallowed me whole.

FIVE

HORSEPLAY

It is easy, when you are young, to believe that what you desire is no less than what you deserve, to assume that if you want something badly enough, it is your God-given right to have it.
- Jon Krakauer, *Into The Wild*

As I rode up an empty valley, I was daunted. I still knew next to nothing about caring for a horse. *What do I do if Nicky escapes?* I fretted. *What if he throws me off and I break a bone, miles from help? What if he dies? What if he's stolen?*

It was going to be a steep learning curve. Trying to shelve my fears I rode on, dismounting for the steeper climbs. I pushed Little Nicky hard and, aiming to establish my dominance, prevented him from grazing as he walked. It seemed to irritate him and he eventually bucked, throwing the saddlebags and me to the ground. It was a messy start to our partnership.

Camping brought new challenges: finding ample grazing, and tethering and hobbling Nicky. Kneeling by his front legs was the last place I wanted to be. I gladly laid my sleeping bag a few yards away on the edge of a small pine grove. It had been an exhausting first day and I soon fell asleep, lulled by the gentle clink-clank of the hobbles as my grumpy pony grazed.

In the morning I was almost surprised to find Little Nicky still with me. I packed up and we climbed a steep slope at the head of the valley, weaving a path through dense, gorse-like undergrowth. The rocky hilltop revealed a wide valley on the other side, dotted with scruffy brown herds and *gers* gleaming white in the sun. We made the tricky descent and I was soon waved over to a *ger* by a bustling mother figure. And so began the rough routine for the next week. Every time I passed near a *ger*, I was summoned in and offered a meal. Mongolia's summer diet is known as 'white food'. Besides the year-round mutton, there was seasonal cheese, yoghurt, bread, white tea (salted with rancid butter), curd biscuits, and *airag*. So ubiquitous and generous was the hospitality that the four days of food I set out with lasted for ten.

Herdsmen often spotted me with their binoculars and rode miles across the steppe to demand I visit with them. I soon learned the basics of horse care by observing a new trick or technique from everyone I met: tying different knots, whistling softly to encourage them to drink at streams, loosening saddle straps to allow the horse to take on more water, and temporarily hobbling with the lead rope.

Apart from his habit of regularly sitting down and refusing to continue, Nicky and I cooperated increasingly well. Except for a short gallop without the bags after pitching camp each evening, we went at a walk and covered at least twenty miles a day. I walked a quarter of the time at first. However, this grew to more than half the time after a week, as I wanted to conserve his strength and we walked at the same pace regardless.

My life as a nomadic horseman was full time but idyllic and uncomplicated. When not on the move I was busied with firelighting, cooking, eating, and dealing with Nicky. There was plenty of time for daydreaming though. As I was unburdened by a backpack, walking through the sweeping scenery was conducive to idle contemplations. The days were a medley of wide blue skies, rolling grass hills, small forests, glittering streams, and a warming glow of gold and purplish-red at sunrise and sunset.

The landscapes were truly vast. Mongolia is larger than Germany, Spain and France combined but with a population of just 3 million people, half of whom live in the capital. The rural Mongolians live much as their ancestors did 1,000 years ago. They ride their sturdy ponies, maintain their flocks, and wear the traditional *del*: a long-sleeved robe, usually belted with an orange silk sash. They eat the same food as the subjects of Genghis Khan did, live in the same style of tent, and adhere to many of the same customs. I felt I had slipped through time and enjoyed that feeling.

The lands I crossed were riotously alive with summer. Each footstep would disturb a dozen fat grasshoppers, and countless thousands of butterflies flapped clumsily around small wildflowers. Siberian chipmunks scurried through the grass and marmots bounded over it. Eating marmot is illegal in Mongolia because the creatures can harbour the bacteria responsible for the Black Death. The rule is often ignored, however, and there are small outbreaks of bubonic plague every few years.

Many herders warned me of the country's burgeoning wolf population and at night I often heard howls nearby. I lit a fire every evening and tethered Little Nicky close by. During the Soviet era there was an annual minimum hunting quota of two wolves per adult male, but since independence they have proliferated again. One evening, while a stoic herder rode alongside me, a black shadow skulked along a treeline fifty metres ahead. Its movements were confident yet wary. It stopped and stared at us. The man grunted in Russian, '*volk*'. I took the axe from my bag and we rode on.

I was wrenched from my slumber early one morning by the threatening crack of thunder. Five minutes later I was wet through, with my secondhand bivvy bag proven to be far from waterproof. The rain lasted ten hours and I plodded through the mud, shivering, while Nicky squelched along unhappily behind me. The evening sun finally chased the weather away to reveal the usual grassland spectacle of golden greens with the silver ribbons of streams glinting in the rich light.

The following day I had lunch with a young family while my kit dried in the sun. The mutton in a curdled milk soup tasted dangerously past its prime but, not wanting to offend, I ate it regardless. As I pushed on that afternoon my stomach started groaning and I could tell trouble was stirring. A smudge of colour on the far side of an open plain told me I was approaching the village of Zaamar. The plain looked about four miles wide, but Mongolia's enormity can be deceptive. It was ten miles before I reached the village, under another angry sky with forked lightning splintering all points of the compass. The tempest was nearly upon us and my stomach was still doing summersaults.

The wind whipped up and the rain sheeted in horizontally as I approached some construction workers. The men gestured for me to follow and we ran to a concrete building. I tied Nicky to a fence and rushed inside. Laughing, we all shook hands and they began wringing out soaked shirts. However, the running had catalysed the revolt in my stomach. I lurched towards the door with bile rising in my throat. I wrestled the fiddly lock for a few seconds, not registering the frantic knocking coming from outside.

I wrenched the door open, and rushed forwards just as the small, elderly woman on the other side did the same. Her head impacted with my stomach sending a spout of vomit from my mouth. I caught her terrified eyes for a second before shoving her aside and executing a few more heaves. The wind caught and carried my lunch wonderfully. Feeling slightly relieved, I went inside to apologise. The woman was shaken but sympathetic.

After dark, I took advantage of a lull in the storm to go outside and tether Nicky on some good grass. Having hammered the stake in with my axe, I rushed back to the building. Just outside the door I lost one of my flip-flops in a puddle of vomit-sprayed mud. I hopped up and down on one foot with my axe-hand raised for balance. At just that moment, two things happened: a brilliant flash of lightning rent the sky and the little old woman opened the door. Horrified, she screamed and fled into the night. She'll probably be telling the story of the projectile-vomiting, axe-wielding white man in the storm for years to come.

Beyond Zaamar there was an arid, desert-like area to cross, but still it stormed for part of each day. For the next month there were only a handful of days when I didn't encounter thunder and lightning. Burned-out, lightning-struck trees became a commonplace sight, their bare and blackened trunks listing sadly to one side.

Each night I fell asleep hoping it would be stay dry and trying to ignore the sound of mosquitoes whining past my exposed face. Despite this, the joy of being outdoors thrilled me daily. It felt good falling into a new routine of simplicity and exercise.

One morning I woke just after sunrise and lifted my head. Arching over my feet was a shining double rainbow. A perfect semi-circle of all-coloured brilliance stretching from the earth into the sky and sweeping gracefully back to the luminescently glowing grass. I stared in silence for as long as it lasted while the storm creating the effect approached. I still didn't move when it swept overhead and soaked me. There were no *gers* for miles around and it was 5 a.m. It was *my* perfect rainbow.

After two weeks I reached the provincial capital of Bulgan on the first day of Naadam, the annual festival of the 'Three Manly Sports'. This tournament of wrestling, horseracing and archery has existed since before the time of Genghis Khan. I walked Little Nicky to the small tournament ground on the south side of town. There were already several drunk men stumbling around topless in jeans and cowboy boots. Some were play fighting, others were actually fighting. I tethered Nicky on some good pasture in sight of the tiny grandstand and slung my axe through the front of my belt hoping to ward off any aggressive alcoholics.

Taking a seat, I watched the people slowly gather. Bulgan is a town of only 12,000 but hosts games for the whole province. Droves of people drifted in from the surrounding countryside by bus, minivan, motorbike, and horse. The elderly wore intricately pattered silk *dels*. The youth opted for denim, t-shirts, dresses, and hot pants. Children darted around shooting at each other with toy AK-47 rifles. A general holiday atmosphere prevailed.

The proceedings were relaxed and disorganised to the point of hilarity. Several bottle-wielding drunks wandered accidentally through the opening procession, scratching bare bellies as they went. The performers in traditional costumes of Buddhist demons got too hot so took of their masks and sprawled on the grass panting. The man on the PA system was slurringly drunk and the dancers were wonderfully out of time. I thoroughly enjoyed the whole atmosphere.

Wrestling was the first event. Most of the men had the signature Mongolian stoutness. A few were muscular, a couple were obese, and some were beanpole teenagers as young as fourteen. They wore small, embroidered pants of red or blue, knee-high boots, and patterned sleeves joining across their backs and rope-tied across their chests. Before and after each round they all performed the *devekh*, a traditional, eagle-inspired dance with circling and arm flapping that has its origin in shamanistic ritual.

Four fights happened at a time, each consisting of one round, with the first to be forced off their feet losing. Some bouts lasted for less than a minute and some lasted half an hour. Men of eighteen stone sometimes faced boys of less than half that. The audience chatted happily among themselves, often seeming more interested in their bottles of homebrew.

Afternoon saw the archery taking place, with men and women in traditional silk garb firing arrows from wooden bows at a target of wood blocks seventy-five metres away. Their accuracy was impressive but didn't draw a big crowd. This was followed by horseracing. About fifty boys and a couple of girls aged under twelve sped off bareback on the biggest, fastest, strongest horses in the province. After a full-speed gallop of twelve miles, an approaching dust cloud heralded their return. The riders blazed across the line and were met with rapturous applause; the winning horse's owner won a minivan, with the first few runners up securing large cash prizes.

The day's events were over by mid-afternoon and the crowds began a long, loud night of revelry, but Nicky and I left town and climbed a hill to camp. The second day saw the goat anklebone tossing competition, exclusively for elderly men, and the wrestling finals. Another minivan was awarded to the bull-like winner and another night of heavy drinking followed. I retreated to my hilltop once more with an unusually contented Nicky, who had done nothing but graze for two days.

Heading out of Bulgan, I followed a braided trail of tyre tracks for half a day before turning north. I had seen a 100-mile 'short cut' running along a river on the map. The narrow, overgrown valley was deserted, and for good reason. Herders would have been mad to graze their livestock among the tenacious horseflies and twenty-four-hour mosquitoes living by the river. Nicky was plagued day and night, growing more agitated and shakier each morning.

We often had to cross the frigid, knee-deep river and I walked mostly barefoot, glad for the cushioning of waist-deep grass. Despite the trials of the wild valley, it was an unkempt paradise. There were vivid wildflowers of red, blue, purple, and yellow, birds of prey wheeled overhead, and groves of birch trees oozed mint-scented sap.

After five itchy days I was relieved to exit the valley and reach Khutag-Öndör. I had emailed Sancho from Bulgan and we had arranged to meet in the small village. Our plan was to continue the journey together using Nicky purely as a packhorse. I was rarely riding him by that point, preferring to walk instead.

Khutag-Öndör's inevitable cluster of feckless drunks were already deep in their cups when I arrived mid-morning. They began following us and taunting Little Nicky. One threw a crushed beer can while others shouted and swung their arms around his face, trying to break his indifference. I tied Nicky to a sturdy wooden post outside the only shop and went into buy supplies. Within two minutes he had wrenched the post from the dirt and bolted. I spent twenty minutes racing after him, the drunkards' laughter ringing in my ears. I was thankful when Sancho arrived and we hurriedly left the village.

Sancho quickly got into the swing of things and we passed the long walking hours getting to know each other. Perhaps the only teetotaler in Mongolia, he had recently graduated in architecture and was now drifting across Asia with the vague plan of ending up in New Zealand. We had very different areas of knowledge and took turns to deliver mini-lectures.

We progressed north to the fringe of the great boreal forest that stretches unbroken from the Pacific to the North Atlantic via the breadth of Siberia. Each night we camped among trees and made a smoky fire with sappy pine branches to keep the insects off. In the mornings we rekindled the fire to toast bread. We entered another remote area and saw very few people. On my map there was a dotted line along a mid-sized river avoiding habitation for at least a week of walking. We had just about enough food and so made our way into the valley.

It soon became clear that the dotted line was a winter route: simply the river surface when frozen over. We found ourselves battling through dense undergrowth with yet more round-the-clock mosquitoes. Being bitten throughout the day was tough, but seeing the pests bloating on Nicky's belly, hundreds at a time, was doubly difficult.

For several days we crossed rushing, waist-deep waters, circumnavigated vast, lightning-felled trees, and coaxed Nicky along sharp, dangerous ridges climbing steep mountainsides above the river. There was no one to be seen, but we saw bear prints, occasional snakes, and a few wild gazelles.

We pulled long, exhaustive days and were down to half rations of plain pasta by the time we reached a village. Zerleg turned out to be little more than ten cabins with sleepy inhabitants and no shop. Thankfully a small family interrupted their cheese-making to feed us and sell us enough food to reach the next town. A small, fox-like dog followed us from the village and was quickly absorbed into our gang. We named the snow-white creature Albi. She slept by my side at night and stalked grasshoppers while we walked.

The four of us continued through sweet smelling pine forests. Nicky had become a calm, obedient horse, content with his role in our operation, and we had developed a slick routine, taking great pleasure in the simple yet arduous lifestyle. We drank river water and ate plain bread.

On a heat-hazed afternoon we caught our first glimpse of Lake Khövsgöl, the 100-mile-long freshwater jewel in Mongolia's forested northern crown. We walked around the southern shore to Khatgal, a dowdy tourist hub from where groups set out on guided horse treks. We ate and rested for a couple of days while I found a buyer for Nicky. However, we decided to walk a few more days along the lakeside before returning and selling him.

Travelling light enough to take turns in riding Little Nicky, we hugged the shore and swam often. It was the perfect swan song for my time with Nicky. We had walked the equivalent of London to Berlin across vast, fenceless tracts of the most naturally beautiful country I knew. I felt a hard-won closeness between the stubborn little pony and me. Sancho had grown fond of him too.

On the last night before returning to Khatgal we camped in a forest clearing, talking by the fire until midnight. I padlocked the hobbles above Little Nicky's front hooves before crawling into my sleeping bag under a vivid full moon. My friend was nearby, my horse was seven yards from me, my dog was curled at my feet, and my mind was at ease.

Sancho woke me at 1 a.m. saying simply, 'Nicky's gone.' His tether was untied. We sprang into action, hurtling off in different directions to scour the area. After two hours of running through the moonlit forest, with cooking knife drawn and Albi at my side, I returned to the fire defeated. I had found the lock-picked hobbles. Nicky had been rustled.

It was a hard pill to swallow hours from the end of our journey but I couldn't complain about the wonderful and varied experience I had had with Little Nicky. Mongolia's wilderness had humoured me for several weeks and it now unceremoniously spat me out: bug-bitten and robbed, but happy. It was time to remount my bicycle.

SIX

RACING

I had to crack on. It was my job to crack on. It may have been the most happy-go-lucky job in the world, but I still had to see it through.
- Tom Freemantle, *Johnny Ginger's Last Ride*

With sadness, we left Albi with a friendly herder and boarded a bus to the capital. The driver was drunk from the outset and his wheezing vehicle was crowded with people perched on plastic drums of *airag* in the aisle. For thirty-five hours, the bald-tyred bus bounced and bumped along dirt tracks. I lost count of the number of times we broke down.

My three days in Ulaanbaatar were flat out. I washed and repaired kit, sold horse gear, collected Old Geoff from Dashkar, and hurriedly prepared him for the road ahead. With my Mongolian visa's expiry fast approaching, I had to work out my route to Kazakhstan.

Mongolia and Kazakhstan together span over 3,500 miles from east to west. They almost meet in the middle but are narrowly separated by a twenty-five mile stretch of Russia–China border. I would have to transit through one of these two countries. My first choice was Russia but the embassy rejected my visa application. I hurriedly forged the requisite flight and hotel bookings for a Chinese transit visa and an old colleague in Beijing drew up a fake letter of invitation. The visa was granted and I boarded the long bus back to Lake Khövsgöl.

I started riding on my twenty-fifth birthday with a daunting race ahead of me. I hadn't cycled in almost nine months but the looming visa deadline didn't allow for a gentle reintroduction. I had only twelve days to ride 900 miles. During the eighteen months it took me to pedal 18,000 miles on my journey to Beijing, I had aimed for sixty miles a day on sealed roads. I now required a daily average of seventy-five on a series of dusty, sandy, rocky trails. As ever in Mongolia, the numerous tyre tracks tangled in and out of one another, splaying all across the landscape. Using my compass I did my best to keep a direct westward route.

The going was slow; I struggled to top six miles in an hour and so often rode through all twelve hours from dawn to dusk. I allowed only thirty minutes for lunches and occasional five-minute water breaks. The previous three months of walking suddenly seemed leisurely as I tried to ignore the pain where my formerly leathern buttocks strove to redevelop their thick skin. I forbade myself from even considering stopping to camp each evening until shadows had pooled heavily in the ruts on the tracks I followed and the sun was nearly lost. Every night was colder than the last, and in my familiarly cramped tent I enjoyed great unbroken slabs of black, dreamless sleep.

Mongolia's scenery continued to stun me, but I largely kept my eyes focused on the rutted tracks, promising myself rest in China. There were daily knee-deep river crossings with icy, rushing water and on the fourth day the path plunged into a more formidable river. It was chest-deep in the centre and had a frightening strength. It took four return journeys to carry my kit across. I bore each bag on my head, half-swimming, half-skipping across the river's uneven bed of rocks. Each crossing swept me a hundred metres downstream.

A couple of miles on I saw a *ger* and dried myself by the stove of a young couple. I first mistook them for siblings as they were both about sixteen years old but then I noticed their slim silver wedding bands.

A shimmering turquoise band appeared on the horizon. Uvs Nuur is a salt lake the size of Samoa that freezes over for seven months of the year. Keeping it to my right and watching the snow-dusted Altai Mountains rise over the opposite horizon, I pedalled doggedly towards the dowdy city of Ulaangom. When I arrived several spokes were broken and my dust-coated, oil-starved chain was grinding loudly. I found a cheap hotel, tended to Old Geoff, and slept for twelve hours.

In the morning I ate breakfast with a German professor of modern Mongolian history who had been visiting the country for twenty years. Her summary of the nation's social trajectory was depressing.

'Alcoholism is crippling this country. And there's a free-for-all land grab. There were no fences here only a few years ago but now people are greedily building them all over the country, staking unfounded claims. It's like the American Wild West. All this land is supposed to be common. It's ancestral land, but only in the sense that everyone's ancestors used to share it.'

'I read that Mongolia had the world's fastest growing economy last year,' I said.

'Yes,' she replied, 'the economy is technically "booming" because of foreign investment in mining. A huge gold and copper mine has opened in the Gobi and has almost doubled the GDP. But, of course, the foreign money coming in has led to corruption. This was a Soviet nation after all. None of the nomads see a pfennig of it but they hear fabulous stories of wealth. So, they move to the towns and cities hoping for work, but there is none, and they lose their traditional lifestyle. It's getting really serious. The culture is disappearing and Mongolia is in social crisis.'

As the professor finished speaking, the waitress delivered a second bottle of vodka to four men at the next table. It was 8.30 a.m.

I rode south on a gravel road that plunged through twelve knee-deep rivers in three hours. Some calculations that morning persuaded me of the need to catch a lift for some distance to reach the border in time, as I had fallen short of the requisite seventy-five miles a day.

Late afternoon brought the approach of a flatbed lorry, the first vehicle on the road in eight hours. I waved the driver down and he agreed to take me 100 miles to Khovd for £3.

We climbed into mountains in darkness and I was deposited early the next morning with more rugged roads to contend with.

On the second-last day of my visa I reached a Chinese-built tarmac road. I pedalled until long after sunset before slumping into my sleeping bag for four hours. The pre-dawn chill forced me to ride fast through the half-light and the immaculate road helped my flight. I wound down from the mountains onto the fringe of the Gurbantünggüt Desert with the support of a steady tailwind. I had covered the 140 miles to the border by late afternoon, rushing across no-man's land with minutes to spare before the Chinese side closed for the day. Half a mile inside China I pitched my tent in the dying light: too tired to eat, too tired to think.

I woke to a stifling tent. The sun was already high and a cock was crowing. During three months of travel in Mongolia I hadn't heard or seen a single chicken. I looked out and saw everywhere the signs of Chinese industriousness. The slim trickle of river I had followed on the dry, uninhabited Mongolian side of the border had been turned into an extensive series of irrigation channels. A mandarin grove nearby heralded the triumph of the Chinese over the desert's aridity.

I ate breakfast slowly, greedily squelching juicy mandarin segments between my teeth. The tension drained from my body. I could now pick my pace and enjoy the ride. The race was over.

The days were warm, the cool nights were dry and I slept under the stars once more. People were exceptionally surprised to see a westerner. Few foreigners visit the far north of Xinjiang Province and the police checked my passport at least twice a day. After three months of Mongolia's lamentable diet with almost no fresh produce, I revelled in the excellent and varied Chinese cuisine. In the first town I went to the first restaurant I could find, hailed the waiter, and pointed at the plate of the closest person to me. I was soon brought a vast pile of noodles topped with vegetables fried in oil, garlic and chilli. I ate two platefuls which a friendly policeman who had come to check my papers insisted on paying for.

After a couple of days the hub on my rear wheel gave out. It had lasted for over two years but had come to the end of its natural life. The wheel wobbled wildly from side to side, the chain shifted gear every quarter pedal stroke, and the tyre rubbed hard against the frame. I was stranded in the desert with an unrideable bike and a thirty-mile backtrack to the nearest town.

The road was busy enough, with a vehicle roughly every minute. I stood unsheltered in 30°C heat trying to wave down motorists with my broken wheel detached and displayed to exhibit my predicament. In two hours not a single car stopped. Many people waved and smiled, or even slowed down to get a better look as they passed. Some even took photos but none offered to help. Eventually a policeman pulled over to check my passport. He had got into his car to leave before I managed to persuade him to give me a lift. He made a call and I was soon conveyed to Fuyun police station in a convoy of five police cars.

Fuyun was another homogenous collection of buildings plopped out of the government's template for a modern Chinese town: a pleasantly spaced spread of state-owned banks and shopping malls with the nascent tree-lined Irtysh River flowing through on its 2,600-mile journey to join the Ob en route to the Arctic Ocean. I found Fuyun's only bicycle repairman with a small trolley of parts. While waiting for him to patch an old man's puncture, I watched an attractive young woman nearby casually roasting a pig's head with a blowtorch. The mechanic said he could build a new wheel and showed me a collection of secondhand parts. I left him to it for the afternoon and wandered around the city. He had a triumphant grin when I returned. He held up the 'new' wheel by its axle and spun it to show there was no warping from side to side. However, it was absurdly egg-shaped in the other direction with the diameter varying by over two centimetres. The mechanic didn't see this as a problem and was proud of his work.

The next 160 miles were extremely uncomfortable, with an abrupt bump for every wheel revolution. I entered Burqin with saddle sores and quickly sought refuge in a fancy mountain bike shop. The charming, underworked brothers running the place greeted me like a long-lost friend and took me under their wing. Through a translation website they asked how they could help. I typed into the computer that 'my wheel is egg-shaped ... and it hurts my eggs'. When the translation appeared, they laughed harder than the joke deserved. The brothers replaced my wheel with good quality parts at factory cost and gave my bike a full service.

I spent the day eating and working with my new friends in the shop. We went for dinner at a night market and ate the local speciality of barbecued fish. They ordered round after round of beer and then offered me their sofa for the night.

In the morning I rode away on a rejuvenated bicycle with functioning gears. The miles felt effortless and I camped just short of the Kazakhstan border. About eighty miles to the south lay the 'pole of inaccessibility' – the world's remotest point of land from any coastline, 1,644 miles from the nearest ocean.

The border was chaotic. Busloads of ethnic Kazakhs and Mongols lugging unwieldy boxes of cheap Chinese products jostled with coachloads of white Kazakhstani tourists[1] with bulging bags of souvenirs.

I was directed away from the bustle and held in a room for two hours. Kazakhstan's immigration officials studied my passport while customs searched my bags repeatedly. They tried to read the crabbed handwriting in my journal and scrolled through hundreds of photos on my camera. They half-heartedly accused me of being an active journalist – a grave accusation for a foreigner travelling on a tourist visa in

---

[1] *Kazakh* denotes an ethnic type indigenous to the region within, but not limited to, the borders of modern-day Kazakhstan. Whereas *Kazakhstani* denotes any citizen of Kazakhstan, whether ethnically Kazakh or Russian or Chinese or Uzbek or even Korean. The same distinction is true of *Kyrgyz* and *Kyrgyzstani*, *Uzbek* and *Uzbekistani*, etc.

a former Soviet Republic.

Finally cleared, I wheeled my bike out of the immigration building where a young soldier manning the gate stopped me.

'Passport!' he barked. I was exasperated, handing it over with a surly snort. He pretended to check the document before shaking me warmly by the hand.

'Welcome to Kazakhstan, Mr British!' he said in English.

'Oh. Well, umm … thank you, Mr Kazakh!' I replied.

SEVEN

GOLDEN TEETH

Every day on a bike trip is like the one before – but it is also completely different, or perhaps you are different, woken up in new ways by the mile. If anything, the world grew more inscrutable the longer I looked at it, and the less focused I was on the brute mechanics of pedalling – aching legs and lungs, miles covered and miles to come – the more awake I could be to the world around me, its ordinary wonders.
  - Kate Harris, *Lands of Lost Borders*

Riding from a recently developed region of China into a neglected corner of the former USSR was like crossing the Iron Curtain from west to east. The roads were broken, the buildings were lopsided and rotting, and the people wore clothes seemingly designed and manufactured in the 1980s.

I rode out of the desert basin and into a town called Zaysan just as a thunderstorm broke. Taking refuge in a half-built house, I met Lojnia, a mechanic with several gold teeth who was welding a bannister onto the staircase. It was his house, a weekend project that would eventually be his home and workshop. Lojnia quickly invited me to stay with his family in their nearby flat. I followed his car through a heavy downpour and soon found myself in a hot shower with a dinner of boiled vegetables waiting for me. Lojnia's five sons, all under eight years old, crawled all over me with riotous giggles while Disney cartoons dubbed into Russian flickered on an antique television.

As I rode on I observed Kazakhstan's mixture of eastern and western faces. In every town were billboards bearing posters of Nursultan Nazarbayev, the popular dictator-cum-president since Kazakhstan had gained independence from the Soviet Union. He visited schools and sat astride a horse and inspected a wheat field while holding the hand of a young girl. The benign-looking elderly man had almost chanced upon his premiership.

Kazakhstan and the other four Central Asian states were all wildly unprepared for the independence that was thrust upon them. In December 1991 Russia, Belarus and Ukraine signed the Belavezha Accord that officially broke up the Soviet Union and created the Commonwealth of Independent States (CIS). None of them had ever been true nation states and had existed under the Russian aegis since Tsarist conquest in the nineteenth century. Equally, none of the new inadvertent 'founding fathers', Nazarbayev among them, had fought for independence and won the high regard of their people. They were drawn from the Soviet elite and had enjoyed positions of minimal power with little to no responsibility.

Coming from humble roots, Nazarbayev's ascent was an archetypal Soviet story. He politicked his way through the Communist Party ranks throughout the 1980s and won the first Kazakhstan presidential elections in 1990: not a huge achievement as he was the only candidate. After independence Kazakhstan remained a close ally of Russia and prospered compared to its Central Asian neighbours, but this was due to its wealth of natural resources rather than good management. Nazarbayev grew to act increasingly like a despotic eighteenth-century khan and allegations of corruption and human rights abuses swirled thickly about him. He was even rumoured to bath daily with young virgins to maintain his vigour and virility.[2]

Cars regularly pulled over to see what I was doing. Grinning, gold-toothed men greeted me beside the clapped-out cars of a crumbled communist empire: the Lada Niva. I have always thought the profile shape of this ubiquitous Soviet vehicle looks like a child's crayon drawing of a car. Collaborating with

[2] In April 2015, Nazarbayev held another sham election where he won 98 per cent of the vote and Kazakhstan's record of never having held a free and fair election remained intact. Much to everyone's surprise he stood down in March 2019 but the new president, Kassym-Jomart Tokayev, is widely believed to be a puppet leader with strings firmly pulled by Nazarbayev. Since his abdication, the Kazakhstan parliament has chosen to rename the capital Nur-Sultan after the former president.

Fiat, Lada was the Soviet Union's only automobile manufacturer. The Niva is essentially a reinforced Fiat 124 built to withstand the USSR's harsh winters and ruinous roads. It looks something like a rusting seventies refrigerator perched awkwardly on wheels.

When chatting with the friendly motorists I enjoyed exercising my fledgling Russian language, having listened to audio lessons for the past few months. Older Mongolians had snatches of Russian but spoke little better than I did. In Kazakhstan, however, Russian was the lingua franca and many people spoke it gratifyingly slowly.

I followed a gravel road over a low mountain ridge and down onto the arid, featureless Kazakh steppe. Occasional ancient Scythian burial mounds known as *kurgans* dotted the otherwise flat plains. It was the beginning of September and the steppe grasslands were tinder dry after the long summer. Fires often broke out, usually after careless drivers threw cigarette butts out of their windows.

While camping one night I saw an orange glow spreading in the distance. It was downwind and I was exhausted so I ignored it and went to sleep. The next morning I found the fire had died, but not before creeping to within 200 metres of me. I rode through a ten-mile wasteland of blackened, scorched earth and acrid-tasting air imagining what might have happened had it spread a little further.

After 600 miles of Kazakh roads I approached Taldykorgan, the first reasonably large city. On the outskirts I met a lorry driver called Nurli who invited me to his home. I stayed three nights with him, his two sons, his daughter, and his granddaughter. Nurli was a weathered man in his mid-fifties with an irrepressible grin and more gold teeth than white. He had lost his wife to cancer five months earlier and fussed over me paternally during my stay. When he saw the battered appearance of Old Geoff he was adamant that I needed a new bicycle. I had to stand in front of his car to stop him driving straight into the city centre to buy me one.

In the evenings we drank beer and ate *shashlik* –

barbecued meat on kebab skewers. Nurli was very worried about my onward travel plans.

'Where do you go after Taldykorgan?' he asked.

'Almaty,' I replied.

'Good. It's a beautiful city. It was once our capital. Where after that?'

'Bishkek in Kyrgyzstan.'

'No! This is a bad thing. A bad place with very bad people. The Kyrgyz are not like us Kazakhs.'

'I'm sure I'll be fine, Nurli. After Kyrgyzstan I will go to Tajikistan and Uzbekistan.'

'No, no, no!' He looked genuinely shocked. 'This is worse. Too dangerous! No law. Life is worth nothing there. They will take your passport and make you build roads. This happened to my friend. Six months he was breaking earth with a pickaxe.'

'Are you sure?'

'Yes! Very sure! You must go to Almaty and take a plane back to your home. It is best. I can pay for your flight.'

'Thank you, Nurli. I'll think about it.'

Nurli introduced me to his friend's son-in-law, Igor, who studied in America and had set up an English language school. We ate steaks together in a silk-draped restaurant filled with affluent, golden-toothed diners. Igor was an ethnic Korean and told me how his grandparents ended up in eastern Kazakhstan. In the early nineteenth century there were growing farming and fishing communities of Koreans living in and around Vladivostok on Russia's Pacific coast, about eighty miles from the modern border of North Korea.

In the 1930s, the Soviets feared that Japanese spies would infiltrate Russia by hiding among the Koreans, so Stalin ordered that they all be deported from the coast. Almost 200,000 Koreans were moved to uninhabited areas of Kazakhstan and Uzbekistan. The transportation conditions were cramped and thousands died in transit. Those that survived the journey were dumped on an unfamiliar landscape with an inhospitable climate and a struggle to adapt. Almost a quarter died from exposure and starvation.

Igor's grandfather, along with many others whimsically suspected of disloyalty, was then sent to a gulag in Russia's far east. He spent eight years doing forced labour on the infamous Kolyma Highway, also known as the Road of Bones as those who died building it were buried in the road's foundations. Incredibly he survived and made his own way back to his wife in Kazakhstan.

One evening Nurli cornered me to talk about circumcision. He had just showered and wore only a small, pink towel.

'Charlie, how long can you fuck for?'

'Umm … with or without beer?' I asked evasively.

'No beer!'

'Err…I don't know. I don't own a watch,' I said, yet more evasively.

'Me? One time is one hour. Bang, bang, bang, BANG!' He pounded a palm on top of a fist with a mischievous, gold-toothed grin.

'OK. Umm … well done.'

'You?' He pointed at my crotch and then at the baby pink colour of his towel. 'Ooooh!' He winced with mock over-sensitivity. 'Me?' He stood up and pulled out his penis. 'Nothing.' He flicked its dark brown end several times. 'Nothing! Ha ha ha!'

'Good for you,' I said uncertainly.

'So … Charlie, I can cut you now?' He asked as though it were a grave honour.

'No, thank you, Nurli. I think I'll be alright.'

'Our secret,' he whispered. 'No problem. Just five minutes.'

'If I change my mind, I promise to call you first.'

Still sporting a foreskin, I left Taldykorgan after a crushing bear hug from Nurli. It was only a two-day cycle to Almaty, Kazakhstan's capital until 1997. As I approached the city, the white wall of the Ala-Too mountains towered ever-higher behind it. The ridge soars to almost 5,000 metres in places and marks the border with Kyrgyzstan.

Almaty was a clean, expensive, modern city. Almost half the residents were Slavs and it felt like a slice of Europe grafted onto the fringe of the Central Asian steppe. Expensive cars politely waited for pedestrians to cross tree-lined streets, and beautiful young people sipped espressos in swanky, artsy cafés. Hotels were dear so I camped on the bed of a dried-up lake near the city centre. A soldier moved me on early the next morning so I took to the road again, tracing the foot of the mountains eastward.

At lunchtime I pulled into a roadside café to find two loaded touring bicycles, one of them a tandem. Three faces peered at me through the window. Juergan, a German, was about to finish a six-week cycling holiday. Keith and Tamar, a British couple, were on a meandering journey from London to Australia. They were also heading for Bishkek, Kyrgyzstan's capital, so we continued in convoy. It was a warm, sunny, still day, and I enjoyed the novelty of conversation while pedalling.

We soon met two more cyclists coming the other way. Mary and Peter from Guernsey were headed east, already a year into a round-the-world ride. We chatted under some trees for a while, exchanging tips and poring over maps. As we rode on, Juergan and I agreed that there was something particularly charming about the couple. They were both so vital and handsome, and clearly deeply in love. They had a bubbling energy and positivity equally admirable and enviable.

Camped on the steppe that night under another sparkling nightscape, we sat out until late sipping Kazakh vodka and Kyrgyz cognac and swapping stories from the varied roads we had ridden.

The border post was at a low pass through the hills and we descended easily to cool, leafy Bishkek. Within thirty minutes of entering the suburbs I was showered and drinking beers with some of the fifteen other cycle tourists staying in the guesthouse. I had met more cycle tourists in two days than over the previous two years.

Time blurred for me in Bishkek as I gathered four visas for my onward journey. I passed the days wandering the city and researching the road ahead. Each afternoon a shouted *adhan* (call to prayer) would blast from speakers of a mosque neighbouring the guesthouse. The pre-dawn *adhan*, however, was sung by a different, younger sounding *muezzin*. His voice was meek, hesitant and melodic as he recited the familiar Arabic words: 'God is great! God is great! There is no god but Allah. Mohammad is his messenger. Hurry to prayer. Hurry to prayer. Prayer is better than sleep…'

Half-asleep, I listened to it happily before slipping back into unconsciousness for another hour or two.

Evenings were spent with other cyclists over heaped plates of rice and warm glasses of cheap vodka. It was nice to finally spend time with some of the other people living the same odd existence as myself. Due to my unusual route I usually found myself seasonally out of sync with, or following less-pedalled paths than, the bulk of the scattered cycle-touring community.

Every year, a hundred or so Europeans leave home and ride east. They often have their sights set on China, Australia, or a round -the-world route with plane hops to Australia, New Zealand, and North America. Central Asia was a bottleneck for these slow travellers. The route through southern Asia was blocked by Myanmar's closed western border and the strict prohibition on independent travel through Tibet. The northern route entails a long and monotonous ride through Siberia made difficult by prohibitively short Russian visas.

The Central Asian 'Stan' republics have also become a cycle-touring destination in their own right, with many flying in for a summer of riding the Pamir Highway or one of the region's many other rugged routes. All of the tourists I met were awaiting either flights home or visas to leave mountainous Central Asia before winter set in. However, I had just arrived.

There was a heartening sense of community among us all. Cycling slowly across the world observing the patterns and rhythms of life in diverse places works wonders for quashing the ego. There was no sense of competition, nobody boasting. Whether people were on two-month summer adventures or gritty multi-year odysseys, there was a simple sense of comradeship that isn't present among all groups of tourists. We all knew how it felt to fight a headwind and want to quit. We all knew the sensation of shifting endlessly, trying to alleviate pressure on a saddle sore. We had all winced when smelling ourselves after several sweaty days without a wash. And we all knew the simple, protracted, hard-won emotional highs after a day-long mountain climb or a cold drink at the end of a week's desert crossing. I felt at home among this ragtag group, where sun-bleached clothes, astronomical meal portions, oil-stained right calves, bushy beards growing unchecked down necks, and outlandish stories were the norm.

After two weeks, I had a passport with all the visas I needed to reach Iran. September was drawing to a close, the other cyclists were dispersing, and it was time for me to move.

EIGHT

MOUNTAINS

For many years, I have been moved by the blue at the far edge of what can be seen, that colour of horizons, of remote mountain ranges, of anything far away. The colour of that distance is the colour of an emotion, the colour of solitude and of desire, the colour of there seen from here, the colour of where you are not. And the colour of where you can never go.
- Rebecca Solnit, *A Field Guide to Getting Lost*

I cycled east through farmland and began the 800-metre climb to Lake Issyk-Kul. Clouds gathered and rain fell as I approached the vast lake, wallowing between two 5,000-metre mountain ridges of the Tian Shan range. Under angry skies, the iron-grey waters looked cold and uninviting. However, Issyk-Kul is warmed by geothermal activity and the heat retention of its almost 700-metre depth prevents it from freezing, despite many months of harsh winter. I pitched my tent on the shore, stripped off and ran in.

During the Soviet era, the Russians used the lake as a naval testing site, trying out their latest submarines and other aquatic technologies. This continued after independence, but at the start of the twenty-first century Kyrgyzstan loosened its Russian ties and the country leased Manas airbase outside Bishkek to the United States Air Force as a launch platform for the war in Afghanistan. However, Kyrgyzstan hasn't leant entirely to the West. In 2008 the Russians leased over 2,000 acres around the Karabulan Peninsula at the eastern end of the lake for further naval testing, and India has also expressed interest in using the site for torpedo testing.

Besides being a military test site, Issyk-Kul was also a retreat for rich Communist Party members. I drifted past the abandoned remains of Soviet health resorts. The once-fashionable destinations were decaying, forlorn and forgotten. Everywhere there was crumbling concrete gradually exposing its rotting skeleton, a twisted jumble of rusted steel rods. A lifeguard's high chair leaned sadly to one side in a complex of boarded-up restaurants and hotels. Shards of window lay at the feet of shuttered shops, and paint peeled from gaudy murals on cold grey walls.

The road swept along the southern shore and through villages where roadside babushkas sunned themselves next to buckets of apples and walnuts for sale. Men straddled tiny donkeys and kids lined up for high-fives as I passed. The trees had adopted the regal colours of autumn and shed a flaming carpet onto the tarmac. The sky was clear, azure, vivid, and vast. The lake was a rich, dark blue and the mountain tops a brilliant white.

I turned away from the water onto a barely discernable track up an almost invisible ravine, which I cycled past twice before spotting. I imagined I was following a secret passage into the mountains. It was rough and steep: sandy in some places, rutted and rock-strewn in others. In my lowest gear I made painfully slow progress. After a while the ravine opened into a gaping valley with flocks grazing on Summer's last grass. The herders were wrapped up in thick woollen layers and wore balaclavas. They told me they were descending to warmer climes for winter and that I was a fool to be heading into the mountains.

The track wound back and forth across the pleasant valley as it climbed higher and higher. The sun was warming but when it set the temperature plunged with it, and my water bottles were thickly iced when I crawled from a frosted tent in the morning.

Towards the head of the valley a couple of 4x4s rattled past me. They soon returned, deeming the pass impassable. They said snow and ice had buried the road, which was dangerously steep and slippery at the best of times. Each vehicle offered me a lift back down but stubbornness drove me onwards and upwards.

The path further steepened and became covered in snow and ice. I began pushing my bicycle, struggling with its great weight on the slippery surface. I often didn't know if I was on a track or just pushing up the mountainside. Snowdrifts lounged across the way and the parallel stream had withered to a trickle between swollen banks of ice. My breath wheezed, my head ached dully and I had to stop every few yards to catch my breath. After seven hours of continuous labour and only eleven miles of progress I reached Ton Pass at a little over 4,000 metres. I had climbed 2,500 vertical metres from the lakeside. I wheeled Old Geoff between two miniature glaciers and an alpine valley came into view beyond them.

Layered up with clothes, I jolted down the rough track into the valley. A stream trickled along the valley floor, tilting ever so slightly downhill in its passage to eventually join some river or other on a journey to the either Indian or Arctic ocean. It was always hard to tell to which distant side of the continent water would fall from the high heart of Asia.

I camped above the snowline and used two sleeping bags for the first time since Tibet, two winters before. Besides a single stray yak, there wasn't an animal or a settlement in sight and my lofty surrounds glowed with patches of snow shining golden in the sinking sun.

I was invited into a yurt to warm up after a bracing river crossing the next morning. Yaks and sheep grazed outside, and a herd of horses grazed nearby, bigger and stronger looking than those in Mongolia. Maryn and her husband, Sovet-Bek, asked me questions over homemade bread, apricot jam and smetana (Russian sour cream) while my socks and shoes dripped dry by the stove. They were in the process of packing up their nomadic summer existence to descend to a village for the winter. They fretted about the inadequacy of my little tent and pleaded with me to turn back with them.

'We are late. Winter has started. Soon everywhere will be snow and ice.'

I tried my best to reassure them before pedalling on. A late-teen on a horse came and rode alongside me mid-afternoon. He asked to try riding Old Geoff. For the rest of the afternoon, Max freewheeled for the downhill stretches while I rode his handsome horse, Tita, and a whippet-like dog bounded alongside. While riding the big, obedient horse, I thought of Little Nicky: semi-wild and stubborn. I wondered where he might be. Probably picking at grass poking through the first snow, unaware and indifferent to his owner, past or present.

Max invited me to sleep at his home in the village of Uzun Bulak and we turned down a sidetrack. The way took us past a rusting Russian train carriage where a friendly old crone and her quick-eyed daughter served us tea. I had no idea how the carriage came to be stranded in the mountains over a hundred miles from the nearest rail track.

Uzun Bulak turned out to be a one-house village. We drank tea in Max's two-room home while a couple of puppies gambolled around our feet. He showed me family photos – faded images with unsmiling line-ups of awkward-looking people. He also showed me a photo of his six-month-old daughter, who his parents were unaware of. He was due to marry her mother soon but seemed reluctant at the prospect. Max lived alone in the mountains with his dogs and his horse and seemed to like it that way.

I woke in the morning to Max's face leaning over my spot on the floor.

'Snake idiot!' he said.

'Excuse me?' I asked, bleary eyed.

'Snake idiot!' he repeated.

'I don't understand.'

'*Snyeeeeg idyooooot.*' He was speaking Russian. Apparently it was snowing. 'Are you sure you want to go today?' he asked with a smirk. I peered out at the ankle-deep snow. Heavy flakes were still falling.

'It's not good for cycling,' I conceded.

'Stay here today. We will hunt the wolf. We will see his footprints in the snow.'

While I ate breakfast, Max carefully packed ten cartridges with gunpowder and shot. We both mounted Tita and set off in search of wolves. I sat behind the saddle on a thin scrap of blanket with my legs dangling free and the gun slung over my shoulder. Tita's spine ground uncomfortably against my tailbone. It was going to be a long day.

The snow-muffled silence was broken only by Tita's hooves. I flicked my eyes around constantly, scanning for the prowling black smudge of a wolf in the distance. But I saw none and Max seemed to lose interest quickly. He decided we would visit his friends instead. We trotted from valley to valley, stopping at several huts and yurts to drink vodka and discuss sheep. We returned to Max's house after dark with numb fingers and toes. It was still snowing when we sat down to boiled potatoes and another bottle of vodka.

The snow was shin deep by morning but had at least stopped falling for the time being. I thanked Max and pushed Old Geoff towards a small pass at the end of the valley. I floundered in the snow, slipping and falling as it got steeper. It took ninety minutes to cover the final mile before I could skid down into the next valley.

Fat flakes of snow began falling again and a blizzard formed. A family invited me into their ragged yurt where they had packed most things into wooden chests. These would be loaded onto the three camels sitting outside, nestling in the deepening snow. I drank tea, chatting with the babushka, while the short blizzard did its worst. A delicate gyre of snowflakes twisted down from a hole in the roof, melting before landing.

The sun appeared fleetingly late in the day and lured me back to the path. However, I was soon fighting through yet more snowfall in a narrow gorge with the glacial blue Naryn River running below me. The road was cut from the sheer rock walls and it was hard to find somewhere flat to camp.

When I woke in the morning my socks were frozen into flat boards and had to be stuffed down my pants for half an hour before I could pull them on. As I continued to descend the chill receded, and I happily left the snow behind. In a wide valley I passed a swastika-shaped forest on a distant hillside. It's believed to have been planted by German prisoners of war in the 1940s unbeknownst to their Soviet guards.

I rolled through the town of Naryn wearing a t-shirt in warm sunshine. The contrasts in a Central Asian day can be wild and disorienting. Soon I was rounding hairpin turns on a series of switchbacks that took me up and over a 2,800-metre pass. As at all road passes in former Soviet republics, the top was marked with a large concrete animal that had seen better days; this one was a crumbling eagle.

I wiggled down to another valley floor and camped among vibrant autumnal trees before starting yet another climb. As I neared the pass my stamina fizzled and I found a rock ledge to sleep on. Camped above 3,000 metres, I used snow to insulate my tent and put a bottle of hot water in the foot of my sleeping bag. The vista from my perch was spectacular and far reaching; a series of reddish-brown hills, stacked one behind the other, rose to mountains in the distance that later glowed white in the darkness.

Another long descent brought me to a hard-up family who invited me for a potato lunch in their yurt. They were dressed in layers of patchwork rags. The mother was two years my senior but looked closer to forty. She spoke little but smiled constantly while her five young children ran around the tent, laughing joyously. I slipped some banknotes under a pillow before leaving.

A little later I stopped at a fork in the road. Both gravel tracks looked identical and there were no signposts. I sat down and waited for an hour before a horseman arrived and set me on the right path. I cycled through apple orchards and walnut groves on my way down into the temperate Fergana Valley. The valley's fertile floor was a sun-kissed landscape of swaying, mid-harvest wheat fields.

I pedalled through the city of Jalalabad then had to make a forty-mile, three-sides-of-a-square detour around an awkward three-mile-wide piece of Uzbekistan projecting into its neighbour. When the Soviets moulded the Central Asian Soviet republics, they did so out of previously indistinct regions with complicated ethnic population spreads. The Kazakhs and the Kyrgyz were predominantly nomadic peoples but within their pasture lands there were cities with principally Uzbek and Tajik populations. Both Stalin and Lenin believed that 'backward peoples' could never attain socialism without a nationalist framework. Thus, their border drawing process involved trying to place the majority of Uzbeks within the newly defined Uzbekistan, Kazakhs within Kazakhstan, and so on. This resulted in farcically complicated borders in the Fergana Valley where Kyrgyzstan, Uzbekistan and Tajikistan meet. The confusingly zigzagging borders frequently double back on themselves and give mapmakers a headache. In Kyrgyzstan's territory there are two oddly shaped Tajikistan exclaves and five more Uzbekistan exclaves, one of which consists of just two diminutive villages with less than twenty square miles of land.[3]

During my detour round the jutting Uzbekistan territory I saw a billowing dust cloud a little way from the road with a small crowd gathered beside it. Scrambling down a slope and crossing a field, I discovered it was a game of kökbörü, known in surrounding countries as buzkashi. This sport is hard to describe but is loosely akin to rugby played on horseback. However, there are no boundaries and a recently decapitated goat is used in lieu of a ball. At the centre of the dust column were about a hundred horsemen all in a frenzy to get hold of the *buz* (the goat). They thrashed their mounts and often each other with small handmade whips. Every now and then, someone made a break from the mob and galloped towards an ill-defined goal. When a goal was scored, the scorer was presented with the prize of a carpet or a Chinese television. Some of the men wore homemade padded headgear and many had bloodied noses. There wasn't a woman in sight.

I stood with the crowd at what felt like a safe distance.

[3] There was a similarly strange case with the border between Bangladesh and the state of Assam in India after partition. There, among almost 200 exclaves, was the world's only 'third-order exclave': a piece of India within a piece of Bangladesh within a piece of India within Bangladesh. In 2015 the two countries exchanged the exclaves to simplify matters.

However, we frequently had to dart away as a scrum of snorting horses ploughed towards us. Before long I was offered a horse and asked to join in. I was unlikely to have another opportunity to play kökbörü in my life so I climbed into the saddle, my brain flooded with adrenalin and testosterone. Feeling conspicuous on a white horse shining with sweat, I drifted around the fringe of the violently seething throng. I had no real intention of actually getting involved. However, someone must have spotted the hesitant white man hanging back because suddenly the *buz* was plonked across my lap and the melee engulfed me.

The carcass had a mud-matted fleece and was unexpectedly hard and heavy. I looked up with horror as the frenzied horses and their indiscriminately whipping riders closed in on me. Someone must have whipped my horse's hind because he sprang into action and charged through a gap in the mob. After a few yards I had space enough to fling the headless corpse over my shoulder.

The crowd were amused by my unmanly conduct. I had to shake many hands and pose for many photos. A little group of men sitting in the shade of a tree invited me to drink beer with them. Ibek was getting married the next day and we toasted him several times. Someone walked over leading a limping horse. There was a deep gash on its right fetlock and the men took turns to hose the muddy wound down with their urine.

Ibek asked me to be the 'official photographer' at his wedding and we were soon loading my bike into a car to go and wash up for his bachelor party. While doing this, an intimidating man in a leather jacket and dark glasses approached. He had semi-Slavic features and barked curt questions at me in English.

'Who are you? What do you do here?'

'I'm a tourist. I'm going to this man's wedding.'

'Where are you going with your bike?'

'London.'

'No! Where *on* your bike?'

'Lon-don. I'm cycling to London."

'You go to Osh next, yes?'

'Yes.'

'Go now! You are not welcome here,' he commanded.

'Why? What's the problem?'

He said no more and stared impatiently at me. My new friends were silent, head's bowed. Ibek muttered 'secret police' in my ear. I said an apologetic farewell and good luck to Ibek and pedalled away.

NINE

HUBRIS

He lacked wisdom, and the only way for him to get it was to buy it with his youth; and when wisdom was his, youth would have been spent buying it.
- Jack London, *A Piece of Steak*

In Osh I lazed with a book and overate for a couple of days. As always, my weight was yoyoing wildly from week to week. Many kilogrammes were shed with each period of riding as I was simply unable to eat enough to replenish the calories burned by cycling all day and living outdoors in a cold climate. Whenever I found myself resting in a city I ate four or five large meals a day and still felt hunger.

Osh was a conservative and predominantly Uzbek city ranged around a rocky outcrop known as Suleiman's Throne, where local legend places Mohammad in prayer. The manager of the hostel I stayed in was an Uzbek and an anti-Semite. He spouted vitriolic doctrine and conspiracies about 'the Zionists'. He also ranted about the government marginalising his fellow Uzbek citizens in Kyrgyzstan.

Walking around town, it was easy to distinguish the Uzbeks, who had noticeably fairer skin and fuller beards than the more eastern-looking Kyrgyz. The city seemed calm but had been the site of fierce ethnic violence just two years earlier during Kyrgyzstan's 2010 'Melon Revolution'. Kyrgyz nationalists resented growing Uzbek political representation and Uzbek prominence in local business. In a week of rioting, looting, rape and torture, over 1,000 people, mostly Uzbeks, were killed. Kyrgyzstan's authorities were accused of doing nothing to protect their Uzbek citizens and are even reported to have taken part in the anti-Uzbek attacks.

I continued south on a new Chinese-built tarmac road that took me up a 2,400-metre pass where the temperature dropped below -10°C. I then shadowed a turquoise river running through red mountains punctuated by quaint villages. In a district still bearing Lenin's name, I cycled through a village named after Yuri Gagarin, the first man in space. Although the settlements and the people were distinctly Kyrgyz, the traces of a century of Russian rule were all around. Samovars steamed in roadside teahouses, all writing was in Cyrillic, and every settlement had a memorial to the twenty-something millions of USSR fatalities during the 'Great Patriotic War' against the Nazis.

From the snowbound 3,600-metre height of my final mountain pass in Kyrgyzstan I descended to Sary Tash. The windswept outpost village sits on a crossroad between Tajikistan, China, and Kyrgyzstan. The Kyzylsu River flows past, describing the bed of the enormous Alay Valley on its journey to join the Oxus in Afghanistan. Across the Alay is the Tajik border, where the Pamir mountains stand tall and imposing, dwarfing the little village. Just 150 miles to the east, in China, was Kashgar from where I'd set out on an illegal crossing of Tibet two years earlier. My loop of Asia was starting to close in on itself.

At a reduced price, I stayed in a guesthouse that was closed up for winter. There was no heating and I used an axe to hack through several inches of ice in the water butt. Inside, my breath billowed visibly into the frigid air.

I initially planned to cycle the Pamir Highway; the famed road running through the mountainous Gorno-Badakhshan region of Tajikistan that separates China, Afghanistan and Kyrgyzstan. It was the final frontier in Britain and Russia's 'Great Game' where marching armies and mapmaking spies carved away at Central Asia until all was colonised. The special permit required to visit the area was usually easy to obtain. However, when I'd arrived in Bishkek a number of the cyclists had told me of the events in Badakhshan's capital, Khorog, earlier that summer.

In late July a Tajik general was pulled out of his car and stabbed. Tajikistan's government blamed a local warlord, troops were sent in, and fighting started. After a couple of hours there was a one-hour ceasefire to evacuate civilians. During this short window, a convoy of about twenty western cyclists pedalled nonchalantly out of the town while soldiers reinforced their positions and helicopter gunships hovered overhead. The Pamir Highway had been closed to foreigners ever since and I would have to take a more direct, northerly route through to Dushanbe, the Tajik capital.

I turned west on a road following the northern boundary of the Pamir mountains where winter was well advanced. There were excellent views of the intimidating peaks throughout the day. I camped near Peak Lenin (7,134 metres) and, after dinner, I went for a short jog up and down the deserted road to warm up before bed. A beautiful moonset gave way to a startlingly clear night sky and plummeting temperatures. I was glad to zip up my two sleeping bags; my two-litre water bottle was frozen solid by the morning.

The border post I headed towards was usually closed to foreigners but due to the Pamirs being off limits the crossing was rumoured to be open. I arrived at the Kyrgyz side and was lead into a room where a grumpy army officer made phone calls and asked me curt questions before saying the Tajik side of the border was closed. I lied that I had called their embassy in Bishkek and been assured it was open. Grudgingly, the man stamped me out of Kyrgyzstan and I cycled a six-mile gravel mountain track through no-man's land with a deadly drop just a metre away.

Having heard stories of Tajikistan's endemic corruption, especially among police and military, I emptied my wallet, hiding all money in my sock except for a crisp $10 note. This I put in my back pocket for a bribe if I received resistance and the border was 'closed'. I approached the border post trying to look carefree and was greeted with smiles. The officer in charge gave me an apple and a bunch of grapes to eat while he processed my passport details and stamped me into the country.

'Welcome to Tajikistan,' he said in heavily accented English. I chuckled at my misguided suspicions as I stuffed the cash back into my wallet that evening.

I took a casual four days to ride to the capital, Dushanbe, that was formerly known as Stalinabad. The road, also new and Chinese-built, undulated alongside a river with almost no traffic. The country was visibly poorer than Kyrgyzstan and the villages were predominantly mudbrick houses with haystacks heaped on the roofs and grubby-faced children, often barefoot, running between them. There was no electricity during daylight hours.

The people had a Persian appearance and their dress was traditional and conservative. While the Kazakhs, Kyrgyz, Turkmens, and Uzbeks are all ethnically Turkic in origin, the Tajiks are an Iranian people and speak a Persian dialect. The old men wore thick, emerald-coloured cloaks, patterned *kallapushes* (skullcaps), and long white beards. The women wore dark waistcoats, skirts, and floral headscarves. The young men opted for fake leather jackets and tight jeans which often, I suspected, were manufactured for women. Without fail, everyone stopped what they were doing and greeted me as I passed. Most placed their right hand on their chest, smiled and said *salam alaikum*, meaning 'peace be with you'.

A lean, friendly faced man called Momei invited me to his home for lunch. It was the day after the Eid al-Adha feast, which celebrates Abraham's willingness to sacrifice his son, Isaac, in obedience to God.[4] In Momei's house was a table spread with leftovers. I sat with him, his brother, and his sons feasting on mutton soup, flatbread, sweets, halva, and fruit. I was not allowed to meet his wife and young daughters, who ate in the kitchen. However, Momei repeatedly insisted that I should return the following year with my family to share his Eid feast again.

Later that afternoon a young boy calmly aimed his toy pistol at me while I toiled up a hill. As I drew level he said in

---

[4] In Islam, Abraham is known as Ibrahim and Isaac is known as Ishaq. Eid al-Adha is not to be confused with Eid al-Fitr, which marks the end of Ramadan.

English with cold intonation 'I love you' before pulling the trigger and pantomiming a recoil.

In the town of Garm I received my first dose of the Tajik government's propaganda. There were roughly a hundred roadside posters of the president, Emomali Rahmon, inspecting Chinese-built roadworks, laughing with schoolchildren, and standing in a wheat field with a solemn expression on his face and a loaf of bread in his hands. There was one particularly fetching poster of Rahmon and Vladimir Putin walking down a tree-lined country lane, hand in hand. They were almost exactly the same as the equivalent posters of Nazarbayev in Kazakhstan.

In the unstable first year following independence, Tajikistan had six different presidents, one of whom lasted less than two weeks. Rahmon took power in early 1992 after a childhood of peasantry, a stint in the navy, a period working as an electrician, and several years as a Soviet bureaucrat. He rode out the civil wars of the 1990s and gradually created an authoritarian regime by removing opposition, rigging elections, and changing the constitution to allow himself unlimited terms in office. He has also kept an eye to the future by enshrining in the constitution his lifelong immunity from prosecution.

I arrived in the capital, Dushanbe (formerly Stalinabad), two days later and pitched my tent under a walnut tree in the courtyard of the peaceful Adventurer's Inn hostel. That night I met Richard and Callie, a beanpole British man and a dark, beautiful American woman. They were also cycle tourists but had left their bikes in Bishkek a month earlier. Just that evening they had returned from Afghanistan and seemed exhausted, frazzled and shaken.

Callie and Richard had decided to visit the ravaged nation after meeting a Canadian–American couple, Joshua Boyle and Caitlan Coleman, who were also planning on going. The four of them collected visas in Bishkek and then travelled down to Dushanbe together. Callie and Richard continued south and crossed the border a day before the others. The four exchanged contact details and loosely planned to meet up either in Afghanistan or back in Dushanbe.

After two or three weeks off the grid, hiking in the Wakhan Corridor (a narrow strip of Afghan territory bordering China and separating Tajikistan from Pakistan), Callie and Richard got to Kabul during Eid al-Adha and checked their emails. The Taliban claimed to have kidnapped a pair of western tourists and both the British and American governments had been frantically trying to trace them. The CIA even contacted Callie's mother saying her daughter was suspected missing in Afghanistan and requesting DNA samples for future identification purposes.

It turned out that Joshua and Caitlan were missing. Caitlan was five months pregnant. Callie and Richard were questioned at length in America's Kabul embassy and then, more than a little rattled, took a taxi all the way back to the Tajikistan border. Their last experience of Afghanistan was the taxi driver demanding double the agreed fare. They refused and the driver said he hoped the Taliban would slit their throats.

For the few days I was in the Dushanbe hostel with them, they both turned their heads reflexively every time the compound gate opened, expecting and hoping that it would be Josh and Caitlan. It never was.[5]

Despite having had a very positive experience while hiking in the Wakhan Corridor, Callie and Richard's story unnerved me. A month earlier, in Bishkek, I had quietly acquired an Afghan visa. Faced with options for my route through to Iran, I had to either go through Turkmenistan or Afghanistan. Turkmenistan was notoriously difficult for visitors. The government only granted transit visas, which required much documentation, costly letters of invitation, and agency fees. Even after all that, I would be granted only a three-day visa in which to cycle across 300 waterless miles of

---

[5] Boyle and Coleman were held captive for five years during which time Caitlan gave birth to three children and miscarried once. They were rescued by Pakistani troops near the Afghan border in October 2017. Boyle has since been charged with physical and sexual abuse of Coleman both during and after their time in captivity.

the Karakum desert.

Afghanistan, on the other hand, was surprisingly relaxed about granting tourist visas. 'On their own heads be it' seemed to be the reasoning of Afghan officials. I knew the war was still raging in the south and that much of the country was unarguably dangerous. I even had two friends fighting for the British Army in Helmand Province at the time. However, some pockets of the country's north were deemed to be safe and I feared that this brief window of relative security would soon close. It was now or never.

Various members of the International Security Assistance Force (ISAF) had recently announced plans to withdraw their troops. With the job of vanquishing the Taliban far from completed, this seemed to many, particularly Afghans, a tacit admission of defeat. The Taliban were widely expected to rally and proliferate as soon as the foreigners left. Germany, the third largest member of ISAF by troop numbers, withdrew while I was in Kyrgyzstan, and the rest planned to be gone within two years.

Spending time with Callie and Richard slowly filled me with a nervous excitement. It was the feeling one gets before doing something illogical but thrilling; skydiving or bungee jumping, for example. Their reasoning for visiting had been exactly the same 'now or never' rationale as mine. Each night as I lay in my cramped tent with the hostel's needy kitten curled beside me, I struggled to achieve sleep. I felt a tide of fear rising within me and, floating on that fear, my excitement at doing something daring and stupid rose too. I recognised the same hubris that had led me into Tibet illegally, where I almost perished in the punishing winter. But I had post-rationalised that bad decision and was now pre-rationalising another one. The problem was that once I had decided to do something, however ill-advised, I knew that I would consider pulling out an act of cowardice.

My plan was to cross into Afghanistan from the city of Termiz in Uzbekistan so I knew that I had roughly three weeks of cycling in which to consider the prospect.

TEN

TAMERLANE'S CURSE

We are the Pilgrims, master; we shall go
Always a little further: it may be
Beyond the last blue mountain barred with snow,
Across that angry or that glimmering sea,
White on a throne or guarded in a cave
There lives a prophet who can understand
Why men were born: but surely we are brave,
Who take the Golden Road to Samarkand.
- James Elroy Flecker, *The Golden Journey to Samarkand*

I left Dushanbe on a clear, chilly morning and pedalled up a winding, rocky valley. The road climbed past affluent, half-built holiday homes with small swimming pools and neat, incongruously green lawns. Fiery, shedding trees lined the increasingly narrow valley and the road grew steeper the further I progressed. After thirty miles I realised I had left my MP3 player plugged into a power socket, so I left my bike with a gaggle of village girls and within two hours managed to thumb a ride into town, collect the MP3 player and hitch back to the village. Old Geoff had been cleaned in my absence.

I continued to climb through a series of short tunnels and passed above the snowline. In a bit of a daydream, I accidentally entered an infamous tunnel I had been repeatedly advised to hitch a ride through. The Anzob tunnel is known locally as 'The Tunnel of Death'. It was an unfinished Iranian-funded project started six years earlier: three miles of unpaved, unventilated darkness with an underground river leaking into it. Several people are said to have succumbed to carbon monoxide poisoning inside the tunnel during traffic jams. Before the tunnel was dug, Tajikistani motorists and goods would have to pass through part of Uzbekistan on an avalanche-prone dirt road to travel from the capital to Khujand, the country's second city. This was another inconvenient quirk of Central Asia's labyrinthine tangle of borders and was especially crippling for Tajikistan due to strained relations with its westerly neighbour.

As daylight shrank to a dot behind me, my low-powered head torch lit nothing but the condensation billowing from my mouth into the freezing air. I rode on, semi-blind in near complete darkness. The ground was covered with brown, running water making the uneven surface an unseen obstacle course. Frequently I shunted to an abrupt halt as my front wheel dropped into another of the many shin-deep potholes. The walls were rough cut mountain and unsecured with cement or mesh so falling rocks were a constant threat. I jumped every time I heard a splash as an unknown-sized chunk of mountain dropped into the water. The growing roar of approaching lorries terrified me but the light they brought was a blessing. Increasingly my lungs burned as I breathed more and more of the noxious air that hung heavy in the tunnel.

For forty minutes I hurried up the sloping hole through the mountain, powered by fear-spiked adrenalin. I was physically shaking by the time I emerged into the longed-for ring of light. The exit was at a height of almost 3,400 metres and the grand, snowy mountainscape that greeted me was a calming salve. Layered up with warm clothes, I made the chilly descent to another valley floor.

In bucolic villages, velvet-cloaked old men basking in the thin autumn sunlight greeted me with enthusiastic waves and toothless smiles. The road climbed again, back and forth around tight switchbacks carved from the near-vertical mountainside. Yet more rangy, rugged views compensated for the toil, and pitching my tent next to a sixty-metre drop provided a spectacular, rage-red sunset during dinner. The next morning, at 2,900 metres, I reached the recently opened, Chinese-built Sharistan tunnel. I shot through all six downhill, well-lit, freshly paved and ventilated miles in a few short minutes. A poster of President Rahmon and Chinese leader Hu Jintao adorned the exit, hands clasped and smiles false.

From there it was all downhill to the arid plains of the country's north. A murky grey-purple haze hovered on the horizon and narrow irrigation channels bordered cotton fields stretching across the land. It was a different world to the mountainous majority of Tajikistan and it felt like I had already left the country.

The following day I entered Uzbekistan and turned west towards fabled Samarkand.

Uzbekistan had a different feel to Tajikistan and Kyrgyzstan. It has twice the population of the other two combined, a supposedly secular government, and a culture born of deserts and steppes that contrasted with its mountainous neighbours. When I stopped and spoke to people they were perfectly friendly, but life on the road felt less calm. Men barked 'Where are you from?' in curt Russian as I passed. Many whistled at me repeatedly to catch my attention. Gone were the respectful greetings, the bows, and the waves of the Kyrgyz and Tajiks.

Young Uzbek men with three haircuts on one head drove small cars dangerously fast and unnecessarily close to me. One man flicked a lit cigarette butt at me, perhaps or perhaps not on purpose. I slapped at the smoking hole in my woollen sweatshirt while the car's engine hammered away ahead of me. Another young man drove alongside me for a minute brandishing a knife and proudly saying 'fuck' over and over again. It wasn't such a Golden Road to Samarkand.

It became warm in the daytime and the mountains of Central Asia suddenly seemed a world away, despite still being visible floating above the desert's dust haze. The land was covered with cotton fields stretching as far as the eye could see. I had never seen a raw cotton plant and I previously had no idea what the source of the ubiquitous material looked like. The harvest was recently finished but the tough, waist-high plants were still dotted with little cloud-white puffs of late-blooming cotton. Donkey-drawn carts were stacked with bulging sacks of these post-harvest pickings. They wobbled along roadsides with drivers lounging on top and the donkeys setting their own leisurely pace. Tufts of spilled cotton lay on the roadside, gathered by wind into dirty brown clumps. In some fields the plants were being uprooted and bundled for storage until being used as winter fuel.

Had I passed through a month earlier I would have seen many thousands of people hard at work on the harvest and endless lorries plying the roads, overloaded with bloated bales. Cotton makes up almost a quarter of Uzbekistan's economy and is a state-owned industry. Every autumn, a million people are conscripted by the government into working on the harvest. They receive little or no pay and are threatened with losing their jobs if they don't comply. Historically, school children were bussed out to rural areas and put to work too. They were taught to think of this annual labour as an opportunity to contribute to their homeland's prosperity. However, human rights organisations have pressured the government to put a stop both to the child labour and the forced labour of adults.

Uzbekistan's huge volume of cotton production was made possible with intensive irrigation during the Soviet era. Water was diverted from its natural course down the Syr Darya river and spread across the country's 4 million acres of cotton fields. As a result of the intensive irrigation from the Syr Darya and the equally diverted Amu Darya, the Aral Sea has withered. Formerly the world's fourth-largest lake, it is now only 15 per cent of its 1950 volume and 5 per cent of its former area. It looks set to continue shrinking as Uzbekistan's government continues to issue Soviet-style production quotas.

I had to rush the 220-mile ride to Samarkand in order to register with the police. So I was puffing by the time I found my way to the city centre and into a hostel just a stone's throw from the magnificent buildings I had gazed at in pictures many years earlier.

I had long dreamed of visiting Samarkand. It cropped up

in so many books that I had read, that it had drifted into the realm of legend. Dating back over 2,500 years, Samarkand is one of the world's oldest continuously inhabited cities. It was already well established and prosperous by the time of Alexander the Great's conquest in 329 BC. The Macedonians founded a dynasty of Hellenic rule that lasted six centuries and left an enduring cultural imprint. It was also during this time that the Silk Roads began to flourish, stretching from the Chinese imperial capital to Constantinople (modern-day Istanbul). As a key hub on this route, where traders with caravans of several hundred camels stopped to water, rest, and resupply, the city grew fabulously rich.

When the 'armies of Islam' drove the Arab conquest through Samarkand in AD 710, the city continued to thrive with access to the new markets opening up in an expanding Muslim world. However, as with much of Asia it was pillaged and razed by Genghis Khan, who arrived with his army of horsemen in 1220. A century and a half later Timur (also known as Tamerlane) made Samarkand the intellectual and political capital of a vast and rapidly established empire. His military campaigns were fast, effective, and brutal; his armies became famed for building towers from the skulls of his enemy's dead. However, he was a patron of the arts and spared the lives of artisans, architects, and craftsmen, sending them to beautify his capital. It was during this Timurid era that the grand epithet 'the Jewel of Islam' was conferred on Samarkand due to the city's remarkable architecture.

The decline of the city began as the 1600s drew to a close and the capital was transferred to Bukhara, a week's march west. Traders started bypassing Samarkand and its grandeur began to fade. Polished tilework tarnished, masonry disintegrated, and the Jewel of Islam lost its sparkle. In 1720 the great Persian ruler Nader Shah sacked the city and it was largely abandoned until its ignominious absorption by the aggressively expanding Tsarist Russia in 1868.

Thankfully the tourist season was over by the time I arrived and the sites were mostly empty. On the first morning I took a pre-dawn stroll around the sleeping city's central feature. The Registan was the heart of public life in medieval Samarkand. Three grand *madrasas* (Islamic universities) stand proudly around a south-facing courtyard, their domes and mosaic facades vying with one another for beauty, splendour, and intricacy. Inside each madrasa was a further courtyard surrounded by the ascetic cells that once accommodated students, professors, and mullahs.

Sitting on a bench, I watched in awed silence as the azure domes were struck by a blood-red rising sun and exploded into a vivid purple. They softly melted through mauve to their actual striking blue, the colour and clarity of a cloud-purged sky. I noticed that a street sweeper nearby had also paused to watch the spectacle.

I started in the oldest building, the Ulugh Beg Madrasa, constructed in 1420 by a grandson of Timur who ruled the city for almost four decades. The courtyard was calm and quiet and clean, with several low trees planted around a shallow pond. Hand-painted tilework depicting intricate geological and astronomical patterns crowned the dozens of arched alcoves leading to cells on two floors. A middle-aged Uzbek man sitting in the sunshine told me about Ulugh Beg, who was a reformer, a scientist, and a mathematician. He invited prominent intellectuals from across his empire to study and teach in the madrasa. He even gave lectures there himself. Under his guidance, it became probably the world's foremost centre of secular science at a time when the Inquisition was at its regressive peak in Europe.

Ulugh Beg also built a vast observatory for him and his hand-picked astronomers to study the cosmos. Instruments included an eleven-metre-long stone-carved sextant, which remains mostly intact. Sadly Ulugh Beg was beheaded on the orders of his power-hungry son while on a pilgrimage to Mecca. It seemed cruelly ironic that this largely secular philosopher king was murdered while performing a religious observance. Within three months of his assassination, religious fanatics had destroyed and buried the observatory, deeming its workings and findings heretical. It was almost

500 years before it was found and uncovered once more.

Across the Registan from Ulugh Beg's madrasa stands the Sher-Dor Madrasa, which was built two centuries later. I walked under the grand mosaic facade on which is depicted an unusual-looking pair of mirrored lions that look decidedly like tigers. The vast majority of mosques around the world are adorned with floral motifs and geometric patterns because of a perceived ban on depicting living things pronounced in the Hadith (a collection of sayings of the prophet, Mohammad). As if the roaring lions and the pair of miniature deer they are chasing weren't enough, the decor further flouts religious mores by portraying a sun rising over the back of each lion. These suns have odd male faces at their centres, which some theorise are depictions of Ali, the cousin and son-in-law of Mohammad. Some even believe them to be representations of the prophet himself.

Between the Ulugh Beg and Sher-Dor madrasas is the Tilla-Kari Madrasa. Elaborate blue and green tilework covers the exterior and its grand frontal arch. Inside I found the most impressive painted plasterwork I had ever seen. The ceiling's circular centre was a succession of concentric rings of gilded feathers and flowers and stars on a rich, blue backing. My neck ached after staring upwards too long.

There was small museum inside displaying a few dozen sepia prints of the city over the last 120 years before extensive restoration began on the Timurid buildings. I felt somehow saddened to realise that a good portion of what I was seeing had been rebuilt and retouched in the last fifteen years. Selfishly, I yearned for the melancholic beauty of decaying ruins as at Cambodia's jungle-bound temple complexes or Humayun's overgrown tomb in Delhi.[6] The madrasa's gleaming, freshly glazed tilework, however ornate, didn't have the same pull on me as forlornly crumbling decay. The inevitable, the entropy, and the relative fleetingness of grand buildings collapsing in the wake of the

---

[6] Humayun, the second emperor of the Mughal dynasty, was the great-great-great-great-grandson of Timur.

civilisations that made them is, to me, part of their loveliness. Their unavoidable demise makes their current survival feel all the sweeter and more special. I often wonder what we would think if the Greeks repainted the Parthenon or their marble statuary masterpieces in the bright colours that once adorned them.

I was aware that my obsession with authenticity and age is a very western trait. The most common questions I overheard from western tourists at attractions across the world were 'How old is this? And how old is that?' I couldn't get away from it. These were also the first things I wanted to know when I visited a site. Perhaps as a European I have grown up spoiled by the relative longevity of historical buildings that haven't had to compete with earthquakes, monsoons, and Mongolians. This fascination with genuine age, however, seemed not to be one shared by domestic Chinese tourists, for example, who obediently visit sections of the Great Wall rebuilt entirely after 1980 and don't care that the flowers on the surrounding trees in winter are plastic and affixed to branches with hot-glue guns.

In the three days I stayed in Samarkand I wandered around the various sites, chatting in my slowly improving Russian to anyone who approached. I twice visited the Gur-e-Amir, the family crypt of the Timurid dynasty. As I walked around the exterior the fluted and pattered dome gave a strobing reflection of the sky's hue. The vaulting of the building's several archways was detailed with *murqanas*, a sort of hanging honeycomb ornamentation, that were painted in the striking golds, greens, and dark blues of a Christmas card's nativity scene.

The Gur-e-Amir houses the remains of the great emperor Timur, his teacher, and four of his progeny, including Ulugh Beg. The uplit interior is a frenzy of elaborate yet graceful plasterwork. Friezes of gilded Koranic calligraphy run around the walls while swirling tendrils of relief vines tangled elegantly together in countless symmetries.

Over the six polished tombstones in their dimly lit

chamber, leans a six-metre-long wooden pole with, as I was told by the custodian, the tail of Timur's favourite horse dangling from its end. His armies marched under the standard of a horse's tail. The custodian also told me about the 'Curse of Tamerlane'. In the summer of 1941 Stalin personally commissioned an excavation of the tomb. A team of Soviet archaeologists uncovered and opened the granite coffins one by one. They saved Timur's until last and found the following warning inscribed on the tombstone: 'Whosoever disturbs my tomb will unleash an invader more terrible than I.'

Three days later, on 22 June 1941, Hitler broke the Nazi–Soviet pact and launched Operation Barbarossa. More than 3 million Nazi troops poured across the Soviet border in a matter of days, opening up an 1,800-mile eastern front and dragging the USSR into a war that would cost them more than 25 million lives.

ELEVEN

PILGRIMAGE

The traveller who elects to go on foot where he could perfectly well ride, or to cycle where there are no roads, is merely contriving hardship. His experiences are only marginally more interesting than those of the adventurer who, failing to contrive a knife edge situation, feels no compunction about inventing it. To such a rascal no indulgence was extended in the great age of exploration.
- John Keay, *The Giant Book of Exploration*

Back on the road I passed the hours watching rural village life unfold. On two separate occasions men asked me if I was a Sikh, and I was mistaken for a Turk several times. With long-neglected hair tied into a topknot, a bushy copper beard and sun-ruddied cheeks, I had become used to leaving a wake of confusion.

Riding slowly onwards to Bukhara, the cotton fields finally ended and the Kyzylkum desert began. Shifting banks of wind-rippled red sand hemmed the road and small herds of camels picked at scant, thorny shrubs. It was mid-November and the temperature dipped below freezing at sunset.

I woke in my tent one night just in time to spare my underwear and simultaneously deposit the thick, dry chunks climbing up my throat into a bush. I spent a nil-by-mouth day lying in the tent wallowing in self-pity. When not dragging my aching body on hourly missions to the bushes, I drifted in and out of fevered dreams. That was the last time I cooked my rice with tainted water from the irrigation canals.

In Bukhara's outskirts my rear tyre went flat and I pushed Old Geoff the last two miles to a hostel in the centre. I was fed up by the time I had checked in, having been forced to haggle a fair rate for a bedroll on a crumb-covered floor. The owner said she had closed for winter and I had to pay extra for my low-season stay. I decided to cheer myself up by visiting an internet café – checking emails was always a welcome method of escapism. The short missives from friends and family briefly whisked me away from my odd lifestyle of sleeping rough each night, sitting on roadside dirt for lunch, and never knowing what the rest of any given day might have in store for me.

I fired off a quick update to my parents and received a response a minute later. It was rare for either of them to be online at the same time as me and so we logged onto Skype and I spoke to my mother for the first time in many months. She caught me up on all the goings-on at home and the lives of my brother and sisters. In response I could only muster that my life had been business as usual: lots of cycling, mostly in mountains and desert, some friendly people met and some beautiful buildings seen. I didn't want to bore her with further details.

'Where are you going next?' Mum asked.

'Back to Iran,' I replied. 'I'll probably take my time there, looping through the south to avoid the worst of winter.'

'I remember you really loved Iran last time. I hope you get to meet some of your friends there again.'

'Me too.'

'And then you'll go back to Turkey?'

'That's right.'

'And are you still planning to go down into Africa after that?'

'I am.'

'So when do you think you'll get home?'

'I suppose it's only about two years to go now.'

When we said goodbye, a lump stuck in my throat. I'd been deliberately evasive about my upcoming route, guessing my mother's Central Asian geography was likely lacking. She wouldn't realise that Uzbekistan didn't border Iran. Over the previous weeks I had thought deeply about whether or not to tell my parents I was going through Afghanistan. I thought about the terror Callie's mother must have endured after the CIA turned up asking for DNA samples. She didn't know Callie had gone to Afghanistan and had feared her daughter dead for the best part of three weeks. And yet I couldn't bring myself to have the inevitable argument with my own parents about the foolishness of going to a country at war. I knew my headstrong nature and that I would still go, even if under a cloud. If they knew then they would be driven to distraction with worry the entire time I was there.

This conclusion made saying goodbye feel like I could be saying goodbye forever. I began to imagine the many scenarios in which I would be killed in Afghanistan: I would be shot by a roadside sniper; I would be struck by a suicide bomb; I would be stabbed covertly in the crowded press of a bazaar; I would be dragged from my tent in the middle of the night, bundled into a car with a sack over my head, and held in a locked room for several months on a starvation diet before my captors grew bored of me, switched on their handycam, and cut off my head in front of a black drape.

As I returned to the hostel after dark with a circuitous wander through the city centre, I felt deeply homesick. I considered my response to the question about whether or not I would go to Africa. It had been a reflex. I was so used to explaining my route and it always ended with pedalling down the east coast of Africa and back up the west. Ambling past a moon-silhouetted mosque, I asked myself a question for the first time. *Do I really want to cycle Africa?* It would take at least another eighteen months, when I could simply pelt back across Europe enjoying an alpine spring and a golden summer homecoming. I could be sipping icy drinks in a British beer garden in just six months' time. It sounded very attractive.

It wasn't that I was having a bad time – I was still enjoying my journey. But would I really gain anything from further year and a half of feral road life that I hadn't already got from the last two and a half years?

Climbing into my sleeping bag that night, my breath visible in the unheated room, I resolved to leave those questions unanswered for the time being. I had almost limitless hours on the road ahead to consider my options.

Once again, with the tourist season over I had the run of the peaceful city. With its mudbrick walls and traditional houses, it had remained relatively faithful to the traditional architecture and looked much as it would have when the Russians marched in 150 years earlier.

I strolled through the Old Jewish Quarter's winding alleys and noticed several weatherworn Stars of David carved into gnarled wooden doors, relics from a time of prosperous co-existence when a large population of Jews lived in the city. They spoke a blend of Persian and Hebrew and, until the first synagogue was built in 1620, shared the mosques with their neighbours as places of worship.[7]

I visited several more Timurid madrassas with architectural elegance and splendid tilework approaching those of Samarkand. Towering over the dust-coloured city is the forty-eight-metre-high Kalon minaret, which has stood for almost nine centuries. There are numerous accounts of criminals being thrown to their deaths from the top of the tower, and legend has it that when Genghis Khan arrived the minaret so impressed him that it was the only thing spared from the 'Year Zero' destruction which flattened the rest of Bukhara.

On my last morning I set out to explore Bukhara's old city, the religious heart of secular modern Uzbekistan. When Samarkand began its decline in the mid-seventeenth century, Bukhara became a capital ruled by a lineage of increasingly murderous and despotic emirs who won the city infamy across Europe. The second-last emir of independent Bukhara

[7] Jewish presence in the area spans two millennia, but persecution and forced conversions in the 18th century caused most Bukharan Jews to emigrate. Russian conquest restored freedom of worship and boosted Jewish populations right across Central Asia. However, the brief renaissance was cut short by the Russian Revolution and subsequent crackdown on religion, until the Second World War saw more Jews fleeing the Holocaust arriving in Bukhara. In 1972 restrictions on emigration from the USSR eased and tens of thousands of Bukharan Jews relocated to Israel, America, and Western Europe. Fewer than 150 Jews remain in Bukhara, struggling to maintain their religious rites and to combat their dwindling number.

was Nasrullah, whose sobriquet 'The Butcher' was won by murdering all his brothers and twenty-eight other relatives to secure the throne.

In the summer of 1839, as Britain and Russia were vying for control and influence in the region, a young English officer was sent to petition Nasrullah. Colonel Charles Stoddart requested the release of several thousand Christian slaves, predominantly Slavs, to undermine Russian excuses to invade and annex the emir's territory. Stoddart was also authorised to offer a treaty of friendship with Britain.

However, Nasrullah didn't take kindly to Stoddart who, on arrival, made the social faux pas of riding into the palace courtyard without first dismounting. The emir took him captive, keeping him in a deep pit deliberately infested with rats and scorpions and only accessible by a six-metre rope lowered through an opening in the ceiling. After two years of futile petitioning by the British government, Captain Arthur Conolly rode into Bukhara on a one-man diplomatic rescue mission. His entreaties were heard politely and then he too was thrown in the pit.

Six months later, on 24 June 1842, the two emaciated prisoners were led to the courtyard in front of the Ark (the emir's citadel) and ordered to convert to Islam. Stoddart and Conolly both refused and were beheaded, dropping into graves they had been forced to dig themselves.

The Ark, with its vast, sloping mud walls, was closed for restoration when I visited. But I stood on the recently concreted courtyard and wondered how those two men, so far from home, must have felt in their final moments before execution in front of a large crowd. I had read of their story many years before and often thought about them when contemplating my journey through Central Asia. They lived at a time when travel in the region was truly perilous and often lasted years. I lived in an age where it was possible to zoom through the area on a bicycle in just a few months.

Peering into the gloomy dungeon prison, I shuddered at the thought of even a single night's incarceration there, rats or no rats. Bukhara was an ancient and holy city which received droves of pilgrims in its heyday. However, visiting the grimy pit near the citadel was my personal pilgrimage.

The morning I left it was -7°C. I wrapped up and traced the desert's fringe into Uzbekistan's southeast where white-capped mountains were again visible. Occasional single-humped camels, the first I'd seen in Central Asia, stood among the scrub and roaring flames danced atop chimneys on distant natural gas wells.

As I approached the mountains the desert buckled into low, dusty hills. Three elderly men sitting at breakfast in the morning sun waved me over to join them. I gratefully tucked into some soup with bread but declined the vodka. They eagerly worked their way through to a second bottle, toasting the health of Uzbekistan, Mohammad, or me with each glass. When I left they were trying to pour more of the cheap liquor into each other's glasses without being noticed, giggling like children each time they succeeded or were caught.

The road wound up and over the Hissar Mountains – a clustered arm of schist and sandstone peaks lunging down from the Central Asian plateau. I camped at a frigid pass then sped down through pastures and villages to the border city of Termez. The city sits beside the Amu Darya river – the Oxus in antiquity – which forms the border with Afghanistan. For a day I rested and mentally drew breath.

TWELVE

PRECIPICE

A ship in port is safe, but that's not what ships are built for.
- Grace Murray Cooper

During the two months when the prospect of entering Afghanistan had hung ahead of me, I largely managed to think about it rationally or not at all. However, camped on wasteland near the border, my imagination finally ran free with vivid hypotheticals that kept me awake much of the night. My parents were still unaware of my arguably foolhardy plan. I had told just one friend, Jamie, giving him a date on which to 'raise the alarm' if I had not emailed again to say I was safely out the other side.

I was already waiting at the border post when it opened in the morning. The Uzbeks searched me thoroughly for an hour before I passed through an intimidating no-man's land. The Uzbekistan riverbank had long been defended by electric fences and a minefield to prevent Afghanistan's troubles leaching across the border. Signs warned of these dangers and kept me following existing tyre tracks in the dust. I then pedalled across the Friendship Bridge, which the Soviets eventually built in 1982 to supply their forces, which were pushing south through the country after their 1979 invasion. The US-armed mujahideen fought back and the demoralised, defeated Russians finally withdrew across the stark steelwork in February 1989.

Things were instantly different south of the river. The road was channelled between two high walls of sandbags topped with menacing razor wire. It looked and felt like a warzone. The immigration official briefly raised an eyebrow at me, but soon stamped my passport and waved me through without search.

I was spilled out into Hairatan. The small border town is little more than two rows of shoddy buildings lining the road.

The signs and text on shop fronts was all in the Persian script and every man wore facial hair and a *shalwar kameez* (loose, pyjama-like trousers with a long tunic). The women drifted along the roadside in pastel blue *burqas*, their world obscured by mesh across the eyes. Somehow there was rising dust everywhere, when there had been none across the river. The Uzbek side had been covered in trees and irrigated crops but the land on the Afghan side seemed barren and abandoned.

I drew a woollen scarf over my head to avoid unwanted attention and began the sixty-mile ride to Mazar-e-Sharif. A couple of people waved me over but I was guarded and cycled on as fast as possible, turning my face away from oncoming vehicles. I was a stranger in a high-risk country; a foreigner with low-awareness and next to no local language. I was afraid and soon started wondering if coming had been a mistake.

Within a few miles I was in desert proper on a road snaking south between five-metre high dunes. The empty stretches of road, walled in by sand, eased my mind and I regained control over my fears. Then, suddenly, an unmarked green 4x4 roared up behind me, overtook, and skidded to a halt fifty metres ahead. There were two huge guns mounted on the open back. Three men jumped down and started running towards me. They were as covered up by headscarves as I was. Helpless and terrified, I jammed on my brakes, put my feet down, and held my breath, bracing for abduction. As they neared, one of their scarves slipped and I noticed he was smiling. They stopped in front of me and reached out to shake my hand. I relaxed and breathed again. They were plain-clothes police who simply wanted to greet me and take photos together.

In the afternoon I reached the turning onto northern Afghanistan's main east-west artery. A convoy of five massive armoured vehicles displaying Swedish flags passed me. The helmeted white faces in the high, bullet-proof windscreens pointed at me and shook their heads sternly. I couldn't tell if it was disapproval or disbelief.

The road ran directly to the city centre, terminating at a

large mosque with magnificent blue mosaic work. I leaned my bike against a wall on a street corner and looked around defensively. A man approached me and asked in English if he could help. Within a couple of minutes I had changed money and bought an Afghan SIM card. I had used Couchsurfing (a worldwide online community of travellers and hosts) for the first time and been invited by cousins Masood and Nasir to stay with them during my time in Mazar. I called Nasir who said he would come to meet me shortly.

Relaxing further, I sat down and enjoyed watching the raw, busy life of the city rushing all around me. Street children sold plastic bags, jewellers haggled over the price of lapis lazuli necklaces, men pushed wooden-wheeled barrows of rubble to and from roadworks, and rows of moneychangers sat on the pavement with small glass cabinets displaying various currencies. I realised that despite the ongoing war in the south it was, in many ways, a country like any other where people went about their daily lives. Several people approached and addressed me in decent English. A carpet seller called Sadaek sat me down in his shop and gave me tea. He had never seen a cycle tourist before and was fascinated. He asked why I had come to Afghanistan. Was I not scared? I had only to look at the interesting and benign scenes around me to find an answer.

Nasir arrived and greeted me in the Afghan custom with a hug and a kiss on the right cheek. He was a twenty-two-year-old journalist and was dressed in jeans and leather jacket. We walked for fifteen minutes to the Barg-e-Sabz guesthouse, which was owned by yet more cousins who generously kept a room free for any 'couchsurfers' who come to Mazar. I was greeted by the jovial, bear-like Masood who ran security for the American consulate, and Stefano, an Italian tourist who had arrived in a car the previous day. Stefano had been roaming Asia as a magician in a small travelling circus until he met an English couple in Kyrgyzstan. They had driven a small white van, the kind a plumber might typically drive, from the UK and had grown weary. They charged Stefano with the task of finding somewhere to deposit their vehicle where it would be needed and appreciated. He took the tired van over the Pamir Highway, which had finally re-opened, and then to Mazar-e-Sharif. Masood had arranged for him to give the vehicle to a local girls' school.

Early in the morning we took the filthy white van to a mechanic to get the exhaust fixed. Masood pointed out a charred hole in the pavement surrounded by cracked paving slabs. He said a tree had stood there a month earlier when a bicycle had been leant against it. The bomb in the bicycle's saddle bag detonated during rush hour killing one man and three boys and maiming many more. I saw a metal electronics box attached to a blackened pylon nearby. It had been blasted violently in one direction and now resembled the hair in a photo of someone sticking their head out of a fast-moving car window.

With the foreign troops largely confined to their bases and awaiting withdrawal, the Taliban were already regaining control of the surrounding countryside in Balkh Province, advancing village by village to within five miles of the city. The ISAF[8] withdrawal loomed ever more ominously in the minds of Mazar's population, many of whom felt they stood on the edge of a precipice.

I waited at the mechanic's garage while Masood and Stefano disappeared to run some errands. My phone rang just as the mechanic was finishing the job. Masood and Stefano had been delayed and would have to take a taxi straight to the school. There would be no time to wash the grime-covered car, which I had to drive nervously to the school. I hadn't driven a car in two and a half years. The clutch was exhausted and the morning rush hour roads manic but I somehow managed to get the thing into the school and embarrassingly stall it in front of a crowd assembled to greet it.

[8] International Security Assistance Force. The coalition of 51 nations that fought in Afghanistan against the Taliban and al Qaeda from 2001-2014. The USA was the largest contingent supplying 100,000 of the 140,000 foreign troops deployed. The UK supplied 9,500, Luxembourg supplied 9 troops, and Iceland sent 2. At the time of my visit, despite being two years from full withdrawal, the ISAF was already drastically reducing numbers.

When the Taliban first seized Mazar-e-Sharif in 1997, they immediately closed The Fatima Balkhi School for Girls, because female education didn't fit in with their fundamentalist Islamic world view. The school was then used as a Taliban military headquarters until 2001, when the US Air Force bombed the school along with 1,500 of its Taliban occupants. It had eventually been rebuilt and was now educating 6,000 students. However, when it first re-opened there were no chairs or tables and the girls huddled together on the floor for warmth as there were mortar holes in the roof through which snow fell. They also had few books as the Taliban burned every non-Koranic book they got their hands on. For the first few years the school had even remained open throughout the holidays, giving the girls a chance to catch up with male contemporaries after the four-year hiatus in their studies.

We were welcomed with a song from ten young girls. They wore pink and black tasselled dresses, traditional garb of the local Hazara ethnic group that was so heavily persecuted by the Taliban for being Shi'ites rather than Sunnis. We were then ushered into the principal's office for a long session of polite formalities. Stefano and I were unkempt, poorly dressed and awkward in contrast to the immaculately groomed governors and city officials sitting opposite, wearing three-piece suits and neat, grey beards.

Masood translated the interminable pleasantries before we went outside and the keys were officially handed over in front of the shamefully dirty van. That evening we spotted ourselves on local television news. It wasn't the low-profile first day that I had intended for my time in Afghanistan.

The following day I walked around the town chatting with Nasir. In a crowded market he was amused by what he overheard people saying of my scruffy appearance: 'I thought foreigners were rich but this one can't even afford shampoo…and look! Look! The rats have nibbled at his shoes!'

Nasir had fled Kabul two months ago, having received numerous death threats over his outspoken writing on religion and politics. He was desperately hoping to emigrate. During the week I passed in Mazar-e-Sharif I chatted with many other educated Afghans and, without exception, they all wanted to escape the country as soon as possible. Most felt certain that it was only a matter of time before the Taliban took control again.

One afternoon, Nasir took Stefano and I to meet a photographer friend of his called Qais. He worked in a little basement studio and served us cup after cup of tea while displaying his striking prints. Among others he had sold his work to the international news agency AFP, and his photo of a raped five-year-old girl in her hospital bed had recently been *Time* magazine's photo of the month.

Qais was quiet and humble in an endearing way and I took to him at once. His modesty meant I had to coax his achievements and extraordinary experiences out of him but this only made me like him more. Many of his photos were from a government orphanage just outside the city which we decided to visit so Stefano could perform magic tricks for the children and Qais could take more photos.

The Balkh Orphanage was one of a bleak little crop of buildings in the desert on Mazar's thinning outskirts. We were shown around the four simple rooms that housed ninety orphans. In the courtyard, the eager children pressed forward to shake our hands and chorus 'What is your name? What is your name?'

Nasir translated while a few spoke about how they came to be there. I heard horrific stories that afternoon. I listened to an eight-year-old boy flatly describe how he was tied up and forced to watch as the Taliban cut the throats of his parents and brother. He was then placed in a madrassa for religious indoctrination by the very people who had orphaned him. I tried in vain to shake the image of a bound boy crying, his kicking feet on the edge of a growing puddle of blood.

Stefano bamboozled the children with his conjuring, wearing a magical looking Kyrgyz *kalpak* hat of pointed and patterned white felt. We played football with the boys in a rising cloud of dust before returning to our room in the Barg-e-Sabz guesthouse to eat dinner with Qais and Nasir. Nasir produced an illicit bottle of revolting moonshine known locally as 'dog sweat'. In an Islamic Republic where alcohol is forbidden one has to make do with what's available.

Stefano took a flight and I wandered around the town talking to anyone who approached me. I bought an Afghan headscarf to cover my clearly foreign face and hair. Most people were incredibly friendly but I did receive a number of overtly threatening stares and scowls. These were mostly from conservative-looking, middle-aged men wearing thick black beards and *surma*, an eyeliner made from coal dust.

I frequently found myself wondering which of the people I was passing or meeting might secretly lament the fall of the Taliban regime. I knew many of those walking the streets must have been relieved when the ISAF liberated the country from medieval theocracy. However, how many thought that the dark days under the Taliban had been preferable to the devastation and collapse of the country since the 2001 foreign invasion? One man told me in halting English that his greatest desire was to sleep with a foreign woman – any foreign women.

'Foreigners *fucked* my country so I dream to *fuck* one of them.'

Despite this I felt relatively comfortable in Mazar-e-Sharif. Many conversations were steered quickly onto the topic of religion by those I met. To avoid offending or potentially attracting dangerous attention, I listened politely and said little during these exchanges. There was a man called Farid with excellent English who worked for the German government's aid programme. Farid plainly stated at the opening of our conversation in a *chaikhana*, or teahouse, that his objective was to convert me. Several of his assertions were so absurd that I struggled not to snort.

'NASA scientists used a world map and *phi*, you know,

the Golden Ratio, the divine proportion, to calculate where the geographical centre of the Earth is. And, you know, they discovered that it is Mecca. Of course it is Mecca! But those NASA men don't release this information though because they are infidels.'

Another young man I met, Zabi, worked as an interpreter for the Norwegian troops up until their withdrawal. He worked on 'hearts and minds' type forays into the villages as well as on interrogations of captive Taliban fighters. In a tremulous whisper Zabi confided his belief that 'religion is cancer'. He liked the central message of Zoroastrianism. Zabi spoke of being deeply disturbed when, as a child, he saw a woman stoned to death 'in the name of Islam'. In the restaurant where we spoke, he was filling out forms from the Norwegian embassy that he hoped would facilitate his permanent emigration.

'I was born in this country, Charlie, but I don't want to live here,' he said.

'Is it because you don't recognise Afghanistan today as the country you were born in?' I asked.

'No. It is because I do.'[9]

---

[9] Zabi moved to Norway with his wife and young family a few months later.

THIRTEEN

SURGEONS

*The Iraqi and Afghan wars have not 'ended.' Only America's
involvement has 'ended' ... When a country leaves a war before
achieving victory it is not called leaving. It is called defeat.*
- Dennis Prager

I sat on a bench writing up my journal and watching
families mill around the white-tiled courtyard surrounding
the Timurid Blue Mosque at the heart of Mazar. The mosque
was built in 1481 as a shrine to Mohammad's son-in-law, Ali.
Some believe his remains were buried there rather than Najaf
in Iraq as is commonly believed.

The mosque's shimmering turquoise tiles quivered with
diffraction under an unusually smog-free morning sky.
Padding around in bare feet, visitors left a chaos of shoes at
the entrance. Many fed the several thousand doves that are
believed to be pigeons turned white by the purity of the site.
A vendor sold handfuls of grain folded into scraps of old
newspaper. Another man with a broom scattered the doves
and swept up uneaten grains to be repackaged and sold again.
The clustered doves swarmed the laughing people throwing
corn, and the birds that had eaten perched on the cables
running between the legion loudspeakers tacked onto tiled
walls.

Young men lounged in groups on cracked marble steps;
faux leather jackets worn over *shalwar kameez*. Groups of
older men with chest-length beards and ankle-length green
and purple robes shook hands enthusiastically in a never-
ending medley of greetings. Uniformed Afghan soldiers
mixed among the citizens, rifles slung over shoulders. There
was an incredible variety of male faces all around me.
Afghanistan has more than twenty distinct ethnic groups
ranging from the pale northern Uzbeks and more eastern-
looking Pamiri mountain people to the swarthier southerners,

such the Balucchis and the various Pashtun tribes.

I couldn't see if the women were as varied, or even whether they were laughing or speaking or frowning: most were simply depersonalised blue fabric shapes.

Nasir and I visited the nearby city of Balkh. It was only fifteen miles away but was not considered 'safe' in the same way Mazar was. Nasir uncharacteristically dressed in *shalwar kameez* and was visibly on edge for the whole day. He repeatedly murmured his regret at the decision to visit, saying that Taliban live openly and freely in the city.

Balkh is perhaps Afghanistan's oldest town and dates back at least 4,000 years. Zarathustra, the prophet of Zoroastrianism, a mystical fire-worshipping religion, is thought to have preached and died in the city around 600 BC. It is also where Alexander the Great married the Bactrian princess Roxana in 327 BC.

A high, curving earthen wall, still grand but much decayed, ran for six miles around the city. Drooping watchtowers sagged at fifty-yard intervals and a claustrophobic warren of waist-high tunnels wormed through the ancient mudwork.

In the centre, where eight roads following and dissecting the cardinal points converged, stood a crumbling Timurid mosque. The ribbed greenish dome and spiral-corded pillars looked neglected and bore the pockmarks of Soviet invasion. Nasir was particularly jumpy in the centre, saying he could spot Taliban at every turning.

'I can see who they are. They are not even trying to hide,' he said.

'Could you point them out?' I asked.

'It is no use. They are all Taliban here.'

We hurried through a couple of crumbling shrines and then stopped into the tomb of Rabi'a Balkhi, the first and most revered female Persian poet. According to legend Rabi'a fell in love with a slave called Baktash and as a result was imprisoned in a hammam by her brother after he partially cut her throat. She composed her last poem on the walls in her own blood. Female pilgrims filed through the low, vaulted building in twos and threes. They knelt at the green-shrouded tomb to pray, each touching their foreheads to the velvet fabric. A thousand years after Rabi'a died, women in Afghanistan still have limited access to education and little say over whom they marry. At the time of writing, the literacy rate for women in Afghanistan is 12 per cent and life expectancy is under sixty-five years.

North of the town stood the Bala Hissar fortress that tried over the years to protect the numerous citadels built consecutively within, but which was toppled by invader after invader. Ringed by ruined ramparts, the uninhabited mud plateau was formed over millennia by hundreds of pulverised castles, each built on the crushed remains of the last. We poked our heads into a small hut within, the only modern structure in sight. It was an opium den with skeletal bodies strewn about in various states of contortion. A row of glassy-eyed men sat along the outside wall, mouths agape.

Last stop was the Noh Gombad Mosque, which had been a Zoroastrian temple until Buddhism arrived and it was converted. Centuries later, after the Arab conquest, it was demolished and the earliest known Islamic structure in Afghanistan was built atop the heathen ruins. No longer a working mosque, it was under tentative restoration by the World Monuments Fund. As I photographed the intricate carvings on a column's capital, Nasir leaned in and pleaded quietly.

'Please, Charlie, there are men outside. They are watching us and they are bad men. I don't like it. We can go now, please, directly to Mazar.'

That evening Nasir became his normal relaxed self again. We sat with Masood and the owners of the guesthouse, Farod and Walid, eating kebabs and drinking smuggled Uzbek vodka with pomegranate juice. An LCD television was tuned into a banned Lebanese channel with Arab girls in figure-hugging clothing dancing awkwardly on a flimsy studio set. Each girl wore a distinctly different colour to the others. Walid explained that the channel acts as a broadcast brothel –

rich Arabs phone in and order whichever dancer takes their fancy, stating the colour as an identifier.

After being told by countless people that the road to Herat passed through Taliban-controlled territory and was unsafe, even for Afghans, I decided to do the sensible thing and fly there. Masood also warned that Herat was not as safe as Mazar. The airport was small, with only a couple of flights a week. The departures lounge consisted of a row of plastic patio chairs on the tarmac where male passengers waited while a few women stood apart. My fully assembled bicycle was wheeled onto the plane and I gazed out of the window for the forty-five-minute flight. We followed the divide between desert plains stretching north to the Kazakh steppe and the snow-covered Hindu Kush that runs to the Chinese border. As we landed, I spotted several US jets and a neatly parked row of attack helicopters in a high-fenced area of the airport.

I called a man called Romal who I had found on Couchsurfing and who had invited me to stay at his home. He sounded surprised when I phoned, as if I had caught him off guard. Romal said he was in a meeting but told me to be at the entrance to Herat's football stadium in twenty minutes. I once more covered my face with a headscarf and cycled into the city. Outside the stadium I waited for an hour before calling again.

'I am on my way to you. Stay there,' came the reply before the line went dead.

Two hours later I was still alone and evening was approaching. I called several more times and eventually received a text message: 'Please stop calling me. I don't know you.'

I felt afraid and alone in an unfamiliar Afghan city. Maybe Romal had decided he was uncomfortable having an infidel in his home. Perhaps he feared the neighbours would talk or that Taliban sympathisers would find out. I had been told by many that Herat was conservative compared to Mazar.

In the dying light I started looking for an affordable place to stay. Three squalid hotels all asked for over $50, which I couldn't afford. Just as I was starting to fret I met an English student called Matiullah. He was on his way home and wasted no time in offering me floor space in the small room he shared with two art students. I accepted gratefully and wheeled my bicycle alongside him. He walked slowly with a heavy limp, thanks to a childhood bout of polio.

'Mati' and his room-mates were all from the city of Ghazni about eighty miles southwest of Kabul. The three of them shared a tiny, bedless room in a complex housing 500 students. We prepared and ate a dinner of bread and stewed aubergines. As we were bedded down in a row on the floor Mati's phone buzzed.

'It is teacher. She says you will be welcome to join our class at the university tomorrow.'

I woke in the dark with dull explosions rocking my stomach. Dinner clearly hadn't agreed with me. My three companions were nowhere to be seen. Hurriedly, I snatched loo paper from my bag, pulled on shoes and staggered down the corridor, clutching my belly. There was a long queue of young men waiting to use the loos and perform their ablutions before *Fajr*, the dawn prayers. There were about 300 people and only eight toilets. After fifteen minutes of wincing and clenching and aching and fretting I finally reached one of the open-plan latrines. By that point I was on tiptoes with my hips thrust forward and my fists whitening by my sides. Judging by the state of the hole in the ground, and the concrete surrounding it, I was just one of many with upset stomachs that morning. My neighbours politely ignored me.

I was the only person in the place with paper. The rest used their left hands in conjunction with plastic jugs of water. This wasn't new to me, however, as I washed my hands at the tap on my way out I noticed that there was no soap provided and nobody carried any with them. The rooms were without taps and I suddenly knew why so many were suffering from digestive complaints – the place must have been crawling with faecal bacteria.

After my three room-mates took turns with one prayer rug we drank a quick cup of tea and set off on bicycle for Herat University. Mati insisted that I fully cover my head and face for the ride.

'This city is not safe, Mr Charlie. Bad peoples must not see your most white face. They will think you not *Musulman*. Stay with me, please. I must be insisting that you not go anywhere by your alone.'

I sat in on a literature class in which fifty-five students folded into an undersized room; forty chattering boys to the left and fifteen silent girls to the right. The male students all met me with handshakes and the greeting: 'Hello! How is your health?'

We listened to the teacher read a synopsis of Beowulf in imperfect English before ordering the class to pick their way through a sample passage. I couldn't understand why a group of fledging English-speakers were being put through the ordeal of a relentlessly alliterative Old English text. The class had the feel of a high school rather than a university and culminated with me being coaxed into reading and explaining a couple of Shakespeare's more saccharine sonnets.

After class Mati took me, again covered, to the Jumah (Friday) Mosque. The 800-year-old white marble courtyard was peaceful and empty but blindingly bright in the midday sun. We then walked hurriedly through the old city's jumbled streets brimming with tailors and booksellers, barbers and cobblers, notaries and apothecaries. I almost jogged to keep up with Mati. His discomfort and manic rush to show me the sites was unnerving and reminded me of Nasir in Balkh. By mid-afternoon he started fearing for his own safety and asked that I tail him, following at least ten yards behind. His fear of being seen with a foreigner watered the vague unease I had harboured throughout my time in Afghanistan.

Our last visit was to the single remaining Musalla Minaret. Formerly twenty-four in number, the minarets were commissioned by Gowhar Shad, the wife of Timur's son, in the early fifteenth century. As with so many things, the minarets were often described as 'Jewels of Islam'. When Herat was under British occupation in 1885, an invasion by a Russo-Persian alliance was imminently expected. The British dynamited nine of the minarets to rob the Russians of cover from artillery fire. But the invasion never came. Although not ideologically motivated, this wanton vandalism has been compared to the Taliban's 2001 destruction of the monumental sixth century Buddhas of Bamiyan.

A further fourteen of the Musalla Minarets fell victim to a series of earthquakes in the early twentieth century. The one sad survivor leans dangerously to one side and is supported by steel cables. Turbaned vendors sold fruit off rickshaws around the base. A busy road ran past giving off vibrations from trundling traffic. Add to this Herat's famously harsh winds and the odds look bleak for the last minaret.

It was only a short walk to the four shorter but equally forlorn minarets that once marked the corners of the long-lost Musalla Madrassa. Robert Byron visited in the 1930s when some ruins remained and eulogised about the lost masterpieces.

> *No photograph, nor any description, can convey their colour of grape-blue with an azure bloom … White marble panels carved with a baroque Kufic, yellow, white, olive green and rusty red mingled with the two blues in a maze of flowers, arabesques and texts as fine as the patterns on a teacup … if the mosaic on the rest of the [Madrassa] surpassed or even equalled what survives today, there was never such a mosque before or since.*

The police had been to the room asking questions about me while we were out and this heightened Mati's discomfort. He would no longer allow me to visit the communal toilet without covering up, for fear of other students spotting me. I offered to go to a hostel but he refused and seemed insulted. The next day when we exited the complex, he asked me to wait a whole minute before following. I was growing tired of this charade, wishing he would let me move to a hostel.

We walked, fifty yards apart, up a hill in the old city to visit the fifteenth-century Ark (or citadel). The imposing fortress with walls several yards thick housed the new German–American funded National Museum. The mostly bloody history of Afghanistan was neatly presented. Beside dusty glass cabinets of rusted jezails and dented flintlocks I read small information cards detailing war after war, including the three nineteenth-century conflicts with the British. The curator gave us free rein to explore the restored citadel so we clambered over its battlements, enjoying the best possible views of the mostly mud-built city.

I returned to the room as instructed, after dark and this time a full hour behind Mati having twiddled my thumbs on a park bench. The police had been again. Apparently they didn't believe I was a tourist and the embarrassed students had been ordered to turn me out. Oddly, the police hadn't cared to see my passport or even question me. I told my new friends not to worry and we shared aubergine soup before I wheeled Old Geoff out into the night. At length I found a grubby men's hostel where the communal squat toilets consisted of doorless alcoves dotted along the corridor.

Wrapping my scarf tightly around my head once more, I cycled out of the city headed for the Iranian border. I took a wrong turn somewhere, ended up on the wrong side of a river, and for a time I was lost in a labyrinth of dirt tracks knitted across a landscape of farming villages where everyone stopped to watch me pass. I was increasingly nervous. My time in Herat and Mati's fears had left me stressed and cautious of strangers. I had been warned of insurgents, or 'surgeons' as Mati put it, on the road that acts as the major Iran–Afghanistan smuggler's highway. I was deeply relieved when I eventually found my way onto the tarmac road and picked up speed towards Iran, which I had started to consider a safe haven.

The road passed wrecked Russian tanks and occasional caravanserai; wallowing, tumbledown structures echoing other eras that were slowly being swallowed by the desert's shifting sands. There were regular military surveillance posts, and at one two friendly soldiers sat me down with a rice lunch before posing for photos in front of their truck-mounted gun and making me fire a skyward round from an AK-47.

Still scared, I pushed Old Geoff deep among some dunes until utterly hidden from view before pitching my tent for the only time in Afghanistan. I had been told the army own the daytime in the area but the night belongs to bandits and the Taliban. I slept poorly, flinching at the slightest sound in a troubled half-sleep.

In the morning I packed up and pedalled quickly, reaching the border at lunchtime. Behind another imposing wall of sandbags and razor wire, an Afghan immigration officer invited me to drink tea. We sat for half an hour discussing his country. It was a representative final conversation with an Afghan: he was charming, he was friendly, and he wanted to emigrate.

FOURTEEN

SUSPICION

To travel is to discover that everyone is wrong about other countries.
- Aldous Huxley

Beyond the military fortifications on the Iranian side of the border my passport was taken away and scrutinised. I sat and waited with a book until, almost an hour later, I was ushered into a concrete room with drip-stained walls. A stern, plain-clothed security officer sat behind a desk. The door shut heavily behind me and the man gestured at the empty chair opposite him. On the otherwise bare desk was a world map and a stack of papers; copies of every page in my passport.

'Where are you going?' he asked.

'Mashhad.' It was the closest major city in Iran.

'Are you from Israel?' The question threw me and I hesitated for a moment.

'No. No, sir, I'm British. Like my passport says.' I was suddenly worried. Israel is seen by Iran as the biggest threat to national security. The Iranian government claims that Israel has spies everywhere and has frequently threatened nuclear strikes against what they refer to as 'The Zionist State'.

'Have you *ever* been to Israel?'

'Never.'

'I don't believe you. I think you are spying.'

'I'm telling you the truth. I know nothing about Israel.'

'Really? Then what country is this stamp from? See, the writing is the Jewish writing.'

I leaned over and looked at the grainy photocopy. 'It's from Nepal. The writing is Nepali. I think it's related to Sanskrit.'

'Nepal? Where is that?'

'Next to India.'

'Fine, well, tell me what country is this visa for? The

writing also looks like the writing of Israel.'

It took me a while to recognise the stamp. 'That visa is for Laos.'

'Laos? Where is that?'

'It's in Asia.'

'You are lying! There is no country in Asia with that name.'

'Yes, there is.'

'I am an Asian man and I know there is not!'

'There is.' I prodded his world map with a shaky finger. 'It's here.'

'Are you Israeli?' He had raised his voice.

'No.'

'You look Israeli. Your nose, your beard…'

'I'm not even Jewish.' It crossed my mind that there was one obvious and easy way to prove this, but it hadn't come to that yet.

'When was your last visit to Israel?'

'I have never been to Israel.'

The officer stared at me for a long while before making a phone call. My bicycle was wheeled in.

'Do I have your permission to look in your bags?'

It wasn't really a question. I nodded. He opened a pannier and reached inside. The first thing that came out was my camera. He started looking for the switch to turn it on. My heart sank. I knew what the most recent photo was and it would not look good.

He found the button to review photos and the image appeared. He looked up at me sharply then showed me the photo. There I was, standing in the desert with dust-covered trousers and headscarf worn like a turban. In my hands was a shiny Kalashnikov with a wooden stock. As well as my bushy six-month beard, I wore a scowl that gave me the air of a determined fighter.

The photo had been taken the previous afternoon by the two friendly soldiers. I hadn't wanted to pose with the gun but they insisted. Its weight shocked me. I had never held such a bulky and aggressive item before.

Unsurprisingly the questions continued for almost an hour and the rest of my bags were thoroughly searched. Another 500 images on my memory card were browsed. With a deep frown the officer flicked through three well-thumbed and annotated paperbacks. He tried and failed to decipher the crabbed writing in my journal which only made him more suspicious. I knew I had done nothing wrong. However, I also knew that mere innocence had never stopped the Iranian authorities from locking up questionable foreigners.

The simple, baseless questions seemed endless and the whole process was exasperating. However, my interrogator finally relented and my story was believed.

'OK, Mr Walker, it is finished. You can go now.'

I hurriedly rode into the desert again, Afghan headscarf still covering my face. A few miles later, I glanced around. There were no cars in sight so I quickly pulled off the road and slumped behind a low, mud wall. My movements were furtive. I wanted to hide. I needed to be alone. The previous month in Afghanistan had gradually worn me down. I had enjoyed generosity and friendship and never felt overtly threatened. And yet, I rarely had time to myself, and the creeping sense of unease that began the moment I entered the country had only grown as time passed. The border crossing was the last straw. But I knew that I was safe now and that the stress would recede. I reminded myself how friendly Iran was, how I had made good friends on my last visit and how I never felt out of my depth.

Sitting behind that wall in Iran, I finally exhaled deeply. My shoulders sank and I relished the knowledge that nobody knew where I was. Feeling completely safe and relaxed for the first time in a month, I pulled off the scrunched and sweaty headscarf. I was free at last.

I stood up and was spotted by a driver who pulled over. I walked confidently towards his car as he jumped out. He greeted me with a hug and triple kiss on the cheeks before shaking my hand warmly. He was a total stranger but I was a visitor to incomparably hospitable Iran and he was excited to meet me. Ali asked me where I was from and where I was going, then forced a bag of fruit and a bottle of juice into my hands before driving off with his hand waving out the window. I was thrilled to be back in Iran.

During the three-day ride to Mashhad kindly motorists continually stopped to chat and force food upon me. The desert days were warm and pleasant but it was already December and the nights were well below freezing. As I pedalled, I gathered my thoughts on Afghanistan. I was glad I visited the country, if only briefly. However, I would not rush to return. I never felt totally at ease; unsettled by the thought that among the crowds there was a hidden minority. Although small, this determined minority would have liked me dead because of who I was and what I believed in. I was left feeling sadness and despair for Afghanistan whose future seemed more uncertain than ever.

There *were* positives though. I met some wonderful, enlightened people and there was a small economic boom happening in the country. But how much longer would foreign countries continue to pump investments into the economy if, as many predicted, Afghanistan slid back into civil war after the foreign forces withdrew? I feared the reasoning that it was my last chance to visit Afghanistan in safety for many years may have been accurate.

I entered Mashhad's sprawl on a gorgeous afternoon and found my way to the small, family-run hostel I had stayed at on my eastward ride two years earlier. Vali, the eccentric owner, recognised me and I was welcomed with a hug. My two-year, seventeen-country, 14,000-mile loop around Asia had gone full circle. Only the Middle East and Africa lay between me and home.

FIFTEEN

MARRIAGE

I know not, said the princess, whether marriage be more
than one of the innumerable modes of human misery.
- Samuel Johnson, *The History of Rasselas, Prince of Abissinia*

Under light snowfall I cycled out of Mashhad and climbed westward into mountains; brown, white, barren and beautiful. I was in no rush. My visa was good for one month and could be extended twice. While the winters in northern Iran are harsh, the south enjoys warmer weather and I vaguely planned to head south until spring, taking my time while avoiding the worst of the weather.

I had emailed Monireh, a friend from my last visit, who lived in a city called Shahrud. She and her family were expecting me in a week or so. The main road to Shahrud was 300 miles but I had cycled that route and so opted for 400 miles of back roads.

The daytime temperatures remained resolutely below freezing and the night temperatures were truly bitter. My punctured sleeping mat deflated three or four times each night and my joints ached each morning from the cold ground. It was dark by 5 p.m. and the sun didn't rise until 8 a.m. As a result, I passed at least fifteen hours in my tent each night. Two sleeping bags and a stack of paperback books – anything in English I could lay my hands on – helped pass those hours confined in the cramped tent. I also poured over my Persian map of Iran and painstakingly transliterated the place names into Latin letters so I could read it more easily.

Each afternoon I found a village shop and picked up breakfast for the following day. Usually coffee, bread, feta cheese, walnuts and fruit. Firing up the stove for coffee warmed the tent in the morning and I read in 'bed' until luxuriously late, bracing myself to face the frigid world outside.

Motorists often pulled over to talk, take photos, and force food upon me. I struggled to eat my way through the vast supplies accumulated in panniers. One man, Mohammad, noticed the poor state of my shoes and shook his head with disapproval. They had hand-stitched repairs and carrier bags worn inside them to keep water out. Mohammad tried to swap a flash new pair of leather boots for my sodden, rotting pair. I had to insist firmly that I was happy with my shoes. He only relented when I promised to buy some new ones in Shahrud and accepted a few crumpled banknotes to go towards them.

One day I woke to an unusually small, dark and warm tent. The cosy cocoon was caused by a heavy, insulating ten centimetres of snow. There was even a couple of centimetres perched precariously on the thin guy lines. That morning I worked my way across the bleak, white landscape on an eerily empty road.

There was a melancholic peacefulness to pedalling the backroads alone across the snow-muffled landscape. In one village, three dogs sat, mournful and silent, around a dog-shaped lump in the snow. In the afternoon the land sloped downwards past snow-dusted sand dunes as I descended to the northern fringe of the Kavir, a desert as big as Belgium.

In a basic, mud-built desert village, a handsome shepherd in his forties ushered me into his low, dark home. He gave me tea and bread before lying almost horizontal and smoking *teriyok*, a resinous opiate from the poppy fields of Afghanistan. He smiled contentedly, watery eyes half-closed, while his three wives and six children studied me with bashful curiosity.

A passing policeman spotted me sitting on the sand patching a puncture one afternoon and asked to see my passport. He was convinced my visa had expired and a soon-to-be-familiar two hours of questions in a village police station ensued.

'Do you have GPS?'

'No.'

'Do you have a camera?'

'Yes.'

'Why have you taken this photo in the desert?'

'It is beautiful to me.'

'Why did you come to Iran?'

'To learn about your country.'

'Are you sponsored by your government?'

'No.'

'Do you have GPS?' …

The next day brought another village police station and two more hours of the same repetitive questioning, this time from a fat man in an undersized shirt with two burst buttons. He treated me like an errant child while his deputy scanned several hundred photos on my camera. They had received a call from the previous day's espionage-busting hotshots. I was eventually released and told to report to a certain address on arrival in Shahrud. Someone there would be expecting me.

On the last day's ride to Shahrud I struggled up a sandy track among the foothills of the Alborz mountain range where the trail abruptly disappeared. I spent several hours pushing past occasional shepherd huts and thorn bush corrals abandoned for the winter with snowdrifts slumped in their shadows. At one point five huge and terrifying dogs had to be literally beaten back with a stick. Later six illicitly drunk hunters in jeeps, the only people I had seen all day, stopped to show off their guns and a sack of small, dead birds before roaring off into the dunes. Lost and without any tracks to follow, I began to despair. It was winter solstice, the shortest day of the year, but it was beginning to feel like my *longest*. I eventually guessed what compass bearing Shahrud might be on and plugged away in as straight a line as I could manage.

Long after dark, exhausted, I spotted the ochre glow of a city's streetlamps on the horizon and soon descended from the hills on a dry riverbed. Twelve hours after starting that morning, I gladly reached the streets of Shahrud and remembered my way to Monireh's home.

The family had taken me in for a couple of nights two years earlier when I was just five months into my journey. Back then I was youthfully wide-eyed and impressionable. And Monireh, with her glowing brown eyes and waist-length hair, had made quite an impression on me. When she answered the door and greeted me with a smile and a demure handshake, I was instantly besotted again. She was even more striking than I remembered. As before, she was the only woman in the family who wore her hair uncovered in my presence.

Monireh's aged mother, tiny and Yoda-esque, was sitting on a sofa and waved me in. The grey-black rings around her deep-set eyes had further darkened, and her creased, brown-toothed grin had widened. Monireh's brother Ali embraced me warmly and helped wheel dusty Old Geoff into the flat. His wife Neda was there too. The stomach bump of two years earlier had grown into an eighteen-month-old girl called Vienna. The baby was so terrified of my appearance that when I was handed a towel and shown to the shower, I shaved off seven months of bushy, copper-red beard. The younger, slightly gaunt face that emerged startled me.

Once I was washed, shaved and dressed in some of Ali's clothes, we sat down to a late dinner of stewed fish and *sabzi polo* (herbed rice). A jug of fresh *doogh* (yoghurt drink with chopped mint) was poured into tall glasses with golden flower motifs. We ate and I did my best to restrain my rampant appetite after a long and physically demanding day.

When we had all eaten and slouched onto floor cushions Monireh started quizzing me about the last two years, translating my answers into Farsi for the family. Her English had improved and she said she had been reading and translating my blogs as practice. At midnight Ali and Neda said goodnight and returned to their flat upstairs. I was to be the sole male for the night in the flat with Monireh and her mother. This was scandalous by Iranian standards. I was a foreigner, not part of the family, and an infidel at that.

The mother smiled, rose with a groan, and shuffled into her bedroom. Monireh and I were suddenly alone together, something that should never happen in conservative Iran. My thoughts raced. She showed me photos of her oil works from the art degree she was doing. I noticed that Monireh increasingly took every opportunity to lay a hand on my arm when talking to me, and gradually shuffled a little closer until our knees slightly touched where we sat on the deep-pile carpet.

By 3 a.m. we were side by side watching a film on her laptop with our hands clasped together, fingers interlaced. When the film finished Monireh awkwardly leaned over and kissed me. Her first kiss was how she had seen it done in films. A fierce pressing together of closed mouths and pursed lips. There was lots loud nasal inhaling and rapid head tilting from side to side; a confusion of replicated passion that left her with stubble rash above her lips.

I offered some instruction and we tried again. She then kissed me on the cheek and tiptoed into the room she was sharing with her mother. I stretched out on some cushions in the living room and was asleep in minutes.

In the morning Monireh drove her mother and me to the address I had been given by the village policeman. They gasped when I first showed it to them. It was the *Vezarat-e Ettela'at va Amniyat-e Keshvar,* VEVAK for short, or the Ministry of Intelligence. Not a place where a foreigner, or indeed any Iranian, wants to find themself. However, I was expected and Monireh said that it was better I showed up to explain my innocence.

Two surly intelligence officers sat in a peeling, beige office with disorderly stacks of papers on every surface. They already had my passport details although it took a while to dig them out. The two seemingly junior men perused my passport for a long while, tut-tutting and shaking their heads. The mostly filled pages of my battered passport were a collage of stamps, visas and entrance or expiry dates illegibly scribbled in fading ballpoint pen. The longer they took the more Monireh's mother grew impatient, berating them for wasting everyone's time.

Eventually a senior officer was fetched and swept into the room in a flurry of impatience. He snatched up my passport and within seconds saw my visa was not yet expired. He was telling the men to let me go when his eyes fell on the camera strap slung over my shoulder. There followed another hour of checking through several hundred photos on my camera's tiny display screen. I was eventually ordered to only take photos of the road and not the land to either side of it. I nodded acquiescence to this absurd request and was allowed to leave.

That evening Ali took me to a public swimming pool. I had no swimming shorts so he lent me an old threadbare pair. They were genuinely indecent and I could have read a book through the fabric. However, Iran's morality laws don't allow men and women to swim together and it was men's night at the pool, so it mattered little.

I swam a few lengths before realising what the pool was actually for. The other men stood in the shallow end or sat around the edge drinking excessively sugared tea in little glasses brought by a portly attendant. I joined Ali in the jacuzzi where he told the assembly of very hairy, barrel-chested men about my bicycle journey. I understood snatches here and there.

A strange thing then happened. The man to my left said something to me. Not understanding, I smiled and shrugged. He placed a hand on my thigh under the water and squeezed a few times. He turned to the group, nodded approvingly and pronounced simply '*bozorg.*' Big. The rest of the men then came forward one by one to prod, squeeze, and generally inspect my leg muscles. They muttered their endorsements, shook my hand and called over the attendant for more tea.

On the way back we stopped into the home of Neda's family, Ali's in-laws, for yet more tea. The newlywed brother-in-law was sitting beside his wife. I asked how they had met and was told casually that they had always known one another as they were first cousins. I later learned that over a quarter of marriages in Iran are between first cousins. In fact, cousin marriage is even seen as the ideal union because the family fortune is not watered down.

Later that evening I asked Monireh for her thoughts on marriage in Iran.

'I have been asked to marry twenty-five times,' she said.

'Twenty-five! You've had twenty-five boyfriends?'

'No. Most of them I had never met. It is not like the West here. You don't need to know someone to ask them for marriage.'

'So they were strangers?' I said.

'Yes. Maybe they know I am from good family. Or maybe not. One of them just saw me in the market and asked the next day.'

'He just turned up here and asked you to marry him?'

'No. The man must tell his parents who will call the woman's family and then we must all meet for tea. It is very rude to refuse to meet, even if you have no interest. We must all sit down together; the man and his parents and me and my mother, and Ali, because my father is dead. There is polite conversation where marriage is not talked about. After they have gone, the father will call Ali and ask if his son can marry me. If the answer is yes then they will talk about the bride price.'

I couldn't imagine going through this socially excruciating rigmarole twenty-five times with a succession of strangers guided by meddling mothers and negotiating fathers.

'So the woman doesn't get to choose?' I asked.

'I am lucky. I am from a modern family, thanks to God. My mother and Ali support my decision not to marry, thanks to God, even though I am thirty-two which is old here. Many women have no choice and must marry who their parents tell them too, even when very young.

'At what age do most people marry?' I asked

'Middle-class women are normally married before twenty-five. And the men can marry very late if they like. They can marry four times.

'But in the villages it is different. The law says boys can marry at fifteen years and girls at thirteen. If you ask the government's permission first, you can even make your daughter marry at nine years.'[10]

'Nine!' I was shocked.

'It is very bad. It was not like this before the revolution. Even for me, from a modern family, I still have pressures. Last year a man threatened to kill me if I did not marry him. I still refused and he tried to kill himself. He is still alive, thanks to God. But I think I don't ever want to marry. I like my life and my art and I love my family and that is all I need, thanks to God.'

After everyone else had gone to bed that night, Monireh and I stayed up watching the nineties romcom *Notting Hill*. Once again we sat hand in hand and she told me the film was a favourite among her friends. Unsurprisingly it is banned in Iran because it shows adultery, nudity and premarital sex. Monireh said her friends all loved western romantic films and there were even some being made in Iran. I had seen snatches of these mawkish creations on televisions in roadside cafés. They were high in schmaltz and all championed the idea of falling wildly in love and, eventually, living happily ever after. I couldn't help thinking these stories painted an unrealistic picture for ordinary Iranians. Most marriages in Iran are arranged by parents. 'Romantic love' is seen as an abstract privilege to most Iranians, despite the abundance of films, television shows, and pop songs about it.

With these unobtainable expectations, it is hardly surprising that the country's divorce rate is one of the highest in the world, rising to over 40 per cent in affluent areas of Tehran. I thought again of Ali's brother-in-law and his cousin bride. It struck me that in Iran marrying a first cousin is not only a way of maintaining family wealth. It is also a safe way of marrying someone you know and trust rather than a complete stranger – perhaps the closest many can hope to get to the ideal of romantic love.

[10] In 2015 the International Campaign for Human Rights in Iran found that each year more than 40,000 Iranian girls under the age of fourteen are married.

SIXTEEN

SCHISM

*Schisms do not originate in a love of truth, which is a
source of courtesy and gentleness, but rather in an
inordinate desire for supremacy.*
- Benedict de Spinoza

We drove 100 miles to Semnan to join the rest of the family for a few days. Monireh had several sisters and a couple of nephews living there, some of whom I had met before. Pooya had grown from a bug-eyed, chubby adolescent to a groomed and gym-going young man. Pouria, now nineteen, had become tall and frowning with excessive hair gel. He had two black eyes and his nose in a cast after a recent nose job.[11]

That night someone in the family noticed that it was Christmas and asked me to sing some Christmas songs. Feeling slightly put on the spot, I struggled through 'The Twelve Days of Christmas', largely with improvised lyrics. Afterwards I thought of my family sitting around the fire with carols playing and scraps of wrapping paper littering the floor. I felt homesick but also glad to at least be among a family that day.

I visited the art school where Monireh and her sister, Mona, studied. I had to walk through the campus gates with a male student, Farzhad, while the girls walked a few yards behind. Men and women cannot enter the university together, even if they've arrived on the same bus. The buses were gender segregated and even had separate stops for men and women, twenty yards apart.

---

[11] Tehran has become the rhinoplasty capital of the world with many people travelling from other countries for the procedure. Every year seven times more rhinoplasties are performed in Iran than in the United States, a country with four times the people. On a short walk around the affluent northern suburbs of the capital, one will likely encounter a dozen people with bandaged noses.

I ended up posing for thirty minutes for a drawing class, who were scandalised when I told them that the last time I sat for art students I was nude. During lunch two officers from the *Gasht-e Ershad*, Iran's 'morality police', told me to leave the grounds immediately as I was eating with women. Farzhad accompanied me to the gates muttering dark curses about the officers. He gave me a pencil sketch he had drawn of me and hugged me goodbye. I then got in trouble from the morality police once again for accidentally standing at the women's bus stop.

Monireh met me in the city centre later and we ordered tea in a café. Fearing further problems with the police we sat in a corner out of earshot, hoping to pass ourselves off as either related or married. Clearly upset, Monireh was repeatedly apologetic about what had happened in the art school. She started speaking darkly about her country then started asking if I could get her onto an art scholarship in Britain. Vainly trying to deflect the difficult conversation, I foolishly asked what she wanted for her future.

'Give me one moment to think about this question,' she said and rested her face in her hands. She remained still for a long while and then her shoulders started to shake. Tears dropped onto the table. After a while longer she looked up, her cheeks a streaky mess of mascara.

'I want to leave this stupid country,' she said. 'I want to go away, to go anywhere. But I can't because of the government and because of my family. If we cannot all leave then none of us will leave. Maybe one day I will find a way to go, please God.'

*   *   *

From Shahrud I rode south out of the Alborz foothills and again into the Kavir Desert. Having lingered with Monireh and her family, I had just five short days to cover 450 miles to the city of Yazd. If I was late to lodge a visa extension application I could expect further trouble from the authorities.

Those five days were solitary and wonderful, with long, hard rides on a quiet road through some of the most featureless landscape on the planet. The heart of the desert was a barren bowl with the low smudge of snowcapped mountains visible through the crystalline winter sky at several points of the horizon. The Kavir was once a large salt sea that dried up tens of millions of years ago. As the water evaporated, a salt crust of several inches was left covering the former seabed of soft, greasy mud below. Over the intervening eons this swamp of treacherous mud has broken through the crust in certain areas creating vast stripes, or striations, of red and white hues resembling the topography of a Martian mountain. I gazed at these swirling rime tides and marvelled at the utter sterility of the land. There was nothing: no scrub, no weeds, no birds, not even insects.

I rode long after sunset each freezing night to hit the required daily mileage, only stopping when the throbbing numbness in my fingers grew too much. In the mornings I ate my breakfast watching the sun rise while melting frost dribbled down the tent wall and dripping icicles of condensation wavered from my canvas roof. Each morning start involved the ache of pressing overworked and cold-stiffened muscles into service. Within an hour my limbs would warm to the task and the sensation of toil would fade, gradually replaced by metronomic peace and, eventually, enjoyment.

As I emerged from the harshest stretch of nothingness, occasional villages began to crop up again. Most were set back from the narrow road; a jarring anomaly of greenery sprouting at the end of an ancient *qanat*. These underground channels carry water from hill sources and facilitate the limited human life that exists in the desert. Some of these channels were dug over two millennia ago and others reach sixty miles in length.

Herds of Arabian camels mooched around village peripheries where the mud walls of former homes sagged with abandonment. I spent one evening hunting among some of these ruins with a village headman's son. Under a fat, red moon, this Jeremy Paxman lookalike and I stalked through stooped archways and over forlornly tumbled walls in search of desert hares. We saw no prey save for the flick of a bushy red tail as a fleeing fox darted around a corner.

The final stretch to Yazd was a three-hour starlit ride on New Year's Day, through rocky hills silhouetted against the night's speckled purple canopy. The road was deserted and the solitude was bewitching. I raised the volume of the classical music in my earphones until I was borne along in a blissful bubble of sound, oblivious to all else.

Arriving late at night, I found a £2 dormitory bed in a hostel and collapsed into a dreamless sleep. In the morning I shuffled sleepily into the dining room with a book and gorged for two hours on the extensive breakfast buffet of bread and dates and nuts and jam and fruit and halva.

At the visa extension office the queue of predominantly Afghan men in *shalwar kameez* and grubby off-white headscarves lined up in the sunshine on the pavement. Each newcomer walked to the front of the queue, greeted the first person in line, and then worked his way back, shaking everyone's hands and exchanging polite words.

Inside the office at last, I paid the £6 fee for a one-month extension and was told to collect my passport in five days. With no urgency to get cycling I relished the prospect of several spare days in a strange city where I knew no one.

The following day was Arba'een, the commemoration of Imam Hussein's martyrdom. Hussein, the grandson of the prophet Mohammad, was the third Imam in the Shi'a tradition. Shortly after Mohammad died in AD 632 there was a succession struggle. Those who would come to be known as Sunnis wanted an election to determine who became caliph, the leader of the fast-growing Islamic Caliphate. A smaller group, the first Shi'as, believed that the mantle of leadership should be hereditary and backed Mohammad's son-in-law, Ali. The struggle went back and forth and three caliphs were assassinated in the following thirty years, including Ali.

By AD 680 a Sunni Caliph, Muawiyah, held power but

was growing old. He had become caliph by a treaty with Hussein that put an end to the ongoing schismatic war. The terms of this treaty stipulated that upon Muawiyah's death there would not be an automatic Sunni succession but instead an election in the Islamic world. This solution seemed a way to satisfy both the Sunni insistence on non-hereditary succession, and the Shi'a desire to have Mohammad's descendants at least *considered* for leadership. It appeared that the half-century sectarian rent through the realm of Islam might just have been repaired.

However, the caliph broke the treaty by appointing his son, Yazid, as his successor. When Muawiyah died and Yazid claimed power, Hussein set out with a small Shi'a company to gather supporters and challenge the upstart caliph. While watering their caravan at Karbala, forty miles south of Baghdad, the Shi'as were intercepted by Yazid's much larger force and defeated in the Battle of Karbala.

It is written that seventy-two of Hussein's followers were slaughtered, including his six-month-old son, and that he was beheaded. The women and children were taken prisoner and force-marched to Damascus with the heads of their sons, husbands and fathers borne before them, impaled on spearheads.[12]

From this point onwards the rift within Islam only deepened. The Shi'as remained the minority and today constitute only a tenth of the world's Muslims, while Sunnis make up around 85 per cent.

The anniversary of the Battle of Karbala is known as Ashura and is commemorated with black-clad mourning processions through the streets. Some men in these funereal processions self-flagellate, striking their backs with chain whips or cutting their freshly shaven heads with big knives. Mourners wail and rend their clothes and the sense of

---

[12] Yazid remained caliph for three years until he died when thrown from his horse, aged 36. His reign is remembered as tyrannical. Among his several actions was the destruction of the *Kaaba*; the black, cubic building at the centre of the Great Mosque of Mecca. The *Kaaba* is the holiest site in Islam and is the location towards which Muslims around the world face during prayer.

grievance seems to run shockingly deep. It is as though a loved one had been murdered a few days earlier rather than a stranger killed in battle seven centuries ago.

However, Arba'een comes forty days after Ashura, at the end of the scripturally prescribed mourning period for Hussein. Unlike the visceral pain of Ashura, Arba'een has an atmosphere of relief, celebration even. After three hours of amplified prayers the crowds spilled out of Yazd's numerous mosques and gathered for communal meals provided by the State. In Iran everyone is fed on Arba'een. Whether Shi'a or Sunni, Jew or Christian, or even hungry cycle tourist, all are handed a helping of rice and meat to eat together in public.

Most Shi'as will try at least once in their lives to make the pilgrimage to Karbala in Iraq on Arba'een. It is thought to be the largest gathering in the world, with up to 25 million Shi'as converging on the city from all directions, most on foot and some after journeys of several hundred miles.

Although the original disagreement concerned the successor to Mohammad, the Battle of Karbala remains probably the biggest fault line between the two sects. The same day that I sat on a street corner in Yazd with a polystyrene plate of rice and mutton chatting to friendly young Yazdi men, Sunni extremists in Iraq detonated a car bomb near Karbala, killing twenty Shi'a pilgrims. The echoes of a seventh-century killing continue to cost lives in the complicated religious tangle of the modern Middle East.

I spent a day getting deliberately lost in the old city's winding warren of narrow alleyways. The squat figures of conservatively clad old ladies shuffled along in twos and threes, some with floral patterned *chadors* but most with plain, black iterations of the shapeless, sheet-like covering. Young boys played football in the few wider spaces. They flattened themselves against the mud-plastered walls whenever motorbikes, driven by young men with fistfuls of gel smoothed through long raven hair, sped through.

I wandered the maze, marvelling at how a city of half a million could exist in the waterless heart of vast, desert-bound Iran. Perhaps even more impressive is that there were already 50,000 inhabitants at the turn of the twentieth century before any modern water-bearing technologies were installed. The world's most extensive system of *qanats* carried mountain melt water underground from distant aquifers to numerous wells spread across the city. The chirpy old curator of the Yazd Water Museum told me that wealthy families had their own branch dug off a major *qanat*, channelling a private supply of cool, clean water straight into their homes.

Yazd Province has over 5,000 *qanats*, many of which still function today. Less affluent members of society living in the old city can still be seen lugging drums brimful of water away from the *ab anbar*, or wells, often on donkey-drawn carts.

One afternoon I wandered up one and then the other of two small mountains south of the city. On each was perched an open-topped, circular walled structure known as a *dakhmeh*. These buildings are better known to foreigners as Towers of Silence or, less poetically, 'putrefaction plateaus'. In the Zoroastrian religion the four elements (air, water, earth, and fire) are thought to be sacred and Avestan (the corpse demon) is believed to take up residence in human flesh at the moment of death. Burying this unclean meat would contaminate the purity of the earth and so the dead were left out in *dakhmeh* to be pecked at by vultures.

The towers were each paved with concentric rings of stone, circling a pit at the centre. Keen to practice his impressive English, a smartly dressed young man called Amir Hussein explained that once the bones were picked clean and sun-bleached to a brilliant white, they would finally be placed in the earth. The rich had their deceased's remains gathered and placed in an ossuary to then be buried elsewhere. The bones of the poor would simply be swept into the vast communal ossuary of the pit.

The earliest known mention of this practice is by Herodutus two and a half millennia ago but the two towers at Yazd date back only two centuries. As the growing city outskirts crept slowly outwards during the twentieth century, the idea of piles of putrefying bodies close to people's homes became a health concern and the government outlawed the use of *dakhmeh* in the 1970s. Today, the city's 30,000 Zoroastrians prevent Avestan from contaminating the earth by interring their dead in concrete-lined coffins in a nearby cemetery.

As Amir Hussein and I wandered back down the hill and through the remains of buildings once used to prepare the bodies for their sojourn in the Towers of Silence, he pointed out an elderly man stooped to the shape of a question mark. He was posing for photos with some Korean tourists in expansive visors.

'That man is a Zoroastrian,' Amir Hussein said. 'He was the last *dakhmeh* taximan.'

'Taximan?' I asked.

'Taximan for the dead. His job was to take the bodies up the mountain and lay them out for the birds.'

I watched the unsmiling old man as he leaned on a walking stick and held out his hand for a couple of banknotes from the Koreans. Minus the desert setting, he could have passed for Greek mythology's Charon demanding two coins to ferry the dead across the river Styx. He beckoned ominously to us with an arthritic finger as we passed.

SEVENTEEN

ANCIENTS

History isn't a single narrative, but thousands of alternative narratives. Whenever we choose to tell one, we are also choosing to silence others.
- Yuval Noah Harari, *Homo Deus*

The road south wound through mountainous desert for several days of icy rain showers and piercing headwinds on a little-used road.

As in all of Iran, the streets of villages and small towns were lined with portrait posters of the men and boys who died in the eight-year war with Iraq in the 1980s. The war's initial spark was a dispute over a cross-border oilfield, but it evolved into a sectarian Sunni–Shi'a conflict as each side consciously conflated religion and politics to acquire internal allegiance and external support. It was a dirty war, with chemical attacks, archaic trench warfare, and half a million dead. Brainwashed volunteer soldiers as young as thirteen fought and died for confabulated causes. Iran's 200,000 dead are referred to as *shahid*, or martyrs, and used to rally nationalism and religious feeling. Grainy sepia images of their young, haunting faces gazed out at me everywhere I went, a constant reminder of the government's unwillingness to leave the past behind.

To shelter from the rain one morning I ducked into an empty breezeblock hut on the roadside, lit a fire and read a book. I was suddenly disturbed by the sickening screech of tyres followed by a horrible grinding sound. I dashed outside to see a pickup truck rolled onto its side with its underbelly facing me. As I ran over I saw the long trail of tyre marks where it had skidded before ploughing off the road and rolling over. The skyward front wheel was still spinning.

I hurriedly circled the wreck, looking for a puddle of

leaking petrol, but it was hard to tell on the wet road. Passing the windscreen I saw a moving confusion of black robes through the fogged glass. I clambered onto the top and pulled the door open. Inside the cabin was a tangle of bodies. As well as the wailing of more than one woman hitting my ears, inappropriately jaunty pop music was rattling from the stereo. The middle-aged male driver stared up at me vacantly for a long moment, making me fear a head injury. A toddler was just visible, quietly trembling below him. Two women were engulfed in black *chadors* at the bottom.

When I shouted at the man he snapped out of his trance and awkwardly pulled the child from beneath him, lifting her towards me. The little girl remained silent while I plucked her up and cradled her, looking for the best way to clamber down to the ground. However, she took one look at my unfamiliar foreign face and erupted into a fit of tearful screaming. At length I set the shoeless child down on a pile of hessian sacks that had spilled from the back of the truck. After I helped the man clamber out he didn't pause to look back at the women or check his daughter, but started wandering around his vehicle, inspecting the damage.

There was thankfully no smell of petrol and he didn't seem in a hurry. Neither did he seem interested in the plight of the two women, who I guessed to be his wife and mother-in-law. They continued wailing but refused to take my helping hand. They didn't seem hurt but were evidently shaken and couldn't calm down while piled in the sideways cabin.

The man's disinterest angered me and the screaming was unnerving, making it hard to think. Eventually I grasped the arm of the tiny, topmost woman and lifted her out. This silenced them both. Her mother righted herself and stood in the empty cabin before sheepishly letting me help her up. They set about calming the child while I helped a newly arrived carful of men to heave the truck back onto its wheels. The damage was only cosmetic and ten minutes later everyone had driven away, leaving only skid marks on the road and an irritation in me that the man was so careless of his family.

The rain still fell, so I returned to the hut to stoke my little fire and dry off. But the incident had sewn the seed of a creeping disaffection that was to grow during the following two months in Iran, watered by things I learned and saw. These were mostly attitudes towards women but also the faith-related aspects of a country which has the death penalty (often public, and allegedly by stoning on occasion) for homosexuality, sodomy, pornography, adultery, apostasy, blasphemy, 'enmity against God', and 'corruption on earth' (a freely interpretable Koranic verse). The government carries out more executions per capita than any other state. In 2015 the figure was 977, compared to just eighteen in the United States.

The day after the car crash the weather cleared and I approached the town of Qader Abad. A few miles before reaching town I was caught up by a small red Renault driven by Ebrahim, an earnest English teacher. He invited me for lunch and drove at bicycle speed for twenty minutes, guiding me to his home. It happened to be *Mawlid*, the national holiday celebrating Mohammad's birthday, and I was introduced to Ebrahim's four brothers who had gathered for the holiday.

My hosts had many questions about life in Europe, most of which concerned sex and relationships in western society. After lunch, Ebrahim retrieved a litre of homebrewed wine in a plastic water bottle from under a rock in the garden. Alcohol is illegal in Iran and it had been hidden there for two years. Ebrahim said it was made with local grapes. This meant little to him but I knew that the city of Shiraz was only fifty miles away and that the grape was the indigenous forebear of the transplanted one put to such good use in France, Australia, and South Africa. Although, judging by the taste I'm not sure Ebrahim's wine had necessarily matured during its time 'laid down' in the garden.

It was Ebrahim's first ever taste of alcohol and in the course of an hour I watched him go from soberly serious to rolling around on the carpeted floor giggling at his frequent hiccups to groaning at an intensifying headache: his first hangover. He clutched the hair at his temples and wailed self recriminations for his perfidy. I suggested he drink some cold water and step outside into the fresh air, cool on a Winter's afternoon. However, he preferred to sit next to the gas heater drinking endless cups of black tea brought in by his disapproving wife.

It was getting dark by this point and Ebrahim insisted I stay for the night, laying out a blanket for me by the heater.

In the morning we drove to nearby Pasargad, the capital city of the most revered Persian monarch, Cyrus the Great. Much to the Islamic government's displeasure, Cyrus is often cited by Iranians as their nation's founder. By 559 BC the Achaemenid king had conquered and unified the kingdoms of Elam, Persia, and Media. He ordered the building of a grand ceremonial capital, meanwhile continuing his exhaustive military campaigning. By the time of Cyrus's death in battle in 530 BC, Pasargad was capital of the largest empire the world had seen, stretching from the Indus to the Aegean.

Little remains of the ancient city today. As Ebrahim and I walked around the site inspecting repositioned column bases and weathered relief sculptures, he told me about Cyrus's human rights record.

'After Cyrus conquered Babylon, he freed the Jews who had been slaves since Nebuchadnezzar destroyed Jerusalem. Cyrus allowed them to go home and rebuild their temple. He also made a promise that all the people of his empire, of many different nations, religions, and cultures, were all equal and all citizens with the same rights. There is a famous clay document where these pronouncements are made. It is now living in your British Museum.'

I vaguely remembered having seen the Cyrus Cylinder on a visit to the museum a few years earlier. It's a surprisingly small object, about the size of a marrow, covered in intricate and tightly spaced cuneiform script. Written upon the conquest of Babylon in 539 BC, in truth most of the text is a self-aggrandising boast of heaven-mandated power[13] and a long-winded royal genealogy. However, it does mention that Cyrus freed all slaves in Babylon and allowed them to take their confiscated statues of gods back to their homelands. Whether this is (as many claim) the world's first human rights charter, or whether it is simply braggadocio in one of the world's first public relations efforts, is open to debate.

Cyrus' impressively well-preserved tomb was the main event at Pasargad and we saved it until last. The twelve-metre-high pyramidal stack of gargantuan limestone slabs glared white in the midday sun, utterly dominating its surroundings. When Alexander the Great passed through 200 years later he reportedly entered the tomb to find a golden coffin placed on a golden bed and surrounded by jewel-studded ornaments. The tomb is said to have borne the inscription:

> *Passer-by, I am Cyrus who gave the Persians an empire, and was king of Asia. Grudge me not therefore this monument.*

Today the tomb is empty, the fabled treasures within long since looted during one of the dozens of conquests that have swept through this pivotal land, where the hinge of Europe and Asia abuts the Arabian peninsula and the ancient trade routes of the Persian Gulf.

Ebrahim drove us another twenty minutes to the abandoned remains of the village where he was born and lived the first six years of his life. The decaying complex of shoulder-high mud walls was enclosed within a thick, circling wall for defence in the event of quarrels with other villages. The entire settlement was only fifty metres across. Ebrahim said there was an imam who led religious life and a chief who dispensed food and justice to the 300 villagers. Each family

---

[13] '*I am Cyrus, king of the universe, the great king, the powerful king, king of Babylon, king of Sumer and Akkad, king of the four quarters of the world...*' Translation by Irving Finkel. *The Cyrus Cylinder: The Great Persian Edict from Babylon* (London: I.B. Tauris, 2013).

had a single first-floor room, roughly three by five metres, built over a space for tightly packed livestock, which acted as underfloor heating in winter. Ebrahim stood, silent and reflective, on the ground below where his family of seven had once lived. A few shards of pottery showed through the milky brown earth at the feet of sloping ghosts of walls.

'I come here every two weeks to think. Only thirty-five years ago I lived here. Maybe half of Iranians lived like this. And now I have a car and a big house with air-conditioning and a widescreen TV.'

From Qader Abad it was only fifty miles to Iran's biggest tourist draw, the ancient ruins of Persepolis. It was a quiet afternoon as I abandoned my bicycle in the car park, paid the six-pence entrance fee, and walked up the 2,500-year-old stone steps towards the jumble of ruins atop the terrace. It was a clear, warm day in late-January and, excepting half a dozen teenage boys taking selfies with their phones, I had the ancient place to myself.

In 522 BC Darius, the son of a Persian nobleman, became the *Shahanshah*, the King of Kings, and built a new capital at Persepolis. It's hard to know the exact circumstances of his ascendancy as he was the author of his own history. Many historians believe Darius carried out a coup d'etat. Either way, he took power, married Cyrus's daughter to lend legitimacy to his claim, and ruled for thirty-six years. His reign was a time of consolidation and reform in the vast but nascent Achaemenid Empire. He built roads, standardised weights and measures, quelled numerous rebellions, and warred endlessly with the Greeks. Darius also launched the first Persian campaign to Greece and was defeated by the heavily outnumbered Athenians at the Battle of Marathon.

The first building I found at the top of the steps was the Gate of All Nations. Its western facade had two monumental columns each bearing a vast *lamassu*, a mythical bull with the head of a bearded man. The Gate of All Nations was a reception hall for visiting satraps – or provincial governors –

from across the empire. Today it is representative of its varied visitors in a different sense: graffiti. Between the forelegs of the left *lamassu* was carved the skull and crossbones seal of the seventeenth Lancers, dated 1810. A detachment of this light cavalry regiment passed through Persepolis when accompanying a diplomatic mission from India to the Shah in Tehran, who was thought to be getting too friendly with the French at the time. The mission travelled through the same troubled area of southern Afghanistan that a friend of mine was fighting in with the same regiment, now called the Queen's Royal Lancers, at the time of my visit. Over 200 years had passed but it seemed Britain simply couldn't divorce itself from Middle Eastern affairs.

Among the hundreds of other names carved into the grand marble columns I spotted the untidily scrawled words: *Stanley, New York Herald.* Henry Morton Stanley was on assignment for the newspaper when he travelled through Persia in 1870 on his way to search for David Livingstone, the Scottish celebrity explorer-cum-missionary who had gone missing in Africa. I knew I'd be crossing paths with Stanley's ghost again if my bike and I made it as far as Central Africa, where he earned both fame and infamy.

Beyond the Gate were spread the ruins of formerly grand, columned palaces, throne halls, a harem, and a considerable treasury. The entire city was built from a dark, highly polished marble that had lightened and lost its lustre as the desert's fine wind-blown dust worked its way into every minute fissure. There were occasional carved details – a lotus flower or the eye of bas-relief bull, perhaps – that modern visitors had run their fingers over and in doing so restored the lustrous dark polish.

The most elaborate and intricate artistry was at the far side of the city in relief carving on the Apadana Palace's staircase. A procession of delegations from all corners of the empire are depicted bringing tribute to the Shah of Shahs, who is flanked by courtiers and his imperial bodyguard. The staircase is a who's who of ancient Persia's subject peoples.

Wearing diadems in their curled hair, the Elamites offer intricately decorated hunting bows. The Armenians wear horseman's cloaks and lead a finely bridled stallion as a gift. The turbaned Parthians bring ornate bowls and a Bactrian camel. The earring-wearing Bactrians from Balkh also offer a two-humped camel. Ionian Greeks in striped robes carry cups and textiles, while the conical-capped Babylonians bring tasselled garments and a humped bull. There are bare-chested Indians with a buffalo, Thracians from modern-day Bulgaria with spears and shields, Arabs with a one-humped camel, Libyans with an oryx, Egyptians with a hippopotamus, and curly-haired Nubians with an elephant tusk and a giraffe.

Perhaps most striking about the procession is that the subject nations, all of which have been recently conquered by the Persians during their rapid expansion, walk hand in hand with their Persian masters. Art from ancient Egyptian, Roman and Assyrian empires all depict the subject peoples as vanquished prisoners of war. It appears that Cyrus' vision of equality across a far-reaching empire enjoying peace, trade, and prosperity endured beyond his death.

The reason for the ruinous state of Persepolis was western aggression. In 330 BC, Alexander the Great sacked and burned Persepolis. It is thought that the uncharacteristic razing of the city was an act of revenge for the Persians sacking Athens and burning the Acropolis 150 years earlier. All Persepolis's cow-hide manuscripts were destroyed, the Macedonian army were allowed to loot and pillage, and it is written by Diodorus that Alexander required 3,000 camels and hundreds of mules to carry off the fabulous wealth of the city.

EIGHTEEN

THE STATE OF IRAN

Americans … are the great Satan, the wounded snake.
- Ayatollah Khomeini, 1979

In Shiraz I extended my visa again. As it was my second extension, I had to undergo a short interview and complete plenty of paperwork. I was asked the full names and occupations of my father and both grandfathers. Mothers and grandmothers details were deemed unimportant. I wrote 'deceased' under occupation for both my grandfathers but my interviewer told me that was unacceptable. I said that they had both been officers in the army. He looked at me sharply.

'Military?' he asked.

'Yes, sir.'

'British military?'

'Yes, sir.'

'Have either of them ever conducted covert operations on Iranian territory?'

'No, sir.'

'Do you have the official documentation to prove this?'

'No, sir. It wouldn't be covert if I did. But neither lived into this century and both only fought the Nazis.'

'The documentation is important.'

'I'm sorry. I don't have any.'

'Will you sign a statement promising that they were not spies against our regime?'

'I will.'

'Very well. Return in five days and you will have your visa.'

I checked into a hostel buried down a maze of alleyways in the heart of the old city. The only other guest in the dormitory was a solo Chinese backpacker called Jeanne. It was baffling to me that in obsessively conservative Iran a unisex dormitory for tourists had somehow slipped under the radar.

Jeanne and I passed a pleasant few days exploring the city together and chatting with the well-educated young Iranians who hang around the city's attractions in the hope of practicing their English on foreigners. They were charming and open-minded people but almost all were jobless and rudderless.

The middle-class twenty-somethings of Iran seemed to complete their degrees and then live in their parents' homes for a lengthy period of prolonged adolescence. Thought to be as much as 20 per cent, unemployment in Iran is highest among the educated who feel they can't (or won't) take jobs beneath their station. Yet they have few prospects among the country's stagnant white-collar work force. Those we met had spoken at length with many foreigners and knew better than most Iranians of the superior freedoms and opportunities that lay beyond their nation's borders. They all had one desperate goal: emigration. Some of them would doubtless achieve their goal and contribute to the chronic brain drain that Iran is suffering. The brightest and best graduates are the most likely to leave and never come back.[14]

I soliloquised about Persepolis to Jeanne and she was interested to experience bicycle travel, so I suggested she rent a bike and we cycle the forty miles there together. We set off late morning and began a ten-mile westward climb away from the city. I tried my best not to pull far ahead but struggled, as cycling uphill has a natural rhythm that is hard to alter. I stopped frequently and waited for Jeanne to catch up.

On the third time she approached she was in tears. Two separate motorcyclists had pulled alongside and groped her as they passed. The second had looped around for another

[14] In 2006, the International Monetary Fund found between 150,000 and 180,000 educated Iranians were emigrating annually. Since the 1979 revolution, emigration has increased 140-fold. In 2000, it was found that 25 per cent of Iranians with higher education were living abroad in OECD nations.

grope but Jeanne waited until he came close before leaping off her bike and hurling a stone at him. I realised that Jeanne was the first woman I had seen on a bicycle in Iran. She said that she had experienced that sort of sexual abuse almost on a daily basis in Iran and relished that she was left alone when accompanied by me in Shiraz.

We approached Persepolis in the dark and pitched my tent among some trees near an odd constellation of large concrete circles.[15] Under a star-studded sky we cooked Chinese-style spicy fried vegetables, eggs, and rice on my tiny camping stove.

After re-visiting the ruins with Jeanne in the morning, I pedalled a few miles to Naqsh-e Rustam, the necropolis of the Achaemenid dynasty. It's a striking site with four funerary palaces of Achaemenid rulers carved in relief on a fifty-metre-high cliff that evoke the rock-hewn glory of Petra. The oldest is the tomb of Darius the Great and depicts him above the portico held aloft by thirty soldiers.

Below the tombs are several reliefs added later by the Sassanids, a dynasty that saw four centuries of near-constant warring with Rome and was eventually toppled by the Arab conquest. The most interesting was a triumphal depiction of the third-century Shapur I with three Roman emperors. Valerian, who was captured in battle, has his wrists seized by Shapur while 'Philip the Arab' kneels in surrender and Gordian III lies trampled under Shapur's horse's hooves, killed in battle.

Jeanne took a bus to Yazd and I set out west into the Zagros

---

[15] I later learnt that these were built as platforms for luxury tents in 1971 when Mohammad Reza, the last Shah of Iran, lavishly entertained 600 of the world's political elite to celebrate the 2,500th anniversary of the Persian Empire's foundation. Presidents, kings, queens, sultans, emirs, grand dukes, cardinals, and an emperor were among the 62 heads of state in attendance. The occasion has been dubbed 'the world's most expensive party'. Estimates in today's money hover around $230m. Commentators speculate that the obscenely extravagant party was a vital link in the chain of events leading to the end of 2,500 years of Persian monarchy within eight years, with the Islamic Revolution.

mountains. As the road wound higher the temperature dropped and I was passed by cars with skis on the roof. For several days I slowly scrolled across lofty, undisturbed snowfields that shimmered a pinkish golden-red in the evening sun. I chose grand, throne-like camp spots with far-reaching views and gorged on dinners of olives, dates, feta cheese and fresh bread. It took a couple of hours each morning to fully regain sensation in my toes.

After a week I descended from the mountains and met Jeanne in the centre of Esfahan. She recalled her adventures as we walked to the hotel where she had taken a room for us.

'Iran men are very sex problem,' she said.

'What do you mean?'

'Because of rules, they are frustrated. On first morning in Yazd, three men grabbed my ass. And another man drove alongside me when I was walking. He opened the car window and I saw he was touching himself.'

'Oh my god!'

'You are man and don't see it, but this happens every day to me in Iran.'

'Are you OK?'

'It's fine, I went to knife shop and now I feel more safe. Also, some Iran people are very racist about Chinese. Someone told me there is no soap in China and that we are very dirty people. They said this to my face ... which I washed that morning ... with soap. One woman asked me if people eat babies in China!'

'I think they just don't get good information because Iran is so isolated from the world.'

'Maybe. How was your journey?' she asked.

'Well, ummm, I cycled a lot. All day every day in fact.'

'Nothing happened?'

'Well, I got a couple of punctures, and I slept in my tent in beautiful places for ten hours a night, I saw a jackal and a couple of foxes, and I warmed my fingers by a fire with some friendly fish farmers one day. But, no, nothing really happened.'

'Do you enjoy that?'

'I think so. I don't know. I feel good when I do it. But it is lonely sometimes. I missed you, actually.'

'I missed you too, *Húzi Shushu*!'

She'd given me the nickname in Shiraz. Jeanne was two years younger than me and Chinese respectfully refer to elder men as Uncle (*shushu*). I was once again becoming unkempt and *húzi* means beard: 'Beard Uncle.' I quite liked the name and called her 'Rice Box' in return; a gentle tease for her impressive appetite. I was growing to like her enjoyable and uncomplicated companionship. In a country where I was viewed as an oddity and a stranger, Jeanne was viewed as even stranger still and this bonded us.

Esfahan was the capital of the Safavid dynasty (1501-1736) and boasts one of the world's oldest and largest public squares. Formerly called *Nashq-e Jahan* (Image of the World), the square is overlooked by balconies of the six-storey, sixteenth-century royal palace. Courtiers once played polo in the square and the sturdy stone goal posts still stand at either end.

However, it is today known as Imam Square and we visited on the final day of *Dahe-ye Fajr*. The event, also known as the Ten Days of Dawn, marks the anniversary of the Islamic Revolution in 1979 and the point at which the country's relationship with the West began to decay. The Iranian people had lost patience with Shah Mohammad Reza Pahlavi. A misguided moderniser desperate to westernise a country he viewed as backward, Mohammad Reza was crudely used as a tool for foreign, largely Anglo-American, exploitation of Iran's significant petroleum wealth.

On 1 February septuagenarian cleric Ruhollah Khomeini returned to Tehran after a fourteen-year exile. Within ten days of Khomeini descending the steps of an Air France plane to a welcoming crowd of several million, revolution was declared, the Shah was deposed, and Khomeini set about creating his vision of a true Islamic Republic.

He installed himself as Supreme Leader sitting at the head of the Guardian Council of Islamic Jurists, with the frequently exercised power to veto any decision made by the 'democratically' elected government. The world's first modern-day theocracy was born.[16]

The laws laid down by a seventh-century Arabian warlord were instituted absolutely. Accordingly, the legal age of marriage for boys and girls was set at thirteen and nine years respectively (it has since been changed to fifteen and thirteen). The conservative dress code of hijab for women was re-enforced, having been previously outlawed by the Shah. All non-Islamic, non-martial music was banned, and the death penalty was installed for conversion out of Islam.

When Jeanne and I arrived, Imam Square was filled with 20,000 people kneeling towards Mecca in neat rows. Loudspeakers projected the voice of an Imam preaching from within the Abbasi Mosque at the southern end of the square.[17] Everywhere were banners and posters of Khomeini and Khameini, the current Supreme Leader. I sat in the square during the climactic prayers of the celebration and chatted with a young man called Ali. He translated bits of the shouted sermon blasting from the loudspeakers:

'We shall tread the American's under the soles of our shoes ... we are on the side of God and he shall ensure our victory.'

Alongside the neatly placed carpets on which the faithful prayed were the tumbling heaps of their shoes. I spotted a few places where several hundred pairs of military issue boots were neatly lined up. Something about an army obediently listening to the hateful propaganda distressed me.

The following day, Jeanne and I took an overnight bus to Tehran to each apply for onward visas and spend a last week together. After checking into a hostel, Jeanne set out for the Armenian embassy. Still not entirely sure of my onward

---

[16] Excepting a small group of celibate, largely elderly men in an enclave nation within Rome with a predilection for ceremonially imbibing 'blood' under the symbolic banner of an ancient torture instrument.

[17] The vast, ornately engraved and tarnished silver doors to the mosque bear pockmarks reputedly from Russian artillery during a nineteenth-century clash.

plans, I set out on a long, pensive walk towards the embassy of Iraq.

Over the previous weeks, doubts about completing the entirety of my original route plan had been fermenting at the back of my mind. Iran had worn me down. As dearly as I loved the country, and as overwhelmingly positive as my experiences had been, other things were rankling. The lack of many basic freedoms I grew up taking for granted and the marginalisation of women stood out among others. They made me long for the relative simplicity of life in my home country.

These feelings were perhaps born mostly of having a totally rootless existence for the last year. I was more exasperated with my ceaseless movement and impermanence than I was with Iran itself. Perhaps this was why I had found it easy to feel so close to both Monireh and Jeanne. Getting to know someone more intimately made me real, rather than just a ghost drifting sweatily from city to city, meeting a succession of strangers and moving on before people quite knew I was anything more than an exotic apparition.

With this sense of momentum exhaustion, the prospect of perhaps 20,000 more miles to Africa's southern tip and back utterly appalled me. Twenty thousand miles of scorched desert and claustrophobic jungle and limitless savannah with dangerous animals lurking behind every blade of grass and dangerous drivers piloting twenty-tonne lorries with ailing steering systems. I had travelled in Africa several years before and had allowed the negative aspects to ossify in my mind. The corruption, the low value on human life, the war, the famine, the senseless violence and the all-pervasive sense of hopelessness. I simply couldn't face it.

But skipping Africa would be giving up. It was arguably the most challenging aspect of my original plan. Attractive as it was, simply cycling back across Europe would be an admission of defeat. The road would have beaten me. Hence I was walking to the Iraq embassy. By the time I arrived I had convinced myself that a one-week dash across the centre of Iraq to the Jordanian border would absolve me of the cowardice of avoiding Africa. It would be a 500-mile sprint though Baghdad, Fallujah and Ramadi in the 'triangle of death'. From Jordan I could continue in safety to Israel and circumvent war-torn Syria with a ferry to Cyprus and then another to Turkey for the leisurely homeward leg across Europe. However, the Iraqi embassy staff saw things differently.

'A tourist visa?' The man repeated, shocked.

'Yes please, sir,' I said pleasantly.

'But, sir, we don't have tourists. It is not safe.'

'I will be fine, thank you.'

'I'm sorry. We cannot give you a tourist visa.'

That evening I considered my options. I was left with no immediate choice but to cycle north towards Turkey. I would at least be able to pedal through Iraq's semi-autonomous Kurdish region in the northeast, which was deemed safe and required no visa. The big decision about Africa would have to wait.

While Jeanne awaited her Armenian visa, we pounded the pavements, picnicked in parks, took lazy lie-ins each morning and cooked indulgent feasts each evening. One afternoon we visited the National Jewellery Museum in a vault under Tehran's Central Bank, where the treasures accumulated exploitatively during the last three dynasties of Shahs are on public display. Hundreds of thousands of diamonds and gemstones glittered in an exhibition both impressive and sickening in equal measure. I had never seen such a show of simultaneous wealth and tastelessness.

Each item – crowns, tiaras, swords, thrones, and globes – had as many jewels crammed onto its surface as possible. It was wealth, not artistry. The government's decision to display the hoarded treasure of a fallen regime is ostensibly a cautionary tale about Iran's past under an oppressive monarchic leadership who sapped all they could from the populace. However, this message seemed lost on the Iranian visitors around us who stared lovingly and longingly at the sparkly stones.

Opposite the bank, outside the German embassy, stood a tall government-erected monument in both English and Farsi urging the people of Iran to 'never forget the German government's complicity and undeniable role' in the 'atrocious crime' of providing Saddam Hussein with chemical weapons which were used against Iranian forces. While it is true that industrial chemicals bought from a German firm were used by Hussein to manufacture weapons, the government's involvement is uncertain and unlikely.[18] And yet, this three-metre-high metaphorical middle finger to Germany neatly displays the Iranian regime's willingness to throw diplomacy out the window and stand opposed to the rest of the world. Of course, other foreign embassies have received much worse treatment. America's was besieged for 444 days in 1979, and Saudi Arabia's was firebombed in 2011. The UK's embassy had yet to re-open after being stormed and looted, also in 2011.

After a melancholy final dinner together, Jeanne boarded a night bus to the north, and I boarded the bus back to Esfahan. We had become very comfortable as a couple and saw each other's company as a refuge from the often-complicated experience of travelling in Iran. 'Rice Box' had become a close friend and 'Beard Uncle' was going to miss her company.

My time in Iran was drawing to an end and from Esfahan I began making quick progress along the 600 miles towards the border of Iraqi Kurdistan. The route skirted the northern foothills of the Zagros range and passed through an innocuous little town called Khomein that was Ayatollah Khomeini's birthplace. I was welcomed into yet more homes as well as being hauled into a few more police stations for vague questioning. At length I reached the fertile farmland of Iran's slice of Kurdistan: a region spread across four nations

---

[18] Ironically, it emerged in a 2018 leak that Iran had purchased similar chemicals from another German firm for the manufacture of deadly sarin gas. During my time in Iran, these same weapons found their way to Syria and were used by Bashar al-Assad's regime against rebel forces in Homs, Damascus, and Aleppo.

and peopled by an ethnic group of 35 million desperately lacking statehood. It seemed a pleasant place worth fighting for. Glowing green wheat fields dotted with grain silos basked in mild weather. Men in baggy black, pyjama-style trousers scattered seeds by hand from the pouches they formed with the fronts of their baggy green shirts.

I received an email from a friend one day with a link to an article. As I read it I felt my stomach drop and I began to cry. Peter and Mary, the charming cycling couple from Guernsey who I met briefly in Kazakhstan, had both been killed in a road accident near Bangkok. Apparently a driver hadn't been paying attention and managed to hit them both, killing them instantly. There was sickening footage of the mangled remains of their bikes and panniers piled up outside the local police station.

What if Peter and Mary had overslept in their tent that morning? Or if they had stopped for a quick rest five minutes earlier? What if the driver had taken two minutes longer at the last petrol station to visit the toilet? What if they hadn't been cycling close to one another and the vehicle had veered harmlessly between them? An infinity of variables had to fall cruelly into place to produce the horrific outcome. How many times had I been just one minor variable away from the same fate?

After several hours of thinking of their devastated parents in Guernsey, and of my parents in England, I decided cycling Africa was unimportant. I had always known abstractly that a single slip from a motorist could be the end of me. But now that fact was more real, tangible even. I had spent years riding on dangerous roads with reckless drivers and I didn't even own a helmet. I had pushed my luck far enough. I would cycle home via the most direct route through Turkey and Europe. I could be home for the British summer and reconnect with the family and friends I had left behind.

With this decision made, the pedals felt lighter and I floated onwards with a strange mixture of grief for two people I hardly knew, and love for so many that I used to know well and would soon know again.

During my last days in Iran I reflected on the country that had been my world for three months. Iran wasn't starving; it was suffocating. The oxygen of progress and prosperity was strangled by paranoid and contrarian leadership. The country's economic isolation had lead to inflation running at 30 per cent and the looming collapse of an economy that, under differing circumstances, could be ranking among the world's largest.

Iran owns the world's second-largest reserves of oil and natural gas and has a pivotal geography at the crossroads between Europe, the Middle East, and Asia. Caspian Sea and Persian Gulf ports connected by railways should position Iran as a beneficiary in the flow of goods between East and West – a modern-day Silk Road. However, modern history has dictated otherwise and Iran remains an international pariah with a population cut off from the wider world.

And yet, internet censorship *can* be circumvented, and the outside world *does* creep in, forcing at least *some* political evolution. Many people, particularly those with education, are discontented. A mild slackening of the rules has so far softened the immovable wall required by any liberal revolution against which to surge and crash.

Things *are* moving forwards, slowly. Many women allow their headscarves to slip scandalously far behind their hairline and Tehran grows ever more cosmopolitan.

Despite the difficulties of life in Iran, or perhaps because of them, it remains home to the friendliest and most hospitable people I've met anywhere in the world. I was shown too much kindness by too many people to recount even a fraction of them. Iran is a beautiful country with wonderful people, and as I prepared to leave I felt certain that a bright lay future somewhere ahead.

The last snow of the season fell heavily as I neared the Iraqi border at the end of a long day climbing switchbacks into the Kurdish Zagros. The snowy flanks of 3,000-metre peaks stood all around me. It was six months to the day since my first snow back in western Mongolia. I pedalled past a long queue of lorries and reached the border post at a pass. Both Iran and winter lay behind me.

NINETEEN

SPRING

Am I doing this because I want to do it, or because I want to have done it? If the answer isn't both, then should I be doing it at all?
- Extract from author's diary

The Kurdish customs officers insisted I drink tea with them and then stood waving until I'd disappeared around the corner. The road was potholed and narrow but it was all downhill. I freewheeled for a couple of miles before pitching my tent beside a sweet-tasting stream of melt water that sang along a bed of smoothed pebbles. The snow stopped falling, the sky cleared, and sunset was a gently fading clash of white, gold, and a darkening blue out of which pinprick stars began to pulse.

In the morning I coasted down the mountain and at a small truckers' stop met a mechanic who had worked in Britain for ten years. We ate lunch together and he reminisced. I didn't catch his name but neither did the immigration official when he arrived at Dover as a refugee with no English language. The officer was asking his name but he couldn't understand and said in exasperation, 'Allah, help me!'

'Ali?' asked the officer. And so he was registered in the UK as Ali.

I followed a gushing river west through a narrow gorge and was spilled out into a scene of lush, green hills flooded with warm sun. Large numbers of expensive, imported cars shot past me on the road, a sign of the economic boom the autonomous Kurdish region had recently enjoyed. The Kurds in Iraq had had a rough history and it was about time something went their way.

In the late 1980s, after decades of fighting for independence from the Arab-dominated government, Iraqi

Kurds were victims of a three-year genocide that resulted in the deaths of around 100,000 people, the displacement of a third of the population, and the destruction of over 4,000 villages and towns.

Saddam Hussein's cousin, Ali Hassan al-Majid (better known as Chemical Ali), was put in charge of Operation Al-Anfal, which used firing squads, aerial bombardment, mass deportation, and chemical weapons.[19] Numerous mass graves have been unearthed, some containing up to 1,000 bodies.

After the First Gulf War, Britain, France, and America began enforcing a no-fly zone in the region, protecting the Kurds from Arab aggression and facilitating some measure of autonomy. However, it was not until the fall of Saddam Hussein's regime in 2003 that the Kurds finally won de facto autonomy. The Kurdish forces, the Peshmerga, aided the US-led coalition in the overthrow of the Ba'ath party then largely withdrew, keen not to be dragged into the internecine fighting that inevitably followed as a power vacuum was created.

Since then foreign investment had been pouring into Kurdistan. Investors were lured by the region's estimated 45-billion-barrel oil reserves. Some started referring to Kurdistan as 'New Dubai' but the local government preferred 'The Other Iraq'. The ongoing problems in the rest of Iraq had left Kurdistan as comfortably the most stable and prosperous part of the country.

My second day in The Other Iraq was a Friday. Scores of families picnicked on the roadside. Long wedding convoys of gleaming, white cars sped past in a blaze of honking horns, fluttering ribbons and joyful shouts. After Iran, where I had been a novelty, people showed relatively little interest in a foreigner on a bicycle. And so I happily stayed in the saddle watching the country roll by.

---

[19] The name is taken from the title of the Quran's eighth chapter and means Spoils of War. Al-Anfal was part of the Ba'ath party's long-running campaign of 'Arabisation' in Iraq's northern Kurdish region. The 'spoils' referred to are the region's vast petroleum wealth.

That evening I bought two cans of Turkish beer in a roadside stall and camped unseen in a crook of the road that was snaking up a steep valley head. I opened the first beer while cooking a dinner of bulgur wheat and vegetables. The valley stretched out before me. Here and there were clusters of evening picnickers enjoying the milder weather of early spring.

I don't remember eating my meal but I awoke at midnight with a pounding headache and a bulging bladder. The tent door was open with my feet spilling out onto the damp earth. Dinner was all gone and the second beer can was half empty. Four months of exercise and teetotalism in Afghanistan and Iran had lowered my alcohol tolerance drastically.

It was a warm morning when I pedalled into the capital, Erbil. En route to the centre I passed through upmarket suburbs with large glass shopping malls, sports cars, and western-style supermarkets. The city centre spread around the Old Citadel that perched atop a steep-sided mound and claimed to be the oldest continuously inhabited place on earth. This raised natural fortress has apparently accommodated people since 2300 BC but was now being transformed into a complex of restaurants, shopping galleries, and nightclubs.

Erbil was heavily policed with soldiers standing guard on most street corners. I had planned to take a rest day there but everything was shockingly expensive; the prices driven up by the influx of international business visitors. After a couple of hours riding around, I stocked up on food and cycled westward. Now that I had made up my mind to ride homeward, any unnecessary days spent idling would only delay reunion with loved ones.

The road was busy with military checkpoints every ten miles. Stretching to the horizon on either side was golden-green farmland. Previously when I thought of Iraq my imagination conjured desert, and when I heard the name Kurdistan I thought of mountains. However, this area looked more like a fertile Midwestern prairie.

Twenty miles short of Mosul I reached the heavily guarded border of Iraq proper, which I had no visa to cross. I was turfed northward onto a quiet side road for two days that took me across more farmland and then onto another busy road. For my last night camped in Kurdistan, I faced my tent southward with a view of the lake formed in the Tigris river by the Mosul Dam and the distant orange smudge of city lights beyond it.[20]

A squat mountain ridge stood before the Turkish frontier and I clung to one of the raised blades of a tractor's plough for the last mile to the pass. A quick descent through thick mist brought me to the border.

At customs, bulging sacks of confiscated cigarettes were being carted away for incineration. The officials merrily offered me a carton before waving me though. I politely declined and rode slowly along the three-mile queue of freight lorries lining the road on the Turkish side. Several drivers flagged me down for tea and bread and it was late afternoon by the time I reached a town called Silopi and took a cheap hotel room.

With the long winter behind me, I took great satisfaction in cutting the lower legs off my trousers and the fingers off my gloves. I took my first shower in a fortnight and used relatively fast internet for the first time in five months. There was an email waiting from Nasir in Mazar-e Sharif. He told me that his friend Qais, the talented young photographer, had died after a brief illness shortly after I left Afghanistan. The sad news and the wasted potential added to my despair at the deaths of Peter and Mary. I felt even more certain that pedalling straight home was the right thing to do.

In the early morning I wandered along the street as shopkeepers drew up their clattering metal shutters and swept yesterday's detritus into the gutter. Rising dust softly

---

[20] Sixteen months later several thousand Islamic State militants seized both the city and the dam, holding them for four years until July 2017 when the bloody nine-month Battle of Mosul was won, in no small part by the Pershmerga. Untold thousands of civilians and combatants lay dead and the city lay in ruins.

stung my nostrils. The chubby middle-aged owner of a furniture store invited me to join him at his breakfast of cheese, tomatoes, olives, and fresh bread. We sat on little wooden stools, smiling at one another and basking in the day's first rays of slanting sun.

The ride to the Mediterranean was an easy, pleasant week. The road scudded along the Syrian border, often just yards from the fortified fence marking no-man's land. Now and then I saw the sun gleam off the nearby Kirkuk–Ceyhan pipeline carrying Iraqi Kurdistan's oil to the Mediterranean for onward transport.

I pedalled seventy miles a day in warm weather across quaint, rocky pastures. There were plenty of sandbagged military garrisons but few checkpoints and it seemed business as usual despite the civil war so close at hand in Syria. But then, in the town of Nizip, I saw the first refugee camp. Tatty, sun-bleached clothes dried on the tall fence and the Syrians inside sat quiet and listless. Many had fled with only the clothes on their backs.

A little further on I reached Kilis, the main border crossing for Aleppo, thirty miles to the south. The place was overflowing with displaced Syrians and I spotted occasional bandaged fighters struggling along on crutches, recuperating from the rigours of war.[21] The official camps built by the government had quickly been filled. Those with money rented accommodation, which drove up prices for local Turkish residents and thereby fuelled tensions. Those without money headed for a makeshift encampment of a few thousand refugees in the town's park. They were being urged by local authorities to move to other newly built camps in the region but were deterred by the bribes apparently required to secure a place and the prospect of moving further afield from family still living across the border. Within three years, Turkey would be hosting 3.5 million Syrian refugees.

---

[21] I later learnt that over the following two years Kilis was to become a popular destination for foreign recruits to the Islamic State who needed a holiday from the war and their atrocities south of the border.

Back on the road, shepherds with red headscarves basked lazily on rocks while their flocks grazed around them. The incongruously loud speaker systems on minarets screamed the call to prayer across an otherwise tranquil landscape. Weathered, nut-brown village men grinned at me over small glasses of sweet tea and young men enthusiastically gabbled at me in German learned during a year or two working abroad. One lunchtime I was invited to join a family's picnic under a gnarled tree. The man told me with blunt sign language how his plump sister's husband had recently hanged himself with his shoelaces. The sister looked on in silence with tears running down the cheeks of her otherwise impassive face.

Each day took me through another mid-sized city, which looked more and more European the further west I went. On the 981st morning since leaving home, unnoticed by me, my odometer ticked past 24,901 miles, equivalent to one lap of the equator.

The last part of the ride along the Syrian border took me through hills of olive groves carpeted with purple wildflowers and I enjoyed afternoon siestas among the fragrant blooms. As I climbed towards a pass I smelled salt in the air, and then at the top was rewarded with a view of the Mediterranean, silvery and vast under a white afternoon sun. I hadn't seen the sea for over a year. For twelve months I had been crossing the frozen mountains and waterless deserts at the heart of Asia. And now it was springtime and I was by the seaside.

I sped down the 750-metre descent to the port city of Iskenderun and was soon in the water relishing the soft sting of brine in my eyes. I felt the accumulated tension and frustration of several months finally dissolve in the cool water. Looking southwards out to sea, at that moment I somehow knew I would be going to Africa. It was a realisation rather than a decision. I simply wasn't ready to go home. I hadn't finished. I feared the nagging regrets that would inevitably haunt me later. Allowing the recent tragedies I'd heard of to deter me was irrational. Peter and

Mary died living their dream, which was as admirable as it was sad.

A few days later I was on a twenty-four-hour ferry running from Iskenderun to Egypt. Most of the passengers were middle-class Syrian refugees seeking lower-cost private accommodation than in Turkey.

We docked at Port Said at midnight and I cycled off the car deck and onto the African continent. The dusty road south was illuminated by piles of burning rubbish giving off the acrid smoke of melting plastic. Twice the length of Africa lay ahead of me, but I chose to focus only on tomorrow, and not tomorrow's tomorrow. Life felt much easier to tackle when there was only one tomorrow.

Walking into the Gobi from Zamyn-Uud, Mongolia

Setting off from Bayanchandmani on Little Nicky, Mongolia

Naadam wrestlers perform traditional eagle dance, Mongolia

Nurli in Taldykorgan, Kazakhstan

Cycling into Tien Shan mountain range, Kyrgyzstan

Buzkashi match, Kyrgyzstan

Author with Nasir in Balkh, Afghanistan

The Blue Mosque in Mazar-e-Sharif, Afghanistan

Author west of Herat, Afghanistan

Monireh and her mother, Iran

Imperial bodyguard depicted on Apadana Palace at Persepolis, Iran

Prayers in Esfahan on the anniversary of Islamic Revolution, Iran

Climbing towards Iraqi border in Kurdistan, Iran

Amhara girl, Ethiopia

Turkana man, Kenya

Cycling through North Eastern Province, Kenya

Author with members of the Burundian Cycling Federation

Livingstone and Stanley carving, Burundi

Road to Mpanda, Tanzania

Cape Agulhas; the continent's southernmost point, South Africa

Fish River Canyon, Namibia

The Wildman of Deadvlei, Namibia

Archie, Zambia

Circumnavigating rapids, DRC

© Archie Leeming

Author paddling down the Lulua, DRC

Author and M'baz, DRC

Author and Archie on the Lulua, DRC

© Archie Leeming

© Archie Leeming

© Archie Leeming

Author recuperating in Kananga, DRC

Cramped transport to Kinshasa, DRC

Road to Sandoa, DRC

Hunter, Republic of Congo

Mud during the monsoon, Cameroon

Road across the Sahara, Mauritania

Arrival in London, United Kingdom

© Chandrika Srinivasan

PART II: AFRICA

Now, being in Africa, I was hungry for more of it, the changes of the seasons, the rains with no need to travel, the discomforts that you paid to make it real, the names of the trees, of the small animals, and all the birds, to know the language and have time to be in it and to move slowly.
- Ernest Hemingway, *Green Hills of Africa*

TWENTY

THE SANDS OF TIME

Egypt's antiquity makes Persia seem young and Europe pre-natal.
- Ralph Bollingscarth

The ride to Cairo took a noisy, dusty two days. Along the roadside white-robed men with bulging bellies slouched astride sturdy little donkeys. Women and boys with sickles worked the fields leaving neat rows of hand-tied wheatsheaves. The breeze carried floating flakes of chaff from villages where labourers threshed by hand.

The tarmac followed the edge of the Nile's green, fertile delta. It occasionally veered away from the farmland and I found myself very suddenly in true desert with fine, soft sand all around, almost too hot to touch. I could feel the dryness in my nostrils. The fiery winds pulsing up from the depths of the Sahara were an unwelcome contrast to the mild spring weather I had enjoyed in Turkey.

Every half hour I spotted another enormous cargo ship, piled high with containers, sailing across the sea of sand to my east, ploughing through the unseen Suez Canal.

The roads clogged as I approached the capital's far-reaching suburbs. Cairo's traffic is a maniacal blend of noise, dust, exhaust fumes, and rusted cars locked panel-beaten bumper to panel-beaten bumper. After nudging my way through to the downtown area, I checked into a hostel in a century-old, seven-storey Parisian-style building. The next day my sister Emily arrived for a fleeting visit. We hadn't seen each other in almost two years and passed three very happy days eating, resting, and wandering through unexpectedly calm street markets.

Our visit was during the seething aftermath of a violent uprising in the early wave of 2011's Arab Spring, which also set in motion the Syrian civil war. Mohamed Morsi had been in power almost a year but his support base was crumbling, with near-nightly clashes between protesters and police. Politics was on everyone's lips and heated discussions were held on street corners over little glasses of sweet black tea.

A British journalism student interning with an Egyptian newspaper showed us his dramatic photos of the street violence. Surging crowds of young men with masked faces shook placards and waved flags while clouds of tear gas billowed thickly from canisters lit by raging street fires.

I thought of the Syrian refugees I met on the ferry. They had escaped running street battles in their own country only to arrive in another nation on the brink of collapse and civil violence.

With tourism numbers down by two-thirds, visiting the pyramids at Giza was not as hectic an experience as we had anticipated. There were no crowds to speak of and it was easy enough to leave the beaten track and scramble around the unmarked ruins poking out of the sand. We stumbled upon, and almost into, a vast pit disappearing deep into the sands and walled with huge slabs of precision-cut stone, doubtless placed several thousand years ago. The opening to the abyss was just a two-metre wide hole in the ground, but the time it took for a dropped stone to hit its bottom suggested it plunged at least forty metres. I wondered what else was yet to be found; which projects of an impossibly ancient people might still emerge from the muffling of the desert's creeping sands, muffled no more and again able to echo their dormant stories.[22]

The largest of the pyramids was also the oldest, at over 4,500 years. It was so high (147 metres) and had such a long base (230 metres) that its enormity was hard to comprehend. The gradient was fairly gentle and the apex so distant that it perplexed all perspective. I finally appreciated its vastness when I overheard a nearby tour guide explain that it

---

[22] In March 2017, an 83-tonne statue of the head of Ramses II (*c.* 1303–1213 BC) was unearthed from the mud of a Cairo slum. The following month, a 3,700-year-old smooth-sided pyramid was discovered 20 miles south of Giza.

comprises 2.3 million limestone blocks, each with an average weight of 2.5 tonnes. He went on to mention that its great height could comfortably swallow Salisbury Cathedral, my local.

On Emily's last day we visited the Museum of Egyptian Antiquities on the east bank of the Nile. The grand, pinkish-red colonial-era building was unceremoniously crammed with hulking statues, sarcophagi and tablets dating back four and a half millennia. However, the museum was poorly lit and offered almost no information to visitors unaccompanied by a guide. Unknown to us, it closed early on Fridays and we were briskly ushered out after less than an hour by an advancing line of men shooing and hissing at us.

Shortly after Emily flew home, I received an email from an Egyptian man I had met on the ferry and who had worked in London's financial district for several years. Osama said he was taking me out to dinner and that I should be outside the hostel at 7 p.m. sharp.

Dressed in my embarrassingly ragged clothes, I climbed into his black, waxed BMW with tinted windows and we drove to a swanky restaurant in an upmarket district. Osama, his two friends and I worked our way through rare steaks and seven bottles of French red. They discussed politics and I listened mutely feeling out of my depth.

'Osama, this Morsi joke has gone way too far, when is your cousin going to do something about it?' asked Nameen, a sardonic beauty in her mid-thirties.

'Patience, my dear,' he replied, 'don't you enjoy seeing *President* Morsi squirm?' His emphasis on the word 'president' was treacle-thick with sarcasm.

'A little. But I also like going directly to my office instead of taking an hour's detour around Tahrir Square.'

I barely recall being dropped back at the hostel late that night. I emailed Osama the following day to thank him but didn't hear back for three months. By that time his first cousin, Field Marshall Abdel Fattah al-Sisi, had seized power in a military coup and Morsi was in prison awaiting trial. A year later al-Sisi became president after winning an election with a questionable 97 per cent of the vote.

I cycled east out of Cairo bearing the glowing embers of a two-day fever. A hard-beating sun rose and my popping ears throbbed with heat. As the sun climbed it bleached the road and whitened the sands like an over-exposed photo. The new three-lane highway towards the Gulf of Suez was almost empty. I was overtaken by dozens of speeding expensive motorcycles, their owners enjoying weekend joyrides up and down the freshly laid tarmac. I soon stopped looking over my shoulder each time the frightful scream of an engine approached from behind. However, one biker slowed and then overtook with a wave. Unlike the gleaming, brightly coloured power bikes that were the norm, this one was a mud-spattered trail bike with a spare tyre and panniers strapped on its back.

The rider pulled over and dismounted as I approached. Unsurprised to see a European face emerge from the helmet, I shook the proffered hand.

'Hello Charlie,' said the tall man of roughly my age. My mind scrambled for who it could be. I have always been bad with names and faces. I didn't recognise the man, but the glare was plaguing my eyes and I didn't have sunglasses so perhaps I did know him after all. My hot, aching head didn't help things. I decided to hedge my bets.

'Hello mate! I wasn't expecting to run into you here …'

'Ummm … where are you from?' he asked, hesitantly.

It seemed a strange question from someone who knew me. I realised that in my sun-stunned state, and with my swollen ears, I must have misheard the man. We had obviously never met before. I mumbled an awkward apology and promised myself I would lie down for a bit as soon as he left me.

The man seemed a little confused but introduced himself as Archie from Scotland, who was biking to Cape Town with two friends. They were further ahead in the south of Egypt but Archie had raced back to Cairo to collect a spare part.

We said goodbye without exchanging contact details and he roared off in a cloud of exhaust fumes. I flopped onto the warm sand in the shade of a road sign and fell into a deep afternoon sleep.

I reached the coast after eighty feverish miles and slept under the stars on a rocky hillside overlooking the sea. The lights of queuing ships blinked out on the water, their prows pointed at the entrance to the canal twenty miles on.

I started awake from my dead sleep in the small hours to see a fox's moonlit face, frozen with fear, less than a metre from mine. The handle of one of my panniers was in its mouth. I grabbed at the bag and after a two-second tug of war the sneak thief fled. The creature had come close to making away with not only food but my passport, cash, and camera.

I followed the Red Sea coast south for three days on a quiet road with a gentle tailwind. There was little distraction from the heat excepting occasional truck stops where lounging drivers invited me to share tea or *fuul*; Egypt's staple of mashed, stewed fava beans with oil, onion, cumin and garlic, eaten in pinches with small, round flatbreads.

There was a forty-mile stretch of wall-to-wall beach resorts, all of them empty. Most were poorly thought out with balconies opening onto the main road that separated them from a narrow beach of dirty grey sand. I was told by a shopkeeper that the resorts usually hosted Russian holidaymakers, but with the numbers of visitors so low only the more attractive beaches across the water on the Sinai peninsula saw any custom.[23]

Past the vacant resorts was a long stretch of road with no buildings but for regular unmanned lighthouses. My first 100-mile day for many months took me through a cluster of onshore and offshore oil rigs with tall gas flares dancing atop

---

[23] Russian flights to Egypt were eventually halted altogether in October 2015 after Metrojet flight 9268 to Saint Petersburg was downed over Sinai by an Islamic State bomb, killing all 224 people onboard, 219 of whom were Russian.

thin chimneys. The noxious smell left me with the nagging sensation that I'd left a hob on.

The temperature rose as I progressed south. I enjoyed using my tent only as a pillow, opting to spend the warm, dry, bugless nights in the open. One evening I turned inland and wove through low, sandstone crags. The road was half built and wrinkled workmen squatted beside the unpressed tarmac, sucking battered shisha pipes. I slept on the sand that night in the moonshadow of an abandoned mosque. Only in the morning did I discover that another ragged itinerant had been sleeping inside. He shook my hand, scratched his face, and wandered off along the road, barefoot and limping.

The last day to Luxor was hard work. I had four punctures in the morning and made slow progress across the utterly empty Eastern Desert. I had no food and little water, and there was no shade to rest in as the temperature climbed to the high thirties. A few dozen shining tourist coaches zoomed past with their overworked air-conditioning units screaming. I began to feel faint and struggled to ride in a straight line.

Mercifully, the hazy band of greenery signifying the Nile finally appeared on the horizon, breaking the desert's monopoly of bleak yellow-browns. I felt some sense of the elation this sight must have brought to many thousands of thirst-crazed caravans over the ages.

I breached the outskirts mid-afternoon after ninety miles, bought an icy Coke in the first shop, and collapsed under a palm tree for an hour. Feeling a little revived, I continued to the centre, found a dog-eared hostel, and stood motionless under the shower's cold trickle for a long time.

Luxor is known for its historical sites so I dutifully took a ferry across the river and cycled up to the Valley of the Kings, where Tutankhamun's crypt was found. To date, sixty-two tombs have been found and excavated in the valley, although most have long since been robbed of treasure. The place was an unpleasantly hot, shadeless, breezeless cleft in the hills. The colour-sapped rocks were blindingly bright in the midday glare and the dust underfoot was like finely milled flour.

My ticket allowed three tomb visits excluding that of Tutankhamun, which cost extra. I picked the deepest, darkest, coolest looking of the tomb apertures, which all plunged, corridor-like, into the rocky hillside. Each consisted of tunnels and chambers whitewashed by the ancients and covered in colourful paintings and hieroglyphics depicting mythological scenes and glorifying the life of the occupant.

I rode back down the valley and locked my bicycle outside the thirty-five-century-old Temple of Hatshepsut, Egypt's formidable female pharaoh who reigned for thirty years. When I emerged, I noticed the odometer had been removed from my handlebars. There was a crowd of touts and young boys watching me from nearby. As I approached they parted and I found myself facing a wizened man with a table of fake relics for sale. I told him I had dropped my bicycle computer and wondered if anyone had seen it. He ushered me into a chair, gave me tea, and said he was sure that one of his young friends would find it. Ten minutes later a sheepish boy came forward and handed me the odometer, muttering as he did so. My host translated that the boy had found it on the road and was very happy to help me. I shook several hands and pedalled off with a smile on my face. In over 25,000 miles it had never once fallen off.

The next day I wandered over to Karnak, or the ancient city of Thebes: a sprawling complex of temples and palaces that was the centre of Egyptian power for 1,300 years. The entrance to Luxor temple was lopsidedly marked with a single grand obelisk on the left.[24] Inside, seemingly endless slabs of engraved stone lay around with grand columns, colossal statues, and cool, sunless chambers covered with intricate hieroglyphs. I did my best to tail tourists with guides, stealing what information I could by eavesdropping,

[24] The 23-metre-tall, 250-tonne obelisk once had an identical opposite number. However, the twin was given to France in 1828 and today stands in the Place de la Concorde on the spot where Louis XVI and Marie Antoinette were guillotined.

but was largely happy to wander wide-eyed through mysterious history.

A few dozen sunburned and harassed-looking Germans and Russians arrived as I was leaving. They seemed uniformly exhausted and irritable. I was shocked by how aggressively the souvenir vendors hassled them, prancing violently around them, following them, yelling, and thrusting things in their faces.

'Cheap cheap price. Goody goody price, my friend ...'

'Madame! *Beauteeful* Maaaadame, I have the earrings just for you. Two t'ousand year old. Just be looking, please ...'

Many of the tourists didn't help themselves with their brusque manner and thigh-flashing clothes. Even I was taken aback by the lengths of fleshy redness on display. Evidently too scruffy to be of interest, I was relieved to be ignored by the touts and vendors, who far outnumbered the scant tourists.

Before leaving Luxor, I visited a clothing shop and treated myself to two new pairs of boxer shorts to replace the two threadbare pairs that had been my sole underwear since walking out of Beijing a year earlier. I also bought a pair of lightweight striped shorts with sailboat patterning, the only pair available, to replace the cut-off trousers I had been living in for twelve months.

The road south traced the river and was prettily decorated with brightly coloured flowers. The desert was never far off, and the road often straddled the abrupt divide between harsh sandy aridity and the almost opulent greenery watered by a series of canals.

Serene rural scenes were enacted between the road and the river. Solitary peasant men in pale blue *gelabiyas* (the traditional North African robe) and white *taqiyahs* (rounded skull caps) squatted in the fields working the wheat harvest with small sickles. It seemed that Egypt was solely producing wheat, and yet it remains the world's largest importer of the grain, which is the staple for the country's 100 million inhabitants.

Donkeys hauled carts of produce and fat men dozed away midday heat under waving palm trees. The men waved and shouted 'hello!' The boys stretched out hands and requested 'Money?' The few women outdoors were mostly in groups sporting synthetic black burqas.

It would have been an idyllic ride were it not for the all too regular *thump-thump* through my saddle of speed bumps: abrupt, unnecessary, and in pairs every half mile.

At the town of Edfu I crossed a bridge to the west bank and visited the Greco-Roman Temple of Horus. This is perhaps the best-preserved shrine in Egypt and was built by the Ptolemaic dynasty, the post-Alexandrian royal line that terminated with Anthony and Cleopatra's defeat by Augustus's army in 31 BC.[25]

The huge edifice of pleasingly angled stone had a cool, dark, faintly mysterious interior of antechambers and shrines. Every surface – literally thousands of square metres – was covered in carvings: histories, legends, reliefs of monarchs and gods, endless echoes of inextricably entwined truth and myth. All the images of gods had had their hands and feet chipped into obscurity by the later Christians to disable the heathen deities.

As I re-crossed the river, I noticed both banks were lined with dozens of ghostly cruise boats, jammed stern to prow and mothballed while the country continued its open-ended convulsions. Empty restaurants, cafés, and souvenir shops lined the roads, their proprietors looking sadly out at the world, patiently awaiting better days.

---

[25] A contributing reason, perhaps, to the downfall of the Ptolemies was their staggering enthusiasm for inbreeding. Most humans have sixteen biological great-great-grandparents. Cleopatra had only six.

TWENTY-ONE

SAMOOM

*I had gotten to Lower Egypt, and was heading south, in my usual
traveling mood – hoping for the picturesque, expecting misery, braced for
the appalling. Happiness was unthinkable, for although happiness is
desirable it is a banal subject for travel; therefore,
Africa seemed perfect for a long journey.*
- Paul Theroux, *Dark Star Safari*

I cycled into Aswan at the end of another long, hot day in
which I drank nine litres of water. A scattering of white-
sailed feluccas drifted tourists up and down the placid Nile
on 'sunset pleasure cruises' as the swollen, sinking sun lit the
river a riotous orange-red. An evening breeze brought dust
from the depths of Sudan and gave the scene an earthy scent.

Aswan sits ten miles downstream from the Aswan High
Dam. The dam was built in the sixties as the 1902 British-
built predecessor, which had been the world's largest upon
completion, was no longer providing adequate flood control.
Variable harvests were a worrying famine risk to the Nile
Delta's burgeoning population of wheat eaters. And so the
High Dam became a symbol of Egyptian ingenuity and
independence in Africa's heady post-colonial era – yet it was
designed and funded by the Soviets, who had stolen a march
on their Cold War rivals.

Lake Nasser, the 310-mile-long reservoir that rises behind
the dam, reaches all the way to Egypt's frontier with Sudan.
There was a road of sorts running down the western side of
the Lake but it didn't cross into Sudan and the whole area
was an off-limits military zone. The only way for me to cross
from Egypt to Sudan was a time-worn weekly ferry that
chugged the length of the lake, depositing passengers at the
Sudanese border town of Wadi Halfa.

It took a couple of days to secure a Sudanese visa and a
ticket to Wadi Halfa. To pass time, I wandered around

Aswan as the rising heat of May pulsed off the pot-holed tarmac. On every corner an opportunistic youth sprang out of the shade to offer me a discounted tour, or a discounted hotel, or a discounted camel ride. The older, more experienced out-of-work tour guides stayed put in their shaded perches, awaiting a less broke-looking tourist.

In an internet café I sat at the neighbouring computer to a young Egyptian man who video-called a succession of western women for about fifteen minutes each. I presumed that he was a sometime tour guide and they were former clients. Each call culminated with the same request.

'Please, beautiful, show me your belly. Only for some seconds … oh my God! Oh my *gaaaaaad!* You are so sexy … the most sexy … a princess!'

I would look up to see the man once more squirming on his creaking wooden stool as yet another globe of fleshy whiteness jiggled on his screen.

'You are the best girl I have ever seen in the world. You are the *only* girl for me. Come back to Egypt, my beautiful, and I will give you very good deal on tour …'

The ferry to Sudan is infamous among travellers. I had heard countless stories of dangerously overcrowded decks, insufficient lifeboats crammed with boxes, and panicked chaos at embarkation. However, the boat had been delayed for a couple of weeks until a few days before, and so the sailing I took was a one-off for the surplus of people unable to cram themselves on the last passage.

I arrived early morning and joined a queue with Mick, a Geordie pub landlord cycling from Cairo to Khartoum. Across the water stood the dam's Monument of Arab–Soviet Friendship: a spiky eyesore of concrete brutalism that was supposed to resemble a lotus flower.

Once processed through the poorly arranged customs and immigration, Mick and I wheeled our bicycles onto the open-air deck that was to be our berth. We strung up a sheet to shelter us from the sun that beat fiercely down on the warped metal floor. Over the following eight hours the boat filled with people and cargo. Everyone claimed a space and strung up their own sheets until the entire deck was sheltered by a colourful patchwork awning reminiscent of a Moroccan bazaar.

The engine choked to life in the evening and the ferry nosed steadily south. Our fellow passengers prayed, ate, and played dominoes with headlamps, before curling up to sleep on the now-cool deck. The floor vibrated softly with the rumble of the engine while a radiant starscape spun silent and unseen above the sagging ceiling of sheets.

In the morning we passed two temples on the western bank dating from the thirteenth century BC. The temples at Abu Simbel commemorated the victory of Ramesses II over the Hittites in the Battle of Qadesh, 1,000 miles away to the north on the border of modern-day Syria and Lebanon. The exterior of the larger temple had four 22-metre-high statues of Ramesses carved out of the rockface. The imposing figures were intended as a show of might by the ancient Egyptians at their frontier to deter incursions from their southerly neighbours, the Nubians.

However, the most impressive aspect of Abu Simbel is perhaps the fact that the original site is now sixty-five metres underwater. The temples were cut into twenty-tonne blocks in the sixties and relocated to save them from the rising waters of Lake Nasser. The final pieces of the giant jigsaw were even cut underwater.

As we slid by, the Egyptian and Sudanese passengers stood side by side gazing at this wonder of engineering, both ancient and modern, that stood as a testament to the centuries-long enmity between their ancestors.

We disembarked in Wadi Halfa with relatively minimal fuss. Mick and I bought a supply of dry foods in a sparsely stocked shop and set out on a new, Chinese-built tarmac road running to Khartoum. A signpost informed us that there was 250 miles to the next town and 600 miles to Khartoum.

Although the heat soared, a firm northerly wind helped us

on our way. Despite familiar depictions of a peaceful sea of eternal sand dunes, the Sahara is a ferociously wind-blasted place. That picturesque landscape of dunes is not a placid sand sea, but rather a slow-moving sandstorm of ever-shifting waves, raging and baking in the tireless wind. The local name for Saharan wind is *samoom* which translates simply as 'poison'. Dunes are always on the move, creeping and shape-shifting. The only thing truly eternal in the depths of the desert is the whistling *samoom*, which mostly blows from the north, softening only at night-time when it inhales, drawing breath for another day excoriating those foolish enough to venture forth.

The wind plagued us when we stopped, but when we rode it blew on our backs, ushering us along kindly. I pushed to the back of my mind fretful visions of having to ride *against* the very same wind in a year or two when limping my way back to Europe on the other side of Africa's daunting breadth.

After forty miles the light faded and the gale dipped a little. We laid out our sleeping bags on the sand and shovelled forkfuls of grit-speckled noodles into our parched mouths. I was kept awake that night by a mouse that found its way into a pannier and nibbled biscuits, noisily rustling the wrapper. Eventually I emptied the bag and dug out the terrified ball of fur with my hand. I walked thirty metres and released it, shooing it away from our camp. However, it hurried back as soon as I laid down and resumed its midnight snacking. With a sigh, I lay back and resigned myself to enjoying the purple magnificence of a moonless Milky Way wheeling before my eyes.

In the first couple of hours of morning riding Mick broke four spokes but had no spares. We stopped at a small hand-worked gold mine where we watched skeletal men with silvery black skin breaking and panning rocks, eyes strained in search of the telltale yellowish shimmer.

Mick had to reach Khartoum earlier than me for his homeward flight and so pedalled ahead while I lazed under a tree. Later in the afternoon I found him on the roadside trying to thumb a lift. His rear wheel had suffered eleven more broken spokes and was warped beyond use. An hour later he waved from the window of a passing minibus with his bicycle tied on the roof. I pedalled on with only the wind for company.

The road across the Sahara loosely shadowed the Nile and saw very little traffic. By noon the temperature in the shade hovered in the high forties Celsius. But the nights were sublime. Long after the sun sank in splendid silence and invested the lunar land with a pinkish glow, I laid down my foam mat for the night. I lay in the open, on top of my sleeping bag and wearing only underwear, gazing at the soporific beauty above and trying to catch the stars moving in the few short minutes before plummeting into exhausted sleep.

I was back on the road long before sunrise each morning to make the most of the cool. Under paling stars I plugged away at the pedals, watching the dark, empty nothingness of the night landscape morph into a lighter, but still empty, nothingness. When possible I ate simple *fuul* lunches in sporadic roadside cafés and dozed away the withering afternoons under trees bent double by a lifetime of wind.

The Nile was often many miles away, but when the road ran closer to the river I would pass small Nubian villages of mud-walled bungalows and little plots of irrigated farmland dotted with palm trees. Some buildings were daubed white, with patterns of rich maroon painted across the walls. Many also had a simple reed-walled hut next to them which would be much cooler to sleep in than the thick-walled houses that had soaked in the sun's heat all day.

If I opened my mouth to the harsh, dry wind, my throat and tongue became paper dry in seconds. I sucked a small pebble, as a Mongolian man had taught me in the Gobi, forcing me to breathe through my nose. Thankfully there were semi-regular roadside shelters with large clay pots of water, fresh from the Nile and brown with silt. I drank at least ten litres of the muddy river water each day. The porous skin of the pots was damp and the water inside was deliciously cool. The wind hitting the moisture acted as a crude cooling system. I began keeping my water bottles inside wet socks.

When the heat became overwhelming I forced myself to remember the biting misery of the extreme cold in mountainous winters. The aim was to make the heat appealing. I knew that in the future, when I looked back at those scorched Saharan days, they would all be the 'good old days', so I strived to treat them as such. But it was a hard bit of self-deception to pull off.

TWENTY-TWO

SAHARAN STING

I think it is the lonely, without a fireside or an affection they may call
their own, those who return not to a dwelling but to the land itself, to
meet its disembodied, eternal, and unchangeable spirit – it is those who
best understand its severity, it's saving power, the grace of its secular
right to our fidelity, to our obedience.
- Joseph Conrad, *Lord Jim*

I took a two-day rest in the mid-sized town of Dongola where I wandered the dusty streets picking up discarded plastic bottles to fill with water. The next leg was a little-used road veering away from the Nile to shortcut part of a looping meander that sees the river describe a stately chicane southward for a few hundred miles before resuming its northward procession to the Mediterranean.

I would have to cross a waterless 120 miles of desert to meet the river again further upstream in a town called Karima. I set off in the early evening, weighed down with 17 litres of water and rode into the night. Thirty hours later, and with not a drop remaining, I rolled into Karima and drank a litre and a half of warm river water in under a minute.

Just to the west of Karima sits a small flat-topped mountain called Jebel Barkal, which marked the southern border of ancient Egypt at its greatest extent during the fifteenth century BC. When the Egyptians retreated they left their gods behind them, and the Nubian kings who took power built a temple to Amun at the foot of the mountain.

Besides a few precariously restacked columns of varying heights and a weather-worn ram sculpture, little remains of the temple. However, there is a cluster of smallish, steep-sided Nubian pyramids dotted nearby. This 2,300-year-old royal cemetery wallows in soft sands and comprises a dozen structures, all under twenty metres tall. Some are little more than triangular piles of tumbledown stones but others have been reconstructed and stand in crisp, straight-edged contrast to their untamed desert home. I had the place to myself and spent a couple of hours clambering around the scattered ruins.

While passing the midday hours under a large tree I was stung on the forearm by a scorpion that had crawled into my pannier. The sting was a sharp jab and took me by surprise, with a burning pain spreading quickly up my arm. It felt like it was being dipped in a bath that hadn't cooled sufficiently. I peered carefully into my pannier and saw the thing guarding a corner, looking back at me with its raised sting quivering, poised to strike again. I looked at my arm as a red rash spread quickly to my wrist before the whole area turned a deathly yellowish-white, like a corpse on the slab.

With no idea if it was serious or not, I was at a loss for what to do. I knew nothing about scorpions except that some kill and others don't. Feeling faint and afraid, I considered my options. I squeezed the skin at the sting and saw a clear, viscous liquid ooze out into a droplet. My mind ran hurriedly in several directions before I clamped my lips to the little red pockmark, sucked hard, and then spat. I vaguely remembered Indiana Jones doing this in a film. He was fictional, of course, but also all I had to go on. I did this several times over then pressed a knife tip into the small, translucent-yellow scorpion's back. I watched as it fought. Its body flailed and its legs kicked wildly while the tiny pincers snapped open and shut. At the end of a broad tail, its fine brown sting stabbed desperately and repeatedly at the blade with violent futility. It wasn't vindictiveness that drove me. I wanted the scorpion in case the sting became a problem and I needed to identify the culprit to a doctor. I didn't fancy taking it alive.

My arm ached with a stabbing throb that pulsed from bad to worse. My eyes watered but the tears evaporated almost instantly. Not knowing what else to do, and with the heat at its midday zenith, I sat down and ate some bread. After fifteen minutes a man passing on a motorbike spotted me and paused a few seconds, thinking. His curiosity won and he approached to shake my hand. I showed him the dead scorpion and my deathly arm, which was goosepimpling impressively. He hurriedly fixed a painfully tight tourniquet above my elbow and pushed me towards his motorbike. Leaving my bicycle unattended under the tree with all my worldly goods except my wallet, we rushed a few miles to a hospital.

I unfolded the page torn from a novel to show an overworked doctor the scorpion I had killed, then presented my bloodless arm. He gave me a local anaesthetic and four other injections and told me to rest for an hour. He refused payment as it was a public hospital for the poor. I had no idea what any of the injections were, but after thirty minutes I grew impatient and stepped back out into the sunlight. The kindly motorcyclist was waiting in some shade, and he returned me to my untouched bicycle, embraced me, and puttered off.

As evening neared I pedalled on with my left hand draped limply over the handlebar. My arm was somehow simultaneously numb *and* excruciatingly painful with occasional bouts of intense cramping. The pain broiled on until I pitched camp and passed out, tentless in the desert, long after dark. By morning there remained only an aching numbness that took two further days to subside.

I later discovered that my attacker had been *Androctonus australis*, also known as the yellow fat-tailed scorpion. It is one of the most venomous scorpions in the world and kills several people each year, although usually children or the elderly. *Androctonus* translates as 'man-killer' and the venom's toxicity is equivalent to that of the black mamba snake. Ninety per cent of scorpion sting fatalities in Africa are victims of the yellow fat-tail. Death is usually from anaphylaxis or respiratory failure three or four hours after stinging, if left untreated. I was glad I didn't know this at the time, and even more glad that my rescuer happened to be passing when he did.

The road ran south along the river for a hundred miles before making another shortcut across the banded orange-yellow desert, this time for the final two hundred miles to Khartoum. I tackled the crossing in two exhausting days. In the three years since leaving home, this was the hottest, driest stretch yet. The temperature soared to 50°C in the shade, and I can only guess at what it may have been under the sun. As I pedalled I watched scars and blemishes on my hands and arms rise and stand out redly as my already leathery skin tanned and burned.

The only life to be seen was the odd camel striding enigmatically over the sands on some unknown errand, hips rolling with the casual gait of indifference. Their slender legs wobbled in the heat haze with a delicate fluidity that belied the beasts awesome hardiness. Every two hours or so I spotted a desiccated camel corpse collapsed beside the road. Bleached and papery skin stretched across broad, collapsed ribs and huge molars sat loosely in exposed jawbones, fixed in the ghostly final rictus of lonesome heat death.

After 115 miles of grinding at the pedals I camped out in the open as usual and was asleep within minutes of lying down. I woke a couple of hours after midnight with the wind picking up and beginning to pelt me with sand. I looked upwind and saw a solid blackness swallowing the stars and the ink-blue sky. I had just enough time to stuff everything into a pannier and encase myself in my sleeping bag before the hard wind wall of sand struck.

I lay foetal and frightened, wrapped around the one loose pannier and wondering if the three bags attached to my bicycle were still there. The fiercest thrusts of the storm lasted for an hour during which I fought to not be rolled over. If I started to tumble it may have been hard to stop.

When the fury abated, I emerged squinting and cautious to find Old Geoff had stoically weathered the storm. A strong and unusually hot wind continued throughout the night. After a while, deciding that the windblown sand was preferable to the sweaty protection of my synthetic sleeping bag, I pulled some clean-ish boxer shorts over my face and lay in the open with drifts of sand gathering around me. By morning my hair, beard, ears, nose, eyebrows, armpits, navel and saddlebags were all filled with sand. Old Geoff was half-buried and had never looked so abandoned and forlorn.

The continuing wind blew a constant stream of sand diagonally across the tarmac as I rode on. It swirled and danced prettily in the wake of overtaking lorries, and I was forced to lean sideways into the wind for balance. When lorries sped past in the opposite direction I closed my eyes and mouth and braced for the slapping wall of sand and air that passed with it.

I stopped to rest at one of the precious few cafés along the way; the only habitations daring to exist in the desert's petrified deadness. I filled my bottles with brackish sepia water from hanging goatskins that were in turn filled from deep and dwindling wells. A lone Dinka man, far from his ancestral home along the White Nile in South Sudan, sat staring stonily at the road. His high forehead was lined with three or four prominent V-shaped ridges formed from repeated scarification. He called to mind a half-remembered character from *Star Trek*.

I was woken with caution in the afternoon by a gentle tug at my shirt sleeve. A tremulous engineer called Mosab stood over me. He wanted to practice his English.

'What is your opinion of our Sudan, sir?' he asked.

'It is big and beautiful. And hot,' I replied.

'Yes, yes, but today is cool, no? The storm last night has pushed the heat away. Yesterday was 55°C.'

'And what is today?'

He consulted his phone for a few seconds. 'It is good. Only 43°C, sir.'

Nearer the capital, the desert relented a little and began to support thorny bushes, beside which goats stood on hind legs to graze the sparse leaves. Nomadic tribes lived in rudimentary reed-walled huts with their herds of white-skinned camels standing listlessly in thorn-branch corrals.

Riding under the hem of Khartoum's blanket of smog, I crossed a bridge just below where the river's two great arteries combine at Omdurman, the satellite sister city to Khartoum. Here the Blue Nile and the White Nile merge their well-travelled waters from the Ethiopian highlands and the East African lakes respectively.

It was just north of here in 1898 that General Kitchener lead 25,000 British and Egyptian troops bearing the latest military technology against a Sudanese army of 50,000 poorly armed warrior tribesmen known to the invaders as 'Dervishes'. The action was a retaliation for the death of General Gordon thirteen years earlier at the end of the ten-month Siege of Khartoum. The Sudanese besiegers had been following a man called Mohammad Ahmad who had proclaimed himself 'Mahdi', the redeemer figure in Islam who is anticipated to rule the world for several years in the run up to Judgement Day.

Much to the consternation of his followers, this particular Mahdi died of typhus five months after the siege. The British sailed up-river and the Battle of Omdurman lasted just five hours, by the end of which 12,000 Dervishes were dead, 13,000 wounded, and a further 5,000 captured. The British, who had lost forty-eight men, proceeded to destroy the tomb of the 'Mahdi'. The twenty-two-year-old Winston Churchill was present at Omdurman as a lieutenant and later wrote an account of the battle. In this book, between numerous unflattering reflections of Islam, Churchill recounts how the British 'carried off the Mahdi's head in a kerosene can as a trophy'.

I was uninspired by the baking and busy streets of Khartoum, which felt claustrophobic after the desert. I visited the National Museum with its wonderful medieval Christian frescos and passed one night in an airless hostel dormitory before riding on southwards. I was also running low on cash. As Sudan was under economic sanction I couldn't withdraw more money, and I set out on the six-day ride to the Ethiopian border with just £8 in my pocket.

Tracing the Blue Nile on a narrow, busy road was little fun and inconsiderate drivers often forced me onto the thorn-strewn verge. My puncture tally rocketed and every morning I awoke to at least one limp tyre. On one particularly frustrating day I suffered nine punctures.

Many Sudanese vehicles ensure ample space on the road with shiny chrome protrusions from their hubcaps reminiscent of the blades on a Roman chariot's wheels. Some of these wheel weapons stick out as far as thirty centimetres. On parked vehicles they looked relatively blunt and inoffensive but on a speeding coach they looked like they could shred a man's leg or turn a cat inside out in the blink of an eye. Dog and donkey carcasses frequently smeared along the roadside paid grim testimony to the ruthlessness of the drivers.

Thankfully I turned away from the river and onto a quieter road after a couple of days. This route was mainly plied by sickeningly fast coaches. Countless road-killed goats festered on the verge. A strong reek of death hung over the road, where clouds of flies swarmed around opened stomachs seething with maggots.

Arriving on the scene of one accident, I saw the damaged front of a coach and six or seven goats dramatically splashed across the tarmac, some still bleeding and one still bleating. The driver was screaming recriminations at the speechless, wide-eyed goatherd.

The road climbed gradually towards Ethiopia and the vegetation thickened. A fat old baboon eyed me dismissively one afternoon, his weary, impassive face following my slow uphill progress. The villages still looked distinctly Sudanese. Women walked along the roadside in conservative yet elegant robes of bright colours, with large water containers balanced effortlessly on their heads. Reclining groups of toothless old men ranged around the twisted feet of ancient trees while their tethered donkeys brayed nearby.

The heat slowly, mercifully eased and the tailwind gradually softened each day until the odd wisp of southerly breeze caressed my cheeks with promises of cooler climes in the highlands ahead.

I reached the border post one fresh morning where the Sudanese police shared their breakfast with me and waved goodbye as I crossed the twenty-metre bridge separating Sudan from Ethiopia. The Sahara and nine months in the Islamic world lay behind me.

TWENTY-THREE

YOU!

Life is like riding a bicycle. To keep your balance,
you must keep riding.
- Albert Einstein

Ethiopia seemed a world away from its conservative northern neighbour. There was no doubt I had passed out of the desert and into sub-Saharan Africa. Metema, the border town, was strung along the road; a lively strip of bars and pool halls with women in tight-fitting jeans, some evidently prostitutes, many of whom had crucifixes tattooed on their foreheads. Jaunty, big band 'African' music blared from crackling speakers and barber shop fronts were adorned with paintings of afros and cornrows. There was a DVD shop with two topless white women painted on the door. There was also a general shabbiness and closeness which registered after the rangy spaces of Sudanese desert dwellings. The buildings jostled needlessly close to one another and plastic litter was strewn liberally across the dusty ground.

The onward road climbed eastward over rippling hills that steepened with each new ascent. Although not many vehicles plied the route, the road was a busy thoroughfare of people and livestock. Weather-worn herdsmen in strangely short shorts and with tattered blankets draped over their heads guided cattle down the road and nodded politely in return to my greetings.

Ethiopians are definitely runners rather than riders. Whereas in Sudan large men slouched astride diminutive donkeys, in Ethiopia spindly herders jogged alongside pack animals laden with fodder or firewood. They ran effortlessly with loose hips up and down hills at altitude for many miles at a time, chivvying along their beasts. It's no surprise that the country boasts four of the ten fastest marathon times ever run.[26]

Some people said 'hello' and others asked, 'Where do you go?', but most people I passed, particularly children, simply barked one word at me rapidly and repeatedly: 'You, you, you, YOU!'

I had heard of this strange phenomenon from past cyclists and had been warned of its relentlessness. The nagging, almost-accusatory nature of it eventually shattered the composure of even the thickest-skinned travellers.

The villages largely consisted of circular thatched huts with flimsy stick fences to enclose livestock at night. Stacked cakes of dung were left to dry in the keen sunlight to be used later as fuel. Each settlement overflowed with small children stumbling busily about.

'YOU! *Youyouyouyou ...*'

Strangely, a large proportion wore shirts but nothing below the waist. Most had a crucifix around the neck. It shouldn't have surprised me how many children there were hanging around. In the last fifty years the country's population has more than quadrupled to 105 million, 85 per cent of which are still village-dwelling subsistence farmers.

Evening arrived with a distinct chill. I pitched my tent for the first time since Turkey and drew my thin sleeping bag tightly around me. Setting off at first light was a joy. Those dawnlit rides became my favourite parts of the journey through Ethiopia. The cool air was fresh and misted with the sweet dampness of night. Sleepy villagers stumbled from their huts to start cooking fires on their yards of hard-packed earth. Semi-somnambulant herders with blankets pulled close about their shoulders traipsed behind their lumbering beasts, avoiding the fresh splats of dung on the tarmac with subconscious nimbleness.

However, the spell never lasted very long. Eventually one bleary-eyed child would spot me and shatter the peace. 'You, you, you!' This call to arms would set off a chain reaction

[26] At the time of printing the other six fastest times, including *the* fastest, were all set by Kenyans.

that raced along the road faster than I could ride. As I stood on my pedals, humping my way steadily uphill, kids far ahead would already have their eyes fixed on me and a stone clutched in their hand ready to launch at the weaving white apparition that moved even slower than the creeping morning mists. Small rocks skittered past my wheels but rarely hit me.

After ninety miles of unrelenting ups and downs I reached the mountain city of Gondar at an altitude of over 2,100 metres. A storm was brewing in the darkening sky and I was relieved to duck into a grubby £2 motel room before the downpour started and the road turned to river. There was no electricity or running water but I lit a candle and I filled a bucket with water cascading off the roof to wash. After the wearisome heckling and the day's exhaustive ride I was happy to chomp on a couple of stale biscuits and sink into the stained mattress, sedated by the white noise of rain rattling on a metal roof.

*   *   *

In the seventeenth century Ethiopia was ruled by the Solomonic dynasty who claimed regal lineage dating back to the tenth century BC. It is written in the bible that Makeda, better known as the Queen of Sheba, visited King Solomon in Jerusalem with a fabulously rich retinue. Ethiopian folklorists claim Makeda as their own and, as legend has it, she became pregnant, giving birth to Solomon's son upon return to the highlands.[27] This child was Menelik I, founding member of the Solomonic dynasty. Ethiopic tradition also claims that Menelik found and brought to Ethiopia the Ark of the Covenant containing Moses' stone tablets bearing the commandments.

Two hundred or so generations later a man called Fasilides was in power and in 1636 built a capital in Gondar. Up to that point the emperors had lived in a roving royal

---

[27] Most modern scholars agree that if the Queen of Sheba existed at all she came from a kingdom called Saba in modern day Saudi Arabia.

encampment, living off the peasantry in one area until local resources became stretched and forced them to move on. Thus, the rulers maintained a presence to citizens throughout their empire, and likely wore their patience thin too.

Fasilides wasn't tentative with this inaugural capital, building an imposing fortified castle on a hill. As I wandered around it and the subsequent surrounding castles built by his successors, I was struck by how much it resembled both a medieval European castle and some of the less-lavish Mughal architecture. There were ramparts and turrets and crenellations and it seemed likely that Indian traders or some of the Jesuit missionaries probing Ethiopia at the time may have had a hand in the design.[28] Stars of David carved over several doorways alluded to the imperial line's supposed descent from Solomon. The castle complex stands impressively intact to this day and has won the glib nickname 'The Camelot of Africa'.

Sitting atop one of the sagging watchtowers in the perimeter wall, I watched a funeral procession pass on the road below. The startlingly narrow coffin was draped in a purple shroud and borne by a dozen huddled pallbearers. Surrounding them were men carrying variously coloured felt umbrellas with dancing tassels. A throng of mourners in white shawls followed slowly, bunched around two men sombrely performing a ritual dance.

On another hill overlooking the small city perched the church of Debre Berhan Selassie. This eighteenth-century structure was the only church in Gondar to survive an attack by the Mahdi's Sudanese 'Dervishes' in 1888. Legend tells that a swarm of bees descended on the Muslim invaders and that the Archangel Michael appeared before the gates and drew a flaming sword.

---

[28] In 1643 Fasilides expelled the predominantly Portuguese Jesuits from Ethiopia after twenty years of religious civil strife. Fasilides' father, Susenyos I, had publicly converted to Catholicism in 1622 and made it the state religion in an effort to secure military aid from European nations against the encroaching conquests of the Ottoman empire. Upon his ascendency, Fasilides immediately restored Ethiopian Orthodoxy as the state religion and burned any remaining Catholic texts.

The church had a striking interior entirely covered in intricate ecclesiastical artwork, much of which brought to mind Hieronymus Bosch. The depiction of hell is particularly memorable, with its painting of the prophet Mohammad astride a camel led by a devil.

Gondar was also where the fascist Italians made their last stand against the invading British in November 1941. After five years of occupying what was then known as Abyssinia, the Italians had dwindled to a garrison of 40,000 men who surrendered after a two-week battle.

I cycled on through more pleasant rural tableaus that I would describe as idyllic were it not for the perpetual screams of *youyouyou* from children. Some also stretched out hands with palms upturned and yelled demands for 'money, money, MONEY!' Ethiopia became the only country where I plugged in my earphones in a deliberate attempt to drown out the mocking sounds of the world.

Broad baobab and fig trees dotted the landscape as well as dense coppices of tightly planted eucalyptus. The tree was imported from Australia in the late nineteenth century to solve the firewood shortage. However, Ethiopians have now become dependent on the thirsty eucalyptus which drains water resources and depletes the soil's nutrients.

I was napping on an untilled patch of roadside one day, sheltering from the midday sun under a grand old fig tree, when a farmer woke me up. He gestured angrily that this was his land and shooed me away by repeatedly kicking dust into my face until I got up, pushed my bike five metres to the road, and left. This unprovoked hostility was unprecedented on my journey but was to become a recurring feature of my time in the Ethiopian countryside. Stones were hurled on an hourly basis and, on slow uphill climbs, children ran alongside relentlessly heckling me and slapping at my panniers.

As soon as I got off the bicycle friendly smiles returned and people mostly acted normally. When not riding I experienced as much kindness and friendliness as I had in most other countries. However, there was something about the sight of a *farengi,* a foreigner, on two wheels that drew out the pest in rural Ethiopians. Perhaps it was simply a mistrust of the bicycle itself in a land where most walked or ran. When the bicycle first reached the country, brought by the invading Italians in the 1930s, it was called *yeshaitan feras*: the Devil's horse.

I slept out in the open one night on a hidden mountain ledge just out of sight of the road and enjoying expansive views. After dark I was woken by two men intent on sleeping there too. They lay down either side of me in their thin blankets and abruptly went to sleep. It was a cold night and by morning they had cuddled close to me for warmth. I made them instant coffee which they accepted with suspicion, unable to take their disapproving eyes off my little stove. They drank the coffee unhappily, wincing with every sip but clasping the hot mug to warm their hands. They never thanked me and when they were finished they placed the mug on the ground and left without a word or a smile. I felt confused and hurt by their ingratitude.

I continued towards the capital, my patience wearing ever thinner. The road had attracted new settlements, creating a corridor of villages which all bled into one another. I found myself spending most of each day in the saddle, as I was soon surrounded by a crowd of begging village children whenever I stopped to rest. My strength and energy waned. I was tired all the time and the exhausting pace trimmed my temper's wick ever shorter.

I passed a crowd of children in a village one morning and a couple of stones whistled past my ear. When I turned to look who had thrown them, a stone the size of a golf ball conked me hard on the side of the head. My bicycle clattered to the ground and I leapt up in a sudden overflow of pain and anger. I scooped a stone off the ground but thankfully I stopped just short of hurling it indiscriminately into the fleeing pack of children who were howling with delight. I had finally risen to the bait and they had won. There were three or four giggling adults scampering away among the gleeful urchins.

I pedalled on with hot anger still coursing through me. Probing the swelling bump above my ear, my still-shaking hand came away with blood on the fingers. I soon ducked into an unlit village café and brooded over my tea. I was shocked at myself; I didn't have a violent or hot-blooded temperament. I had been punched numerous times but never hit back, and I had certainly never wanted to hurt a child before. But for a few red-misted seconds I genuinely did. I wanted whoever had thrown that stone to suffer. In fact, for a sick instant I just wanted someone, anyone, to suffer for the pain and rage I was feeling. Cowering in that café, I felt afraid that I might not be able to pull myself back from the edge if it happened again.

The aggression towards foreigners and the extensive begging was ubiquitous. However, it seemed incongruous in a country that prided itself on being the only African nation to avoid colonisation and extensive foreign meddling.[29] For many centuries Ethiopia was a major imperial power in its own right. However, famines have been periodic in recent history, exacerbated by the dangerously burgeoning population. During my childhood I remember the word 'Ethiopian' being used as a cruel byword for 'starving' or 'skinny'. For several decades now, Ethiopia has been among the world's top five recipients of foreign aid. Every village I pedalled through had signs announcing aid projects funded by foreign organisations. This culture of receiving had arguably contributed to the habit of viewing foreigners as funds rather than people. The reflex of presenting an open and expectant palm upon spotting a *farengi* sat at odds with the nation's pride in a history of imperial conquest, power, and independence.

It was a warm, hazy morning when I approached the lip of the Blue Nile Gorge. This 250-mile-long scar is almost a mile

[29] Ethiopia was colonised by the Italians in 1936 but they were ousted by the British in 1941, who oversaw the country as a protectorate for just three years before restoring full independence.

deep in places and provided a significant obstacle to travel in Ethiopia until bridged by the Italians in the 1930s. I followed a freshly laid Chinese road on its serpentine descent into the gorge's misty depths. At the bottom stood a new Japanese-built suspension bridge. It straddled the fast-flowing brown river alongside the Italian structure, which only herders still used.

The three-hour, 1,000-metre climb was hot and sweaty and grew tougher as the sun burned off the mist. There were no settlements along the road. A small troop of baboons stopped grooming one another to bark threateningly at my approach and I hurried past, preferring their hollow aggression to that of stone-throwing children.

From the village at the top I looked back across ten miles of open air to the other side. Sweat ran down my face, wide-winged birds of prey wheeled leisurely in the void, and I felt at peace. Then a stone hit the tarmac beside me. I looked ahead and saw an expectant huddle of children by a large sign. One was stooping to replace the stone he had just thrown. I cycled towards them with a sigh. The tallest boy demanded money as I neared. When I ignored him he shouted 'fuck you!' repeatedly and with rising volume until I was out of earshot. I assumed he learned the phrase from another exasperated cycle tourist. The sign beside him announced that the village water pump was donated by the EU.

TWENTY-FOUR

KILLING MOON

Maybe when this is over I will only remember the good
times and decide on another journey.
- Extract from author's diary

Ethiopia was the first country I had visited where the urban population was more friendly and welcoming than its rural counterpart. As I breached the outskirts of Addis Ababa the shouts quietened and the stones stopped being thrown.

It was a city of opposing speeds. The half-built pavements were busy with hurried people sidestepping nimbly around dozens of small stools on which calm, elderly men in weathered flat caps sipped coffee in the brilliant morning sunlight and perused the papers.

Making an accidental tour of Ethiopia's early-twentieth-century history, I cycled through the Italian-built Piazza district and freewheeled down Churchill Avenue towards La Gare, the train terminus built by the French in the 1920s to serve the line to their neighbouring colony Djibouti. Halfway down Churchill Avenue I passed the Ethiopia–Cuba Friendship Monument. This fifty-metre-tall obelisk is topped with the Red Star and was donated to Ethiopia by North Korea in the 1980s, during the country's Soviet-backed communist period. It commemorates fallen Ethiopian and Cuban soldiers in a Cold War clash with Somali forces.

Just before reaching the train station I stopped in front of the Lion of Judah monument. The ferocious bronze-gilded statue of a kingly lion wears a crown and holds a crucifix-topped staff. It was sculpted for the 1930 coronation of Ethiopia's last emperor, Haile Selassie. The Judaic lion represents the Solomonic dynasty's fabled but nebulous Israelite heritage, and Haile Selassie was said to be the 225th generation of direct patrilineal descent from Solomon.[30]

I found a cheap campsite and pitched my tent for a week, to rest and fix some problems with Old Geoff. In the campsite I heard a familiar voice say my name. I turned to see Archie, the Scottish motorcyclist I had met in a daze on my ride out of Cairo two months earlier. He was with his two travelling companions, Chris and Balf, and seemed to have forgotten or forgiven my oddness on the Egyptian road. They had been in the city for a week working on one of their bikes, which had engine troubles. After a testing week I was glad for the easy conversation. We met in a bar that evening and compared notes on our differing journeys from Cairo. Their ride certainly sounded more fun than mine; covering greater distances each day allowed them to travel further, see more, and still explore places in more depth while taking days off. They also were never alone and received negligible harassment during their time in Ethiopia.

I started to wonder whether cycling really was the best way to explore a place. It forced me to travel slowly and observe more, but it sometimes exhausted and frustrated me to the point of shutting out the world. When I reached Addis Ababa I wanted nothing more than to hide for a few days. I wanted to lounge around and rest and sip cool drinks and talk to people in English.

I got some clarity on the situation when the bill arrived and I was the only one that winced at the cost of my share, which was no more than a few pounds. I discovered that on their four-month ride from Edinburgh my new friends had each spent roughly double what I had during the fourteen-month journey from Beijing, and I had even bought a horse. It seemed I was cycling out of financial necessity rather than for some grand and noble reason that facilitated deeper

[30] The Lion of Judah statue was moved to Rome by the conquering Italians in 1936 after Haile Selassie fled to live in exile in an ironically Italianate Victorian mansion in Bath, England. The statue was returned to Addis Ababa in 1960, when Selassie was emperor once more. He ruled until 1974 when he was deposed by a military faction and imprisoned. He died a year later aged 83.

understandings of the places I was visiting.

One morning, the Scots and I joined the crowds funnelling into the national stadium for a football game against South Africa. Ethiopia had never made it to a World Cup before, but defeating South Africa would take them to within one game of qualifying.

We each bought and donned the national team's strip on the street before squashing into the frenzied stand three hours before kick-off. The excitement rose to fever pitch before the players even took to the field. Every tree and rooftop surrounding the stadium soon filled with people, and even the floodlight scaffolds filled with spectators perilously clinging on.

The game was scrappy and unexciting but this didn't bother the fans, who chanted and stood on their seats throughout. The most common chant was 'Lucy, Lucy, Lucy!' in reference to the 3.2-million-year-old hominid skeleton that was found in Ethiopia in the 1970s. The 1.1-metre-tall female is seen as the evolutionary link between humans and the great apes. Lucy is an odd point of national pride in a conservative Christian country where creationism is widely accepted.

There was one white player, a defender, on the South African team. The entire 35,000-strong crowd booed gleefully every time he touched the ball. He looked relieved to be substituted midway through the second half and quickly disappeared to the dressing rooms.

Ethiopia won the game 2-1 and the celebrations were euphoric. Fans swarmed over the fence onto the pitch and were opposed by policemen flailing with wooden truncheons. Ninety minutes after the final whistle we managed to exit the stadium, only to find that the entire crowd was outside awaiting the team bus. The bus eventually ran the gauntlet of screaming, chasing fans and the police seemed torn between hitting people and joining their revelry.

The festivities moved into the city's many bars and we followed. In a nightclub I watched the Ethiopians' unique style of dancing. It consisted of moving solely the head and shoulders in a juddering, rotating fashion. The dance floor was virtually static from the chest down except for four limb-flailing Britons who shouldn't have moved from beer to liquor. I woke in the morning along with three very groggy Scotsmen to find my hair had been plaited by some of the numerous bored prostitutes that stalk the city's nightspots.

Before leaving Addis Ababa, I contacted a man through an internet forum who said he could help me get hold of some decent secondhand parts for my bike. Sintayew was a tall, quiet man and carried himself with a regal bearing. On weekends he tagged along for training rides with Ethiopia's national road cycling team and his wife was in the women's squad. Sintayew arrived at our street corner rendezvous with a bag of tools and oil-smeared parts. Together we attended to Old Geoff and soon had him in good working order, although he looked filthy and absurdly clumsy next to Sinta's sleek white racing bike. When the time felt right I pressed a bundle of banknotes into Sintayew's hand and thanked him. He tried repeatedly to force them back on me but I refused, saying he could buy me a coffee if he liked.

'Ok, follow me. My wife will make coffee for us,' he said, and I followed him for twenty minutes to a modest bungalow in the suburbs.

It turned out that 'making coffee' in Ethiopia is more elaborate than kettles and cafetières. Sinta's wife, Nyala, welcomed me into their tiny but wonderfully green garden, where boughs of glossy foliage draped densely from the walls. She ushered us onto small stools and swept the smooth earth floor in front of us. While Nyala spread loose grass on the ground, scattering little yellow flowers among it, Sinta explained:

'In Ethiopia we like drinking coffee, but we like to make it slowly. It is a way to gather the family and be together for some time. We call this ceremony *Bunna Maflat*.'

Nyala proceeded to throw some incense on a little brazier and then slow roast a pan of green coffee beans over the same flame. Once the beans had turned chocolate-brown she worked them with pestle and mortar and then tipped the grinds into an elaborate pot called a *jabena*. She poured in boiling water and placed the *jabena* over the flame for a few minutes while the coffee brewed. The dark, syrupy liquid was then put through a sieve several times before being poured from a height into small, handle-less cups. It was the darkest, most bitter coffee I had ever tasted. Nyala giggled as she saw me stifle a wince and stirred a little spoonful of sugar into my cup.

Coffee is not to be taken lightly in Ethiopia. The *Bunna Maflat* had taken almost an hour and made instant coffee seem almost sacrilegious. I understood why the two men on the mountain ledge had received the Nescafé I made them with such disdain.

It is claimed that coffee as a drink was discovered in Ethiopia. The story goes that a highlands goatherd named Kaldi had one sluggish individual among his animals, always lagging behind the herd. However, one day the idle goat ate the cherry-like beans of a small white-flowered tree and spent the rest of that day skipping ahead of the herd. Kaldi tried nibbling the beans himself and felt energised. He took them to a nearby monastery where a disapproving monk threw them on the fire. However, the aroma that came from the inadvertently roasting beans drew the attention of other monks. They raked the beans from the embers, ground them, and dissolved them in hot water to create the first cup of coffee.

The legend seems apocryphal, but not impossible. Either way, coffee drinking emerged from either Ethiopia or Yemen about a thousand years ago and spread first through the swelling Islamic world and then onwards to Europe. Coffee soon became an integral part of mystic Sufi ritual in Yemen, where it was used as both a stimulant and a concentration aid during sessions spent chanting the name of god for several hours. By the sixteenth century many religious authorities began to view coffee as an intoxicant and it was banned in Mecca and Cairo. Coffee was similarly banned by the

Ethiopian Orthodox church for almost two centuries and was condemned by the Catholic church as 'unchristian' and 'the Devil's bitter drink' until Pope Clement VIII tried it, loved it, and officially bestowed God's blessing upon the coffee bean.

I exited the city wearing the national football shirt, hoping that it might deflect some of the hostility I had come to expect in the countryside. Unfortunately it didn't work and I was threatened by teenage boys with fist-sized rocks while eating lunch on the roadside. They raised their arms, ready to throw, and demanded the small amount of bread that was my lunch. At a loss for what to do as they grew bolder and edged closer, I brandished my cooking knife, slashed it through the air a few times, and hurried off when they momentarily backed away.

The minor road led me through a small majority-Muslim district centred on a town called Butajira. While in this area, where occasional small mosques dotted the roadside, not a single stone was thrown and nobody shouted at me. I was invited into a home for lunch and had an interesting conversation with my host about the marginalisation of Muslims by the overwhelmingly Orthodox Christian government.[31]

From this peaceful enclave I made a long and steep climb to a mist-veiled mountain pass before zooming downhill. Having covered ninety miles since breakfast, I was long overdue lunch and scanned a village roadside for cafés. In passing I glimpsed a young man run out of a house carrying a bottle of water. A second later the bottle flew over my shoulder, brushing my cheek, and crashed heavily onto the tarmac. I snapped. Next thing I knew, I was standing over my floored bike bellowing a furious, wordless war cry at the doorway into which he had ducked. After a few moments of

[31] Muslims first arrived in Ethiopia during the seventh century, escaping persecution on the Arabian peninsula where they were still a minority. The city of Harar, 220 miles east of Addis Ababa, is considered by many as the fourth-holiest city in Islam. Roughly a third of Ethiopian citizens are Muslims today.

awkward silence a chorus of meek shouts arose from various spectators.

'Sorry, so sorry, mister …'

'No problem. No trouble …'

'Please go now. Just go!'

'Where are you go?'

'You, you, you, YOU!'

'Money? Give me MONEY!'

I stood in the road a minute or so, shaking and close to tears, before riding away thinking dark thoughts. I could only channel my fury into slogging up the next climb with my stomach grumbling. I eventually ducked behind a bush and ate a few hunks of plain bread.

It was late afternoon when I approached a town called Sodo beyond the next pass. All the townspeople were out on the road in state of wild excitement, and the streets were congested with screaming, dancing, pulsing throngs of people. The local football team had just won a fixture and been promoted to Ethiopia's premier league.

I gingerly worked my way through the crowds, receiving the odd slap or thump, and rushed out the other side of town. Night was falling and I was concerned by the atmosphere of rising hysteria. It was time I got off the road and pitched my tent somewhere well-hidden. However, the road threaded a route through a never-ending succession of villages and was busy with revellers coming and going. There was no chance I could slip away unseen, even in the dimming twilight, as people continually shouted at me, shattering my cover.

A fat, refulgent full moon bobbed above mountaintops to the east, illuminating the land. I had never seen such a foreboding moonrise.[32] There was true madness in the air and my uneasiness grew as I passed through a village centre every mile or so where knots of people pursued their frenzied festivities. I did my best not to catch anyone's eye

---

[32] I later discovered it had been a 'super moon'. The moon's elliptical orbit results in occasional full moons 14 per cent larger and 30 per cent brighter than normal.

while edging through the crowds, and I stoically accepted the occasional blows that landed on me. The word *farengi* chorused all around.

Eventually, perhaps inevitably, one of these small villages saw me coming. A throng of around two hundred people looked in my direction. I was starkly illuminated by a motorbike's headlamp and the crowd closed around me. A pungent cocktail of sweat and hot breath hung heavily in the air. Pushing back my panic, I put on a smile and tried to ease a passage through.

It happened quickly when it came. The crowd suddenly tightened and I was forced to the tarmac. I balled up, arms around my head, and took the beating. Fists and feet hammered into me as the mob desperately jostled with itself, everyone eager to get at me. I decided I was going to be killed.

It must have been less than a minute that I cowered in the foetal position. The blows landed across my back, arms, and legs but didn't hurt in the moment. From some unknown depth I felt a reaction surging to the surface. The repressed Charlie – the Charlie I was taught not to be – tore forth from some undesirable depth. Survival instinct or indignation or sheer primordial panic? I don't know which, but I lurched into action, fighting my way off the floor with thrashing limbs. I swung wildly around, fists clenched at the circling phalanx of bodies, and gave a guttural roar. It was a cry of fear and rage. The mob, mostly boys and young men, fell back into a stunned silence.

I was alone and still surrounded by hot-blooded aggression. I had bought a few seconds but needed to act quickly. Old Geoff lay beside me, amazingly unplundered. I picked him up and, trying to retain a dangerous unpredictability, I suddenly charged the wall of people. A single elderly man with a stick was trying to clear a path on my behalf. To my relief the wall gave way and a narrow passage appeared: a gauntlet.

I mounted at a run and started pedalling. Two young boys stepped forward and spat at me, one in my face. The hail of rocks and shoes began. I kicked hard on the pedals and made my escape with missiles bouncing off my back.

I was soon alone, the frantic roar fading fast behind me. My hands were shaking on the handlebars. One had blood on it. I hurried on for a mile or so and then very suddenly veered off the road and shot between two bushes. There, with my heartbeat drumming in my ears, I listened for approaching voices or footfall but heard none. I pushed deeper into the bushes and emerged in a cornfield.

In the stark moonlight, I pitched my tent and tumbled in. I began shivering first, then the crying started. I bit down on my shirt and sobbed hard. My shoulders jerked, my eyes streamed and odd staccato groans rose from the back of my throat. Every part of my body started to hurt at once and I missed my parents fiercely.

When the tears subsided, I lay in the dark feeling lonely. A tree next to me was shedding fruit and I flinched every time one hit the ground. I tried to understand what had happened. My most charitable reading posited simple overexcitement and mob-mentality; the liberating anonymity of a crowd in the dark. I knew not to take it personally. How could it be personal when none of my attackers actually knew me? But I was irreversibly shaken and my patience was truly at an end. From then on I was mentally checked-out of Ethiopia.

When cycling in a bad frame of mind there is an obsession with progression; each pedal stroke becomes another futile attempt to kick away the formless demons that haunt the disquieted mind. For two days on the road I looked dead ahead, listened to music, and ignored the world around me. I worried what might happen if I was provoked again. Sure enough, on a dirt road a boy threw a stone that hit my side. Quick as a flash, I dropped my bike, scooped up a pebble, and hurled it at the fleeing figure. It clipped his heel and he went down hard. A chord of joy chimed deep within me for an instant but collapsed into remorse as I watched him get up and hobble away. I was ashamed. He was only a boy with a stone but, in fairness, so was I.

It was a long, gradual descent out of the highlands and into the Rift Valley. A young girl hurled a rock from three metres away as I raced downhill. It struck my head and my speed worsened the impact, but this time I barely registered what had happened. My fury was spent. I rode on feeling sad while a lump rose on my head.

Approaching the Omo Valley, I turned onto a dusty track and soon found myself in a dry, sparsely inhabited land with people little touched by the outside world. They decorated their bodies with colourful beads and fashioned their hair into thick coils using butter. Their homes were circular huts on stilts with conical thatched roofs. Herders stalked nearly naked through the bush behind their herds; some clasped AK-47 assault rifles. They seemed wary of me, often scattering into the trees at my approach. It was a welcome change and I narrowed my focus on the hard toil of sandy, rocky trails.

In Turmi I caught up with Archie, Chris, and Balf. We spent a pleasant day camped in the cool shade of mango trees with some Dutch and South African tourists driving Land Rovers to Cape Town. We talked and played badminton and slaughtered a goat from the market for dinner.

In the morning our routes diverged. We were all avoiding the one main road bisecting Kenya's north. The others were forming a convoy through Sibiloi National Park on the east shore of Lake Turkana. I planned to pedal a seldom travelled route on the lake's west shore.

A forty-five-mile ride with ten punctures from thorns brought me to Omerate. I awoke the immigration official to stamp me out of the country and gave my last Ethiopian coins to a man with a listing dugout canoe. He ferried me across the Omo river and deposited me in a large, wild no-man's land at the intersection of three countries.

I traced a vague mud path through an otherworldly area. There were no tyre tracks so I followed the consensus of barefoot prints. The few people I saw wore only leather loincloths and had hunting bows slung over their shoulders.

Their dark, clear skin was coated in the fine, grey dust that lay light and pillowy on the ground. These people lived in a land overlooked by the great European border-drawing project of the colonial era. Their homeland sat on the smudge of a blurred line between nations and rendered them stateless. I pitched my tent that night, not knowing which country I was technically in, if any.

In the morning I arrived at a thin rope slung limply across the path. Beside it, under a sheet of corrugated metal, was Peter, a lone Kenyan soldier. He produced chapatti and I made us tea while we talked. He asked about Ethiopia and was sympathetic but unsurprised by the hostility. I told him I had only been in the country six weeks but I felt years older. The last thousand miles had felt like ten thousand. Peter stood up and walked a few steps away.

'Come and stand over here, opposite me,' he said. 'OK? Now, you see those mountains in the distance over there?'

'Yes.'

'They are in South Sudan. And everything to your right there,' he pointed, 'that is Ethiopia. Now, you see where your right foot is standing?'

'Yes.'

'Welcome to Kenya! Everything is fine.'

I wanted to hug him.

TWENTY-FIVE

BADLANDS

If there is a road that has not been travelled,
then that is the one that I must take.
- Edward John Eyre

I cycled slowly through a string of villages inhabited by the Turkana tribe. Naked children ran out of reed huts to watch me pass, clouds of dust rising in their wake. The youngest were silent and wide-eyed, while the teenagers giggled and waved. The only two imprints of the outside world were the yellow plastic water containers carried on the women's butter-braided heads, and the battered AK-47s held by some men. The men also each carried a gnarled olivewood *rungu*, a sort of throwing club, half a yard long with an intimidating knob at one end. Most also had a tiny wood-carved stool the size of a small pineapple slung by their waists, which they squatted on to rest. Some of their backs were scarified with stripes and patterns and many had feathers tucked into their elaborately styled hair. The men watched me with wary interest but the women mostly scattered at the sight of me. Clearly the area received few foreign visitors.

Peter had warned me of the current 'high security alert' in the area due to inter-tribal fighting and cross-border raids. He told me that the next 250 miles or so of my route were known for banditry and that I should hide my tent well out of sight each night.

The villages ended where the Omo river spilled into the swampy north end of 150-mile-long Turkana, the world's largest desert lake. A vague set of tyre tracks appeared and I followed their swerving passage across the arid plain between the lake and the Lapurr mountains to the west. The soft sand often required me to dismount and push. The sun hammered down and it was thirsty work, but the area's bleak, eerie beauty more than compensated. I was back in the desert, which provided welcome, peaceful respite after the challenges of cycle touring in Ethiopia.

It was late Sunday morning when I stumbled upon Our Lady Queen of Peace Catholic mission in a village called Todonyang. The track ran right through the small clutch of buildings that hadn't been a village at all before the messengers of God set up shop. My water bottles needed filling but I couldn't see anyone to ask. However, I heard a faint voice and followed it. The voice grew louder as I pushed Old Geoff towards a church with red-daubed wattle walls.

The door was closed so I eased it open carefully to peek inside. Unfortunately it creaked loudly and someone pulled it wide open. The white preacher stopped talking and 200 faces turned towards me. My hair, uncut in almost two years, fell about my shoulders and I had a big bushy beard, thickened with dust. A muttered chorus of the word 'Jesus' swept across the congregation. I hurriedly pulled the door shut and waited under a tree for mass to end.

Some missionaries invited me to join the assembled for lunch afterwards. The congregants spilled out of the service into the baking afternoon. Women and children far outnumbered the men, and the order of exit neatly displayed the stages of conversion. First came the early converts who were wearing bright white t-shirts bearing the church's name and logo. They wore broad smiles and gently ushered the semi-converts who seemed less certain and mostly wore secondhand western clothes. Some still wore the trappings of tribal life.

Last came the new converts in their traditional clothing. They huddled close together and looked around, wide-eyed with uncertainty, occasionally whispering conspiratorially to each other. They had been placed in the front pews, closest to the preacher, who's English sermon would have been incomprehensible to many of them. When lunch was served the new converts seemed more sure of themselves and were first in the queue, clutching paper plates distributed by some

Spanish teenagers on a summer mission programme.

Over rice, beans, and bottled water, Father Albert told me of his ambitious plan to dam the rivers in the Lapurr mountains and irrigate the drought-stricken area. The enormous reserve of water in the lake is just about potable, to the Turkana, at least, but is too saline for agricultural use. The semi-nomadic Turkana spend much of their lives on the move in an exhaustive search for the precious resource. The livestock depend on water and the Turkana depend on their animals.

'How can these people find time to commune with God if they are always searching for water?'

I didn't answer.

The onward track was usually half a mile or so from the lakeside to avoid the strip of marshy reed beds. And so, as the sun rose behind it, Turkana was little more than a shimmering band, a splintered reflection silhouetting the murmurations of untold thousands of small birds mid-migration. As the sun climbed higher – almost vertically, being so close to the equator – the shimmer mellowed into a rich turquoise. A persistent hot wind ensured the water was ever rippling and shifting.

On the hopelessly sandy track riding was hard work, and the dry heat only made it harder. Occasional clusters of round thatched huts dotted the landscape. Each group of dwellings was encircled by a *manyatta*, a fence of thorny branches to contain the goats and camels at night and protect against East Africa's bewildering array of predators.

On the third anniversary of my leaving home I reached the larger village of Lowarengak. I filled my bottles and bought food from the few shops that offered little more than flour, beans, biscuits, and small tins of expired tomato paste imported from Oman; the Turkana region is remote and supplies are irregular. Village children crowded around me chorusing English-language questions learned in school, excited and amused by my arrival. Foreign aid workers, mineral prospectors and agents of God were not uncommon in the area but they arrived in shiny 4x4s or light aircraft. With a dust-covered bicycle, bulging saddlebags, and travel-worn appearance, I was something of a novelty. The word 'Jesus' again echoed around me as I passed.

A few miles later two Land Cruisers came bumping slowly along the rutted trail. They pulled over and several men, mostly Kenyan, got out. It was a seismological research team led by a Brit called Stan and a Chinese man who went by Kenneth. Happy for a break, they gave me a cold, fizzy drink and told me a little about the East African Rift, the activity of which they were there to monitor. For the last 20–25 million years, the African plate has been splitting. The Horn of Africa is tearing away from the bulk of the continent at an annual rate of seven millimetres to form a new tectonic entity, the Somali Plate. This split has formed a series of valleys and elongated lakes that stretch almost 3,000 miles from Eritrea's Red Sea coast to the mouth of the Zambezi in central Mozambique. I would be spending the next few months loosely following this fault line down to the Indian ocean.

In the afternoon I spotted North Island suspended out on the jade water. Tens of thousands of flamingos flock to this extinct volcano to feast from the algae-rich waters of the two crater lakes. Sadly the island is ten miles from the shore, so I couldn't see the massed birds that enjoy one of the prettier collective nouns: a flamboyance of flamingos.

A day later I glimpsed the larger Central Island, an active volcano with a puff of vapour rising from its low peak. For the previous month the island's black lava beaches would have been a hatchery-cum-nursery for the annual gathering of Turkana's 12,000 Nile crocodiles.

In the small town of Kalokol I gorged on fresh fruit from the slightly better-supplied shops. From there a formerly tarmac road left the lakeside and ran across scorched, red desert. The time-worn track was a gauntlet of rubble, potholes, corrugations, and soft sand. Cars were rare and the silence was disturbed only by sporadic screeches from wheeling birds of prey. Feeling the vibrations of my wheels on the corrugated ruts, lizards scuttled off the road where they basked in the sun.

Lodwar, the Turkana County capital, was a desolate outpost but the largest town for at least 100 miles in any direction. It was there that Jomo Kenyatta was held under house arrest by the colonial authorities from 1959 to 1961 for his spurious involvement in the anti-colonial Mau Mau Rebellion. Just two-and-a-half years later Kenya declared independence and Kenyatta became the founding president.

I chatted to various people in Lodwar and was told over and over again not to take the road through Lokori.

'The bandits are there. They all have guns and are wild men!'

'They will kill you for a pack of cigarettes!'

With bags weighed down by food and water, I started in the late afternoon on the road to Lokori. I felt a little apprehensive but over the years had grown accustomed to ignoring overblown warnings about the savagery of neighbouring people.

Termite mounds up to six metres tall stood on the roadside and dark men lazed under knotted trees while their animals stripped tinder-dry bushes of their withered leaves. That night I cooked dinner beside my tent with a view of a nearby *manyata* containing a dozen homes. I watched the gun-wielding men arrive from all directions, herding their goats and half a dozen camels into the little enclosure while the sun sank, fat and red, over the heat-shimmered horizon. Once inside, they pulled thorn branches across the entrance, providing a sense of security for both me and them.

Gradually I climbed out of the Rift Valley towards Kenya's Central Plateau and the desert gave way to greenery. I also passed into an area inhabited by both the Pokot and Turkana tribes. I spent a couple of days weaving and bobbing over an undulating terrain with astoundingly varied birdlife, roaming troops of baboons, and the odd fox. Carpet vipers regularly slithered across the track and I often found their translucent skins abandoned in the brown grass. A mid-sized herd of adolescent camels grazing the bushes casually turned their heads to watch as I pedalled by.

I saw very few people and was relieved, given the area's fearsome reputation. The Turkana and the Pokot have been rustling each other's cattle and fighting over grazing rights since time immemorial; there was a general lawlessness that was palpable. I learned later that whole villages had been burned and scores had been killed in the tribal fighting in recent years alone.

Early one evening I arrived in the hilltop fortress village of Napitorm. It was ringed with high barbed wire and armed men guarded the perimeter in shifts around the clock. I arrived just before they locked the gate for the night. Half the village escorted me excitedly to the wizened headman. He told me how his 400 Turkana villagers moved to the spot seeking refuge and security four years earlier after continued raids from the Pokot in their former town of Lokori. I camped beside his hut and cooked dinner with a hundred-strong audience of curious children.

From Napitorm I struggled southwards on a hilly and broken track, often having to push. For sixty miles I forged on without seeing a single human. Abandoned on the track was the sun-bleached shell of a Land Rover that had been ambushed by bandits a month earlier. It was riddled with holes, and bullet casings littered the ground.

It was with relief that I finally cycled into the village of Kapedo and the end of the bandit country. The village sits on the Suguta River, which flows from hot springs on the slopes of another volcano. The steaming water cascaded down a ten-meter waterfall into an emerald gorge, at a pleasant 52°C. In the crystal-clear water the grime and tension of several sweaty days drained from my body while I chatted with the village boys about their favourite English football teams.

Moses, the resident doctor, invited me to camp by his clinic. He told me of the nightly bursts of gunfire that plagued Kapedo until a tentative peace was struck four months earlier. The village sat on an ancestral boundary of Turkana and Pokot lands so has borne much of the conflict. Moses showed me into a villager's home. They, indeed, most of Kapedo's inhabitants, had dug bed pits half a metre deep. They slept below ground level to be safe from bullets that pass easily through the thin mud walls.

Thirty miles further south I reached the start of a freshly laid tarmac road. The joy of zooming along the perfect surface after 500 miles of tracks is hard to describe. It felt like the bicycle pedalled itself and I had only to sit and admire the far-reaching views.

A day later I crossed the equator and arrived at the farm of Jess and Robin, the aunt and uncle of an old friend from university. They were expecting me but my wild and unwashed appearance still gave them a fright. In no time at all I was whisked away to the *matumba* market to buy some secondhand clothes, shown to a shower, and then seated with the family for a European-style lunch spread of fresh bread and salads, chutneys and cured meats, and frosty beers.

TWENTY-SIX

CONVERTIN'

When the missionaries came to Africa, they had the Bible and we had the land. And then they said, 'Let us pray'. But when the prayer was over, and we opened our eyes, we found that we had the Bible and they had the land.
- Archbishop Desmond Tutu

The 100 miles to Nairobi took me past a string of picturesque lakes before attacking an escarpment on a crumbly road built by Italian prisoners of war during World War II. The top was cold and misty but I soon descended towards the capital and was met by Rod, my friend's father, who had ridden out to meet me. Together we cycled to where he lives with his wife, Deb, in a peaceful suburb and I began a month off the bike while I renewed my passport, which had run out of pages.

After a week in a beach house north of Mombasa being spoiled with Rod and Deb, I took a bus back up to Robin and Jess's home and continued north to the Laikipia plateau, a two million-acre tract of private ranchland that has largely been de-fenced and converted to a haven for wildlife.

Laikipia is the romantic East Africa of films and books. It is the Africa of another era when game still outnumbered people; the sepia-photographed Africa of Hemingway and *White Mischief*. When Europeans close their eyes and think of Africa, forgetting about war and poverty and corruption and disease, Laikipia is what they see: a 2,000-metre-high plateau dotted with flat-topped acacia trees stretching their branches out to the abundance of grazing game, over which they stand sentinel. The savannah is a parched russet palette that twice-yearly explodes into an array of lush greens when the riotous rains arrive.

I was there to help out Robin and Jess's daughter, Donna, and her husband Josh, who run a safari lodge on Mugie

Conservancy, a private wildlife reserve on the northern boundary of Laikipia.

I passed a fortnight hosting well-heeled guests, clearing boulders to create jeep tracks, mowing lawns, and taking the wheel for game drives around the conservancy. The novelty of nosing along the dirt tracks on some errand and suddenly chancing upon a herd of elephants or forty grazing giraffes never wore off.

*   *   *

New passport acquired, I pedalled west out of Nairobi feeling flabby and unfit once more. That night it felt odd to be back in my little tent, eating my simple staples of rice and vegetables. However, cycle touring's monastic lifestyle is one quickly re-adjusted to, and I was soon back into the ascetic swing of things. Chilly mornings gave way to warm afternoons and miles of road gave way to miles more.

My route swept me past the Masai Mara National Park where hundreds of polished safari vehicles shot past me on the road. I glimpsed into them as they blurred by. Well over half carried Chinese tourists – one very noticeable development since my previous visit to Kenya seven years earlier. The boom in Chinese tourism had arisen in tandem with China's massive investment in Africa in general and Kenya in particular. This infrastructure funding is part of the Belt and Road Initiative – a modern road, rail, and sea lane network, reminiscent of the medieval Silk Roads, that links China to the world for trade purposes. This growing web of interconnected nations now spans three continents and sixty-five countries, comprising 30 per cent of the world's GDP and, crucially, 75 per cent of the world's energy reserves. The booming New China rising from the ashes of Maoism requires almost unlimited resources to feed its growth and Africa has rich pickings. At the time of writing, twenty African nations have already signed on to the programme.

After a couple of days I turned onto a mud road through a

hilly area of immaculately kept tea plantations glowing glorious emerald in the late sun. At a loss for somewhere to pitch my tent I asked a villager if I could sleep next to his wattle and daub home. Evans invited me in and we feasted on pineapple-sized avocados from his kitchen garden before sleeping on floor mats alongside his wife and two young children.

A draining ninety-mile day of hills through humid, tropical greenery brought me north of the equator once more and into Uganda. The westward road flirted with but never quite kissed the shores of Lake Victoria until it reached Jinja. I pedalled into the town as the afternoon's heat was peaking and found myself at a popular point on the tourist trail that unfolds through East and Southern Africa.

As a wide-eyed eighteen-year-old I spent a careless couple of months bussing and hitchhiking from Uganda to South Africa. It was jarring being back in some of the same spots seven years later with just a fraction of the money. Where I was once a backpacker blending in with the other Europeans I was now an unwashed pariah, dipping briefly in and out of the fringes of African tourism.

I pitched up at busy tourist campsite with a lawn overlooking the nascent White Nile. Five miles upstream the fully formed rapid-strewn river spilled out of Victoria which, at the same size as Ireland, is Africa's largest lake. The hostel was full of twenty-something American evangelicals, mostly Texans.

Uganda attracts staggering numbers of short-term missionary visitors: messengers of Christ spreading the Gospel during their university summer break. It's a stable and beautiful nation but has seen a concerning rise of the conservative Christian agenda in recent years. Almost a quarter of non-governmental organisations operating in the country are faith-based, and as of 2002 evangelical groups' humanitarian operations in Uganda were worth more than $2 billion annually. This is a mountainous sum and much important work is done, but the aid money is often administered hand in hand with hardline doctrine that filters through to all levels of society.

During my visit, the Ugandan parliament was debating the Anti-Homosexuality Bill (known colloquially as the 'Kill the Gays Bill'), which would institute the death penalty for committing or promoting homosexual acts. The bill was passed into law four months later with the substitution of life imprisonment for the death penalty.[33]

The crowd of fifty or so Texans congregated in the bar, loud and exultantly unaware of others. Many wore bespoke mission t-shirts bearing the name of their bible school. They were largely female, overweight, and sporting recently braided hair. Sunburned seams of flaking scalp glowered angrily from between cornrows. One group performed a laboured aerobics routine on the lawn to 1990s hits by the Spice Girls. I sat near a group of occasionally sniggering backpackers, half of whom were frantically scribbling in journals, presumably also describing the strange scenes unfurling around them.

Then one of the more robust Texan girls yelled across the bar to a friend engaged in conversation with a Ugandan.

'Hey, Michelle! Are you flirtin' or convertin' over there?'

The sniggers turned to groans and I walked back to my tent resolving to leave early in the morning.

More neatly contoured tea plantations and the dense virgin greenness of the Mabira forest lined my way to Kampala. The traffic grew in volume and recklessness as I approached the capital. The most common and dangerous vehicles were the ubiquitous hop-on hop-off minibuses known as *matatus*. One overtook on a blind corner mid-afternoon and veered

---

[33] Eight months later the law was annulled on a technicality, but intolerance and frequent homophobic attacks loom over Uganda's estimated half a million LGBT citizens. Just nineteen of Africa's fifty-four nations have legalised homosexuality and four countries (Mauritania, Sudan, Nigeria, and Somalia) maintain the death penalty. Much of Africa had destigmatised homosexuality in the pre-colonial era but Europeans brought their prejudices with them. British colonies had a law forbidding 'carnal knowledge against the order of nature' and this Victorian-era statute survives in a number of countries with the exact same wording.

off the road to avoid an oncoming lorry. Three tonnes of metal and tightly packed humans ploughed past, missing me by an arm's length before flattening an acacia bush.

As I cycled through central Kampala's blend of dog-eared colonial grandeur, post-independence concrete squatness, and occasional glass-and-steel newbuilds, I couldn't help sensing, or imagining, the echoes of Africa's quintessential dictator who presided there throughout the 1970s. Idi Amin, the towering, insane 'Butcher of Uganda' holds a place in global consciousness as one of living memory's most brutal despots. From humble origins as assistant cook in the British Colonial Army, he made an unlikely rise through the ranks after independence and seized power in a military coup. His rule was marked by ethnic persecution,[34] political purges, frequent assassinations, a predominantly non-Ugandan mercenary army, and rumours of cannibalism.

At the height of his rule Amin claimed the official title of His Excellency President for Life, Field Marshal Al Hadji Doctor Idi Amin Dada, VC, DSO, MC, Lord of All the Beasts of the Earth and Fishes of the Seas and Conqueror of the British Empire in Africa in General and Uganda in Particular.[35] However, when met in person he usually preferred to be called Big Daddy.

After almost a decade of dismantling the state to feed his murderous egomania, Amin finally fled from a Tanzanian invasion and made his way to Jeddah. The usual number of murders attributed to his regime is 300,000. Yet he died peacefully in 2003, having lived out his retirement in exile at the pleasure of the Saudi royal family.

I passed a few days with my friend Archer, mentally steeling myself for the rising heat and humidity ahead as August gave way to steamy, rain-ridden September and I strayed further from Kenya's cooler plateau.

[34] In 1972 Amin expelled 60,000 Asians, most of whom were born in Uganda and owned businesses that were immediately expropriated.
[35] All of these initialisms were self-bestowed rather than won. The VC stands for the 'Victorious Cross' (which he devised himself) rather than the British military's coveted Victoria Cross.

Sticky, swirling, swampy air slowed my departure from the city. Trees dressed in fat moss still dripped with the night's heavy mist. Beads of sweat swelled on my face before filtering through beard and causing a chin drip that splashed repeatedly on Old Geoff's crossbar. I knew the sun seared somewhere overhead but when I squinted upwards I couldn't pick it out from the bleached mass of white sky.

Occasional improvised brick kilns exhaled thick plumes of dark smoke that enveloped the blurred men shovelling charcoal into their makeshift furnace. On a landfill site two dozen marabou storks picked their way through the pungent waste while half a dozen more wheeled ominously above. A grotesquely ugly bird, the bald-headed, burnt-faced marabou stork stands over a metre tall with a three-metre wingspan and a scrotal flesh bauble bubbling from its lanky throat. It's a scavenger known to feast on anything it finds, no matter how putrid. One bird turned to watch me as I cycled passed, a shoelace hanging from its foot-long bill.

For a day the road swept me through a corridor of continuous habitation. Most people smiled and waved as I passed. Some demanded money, but all chorused the same word that visitors hear across East Africa, particularly in Uganda: *'Mzungu, mzungu!'* The word literally means 'wanderer' and was used first to describe the early European explorers of Africa. However, it has come to mean simply 'white man' or 'foreigner' and is often used by children with outstretched hands hoping for a cut of the white man's fabled wealth.

As with the incessant repetition of 'you, you, YOU' in Ethiopia, this simple word, *mzungu,* was to become a torment. It morphed into the trigger that would aid heat, exhaustion, and loneliness in tipping me from happy and positive to frustrated and mentally shuttered. I often pedalled hurriedly through a barrage of roadside shouts, closing my ears to the chant that took on a mocking tone in my mistaken mind. When it was time to stop for lunch I would wait until nobody was in sight and then suddenly duck off the road into the bushes to be left alone while eating. Not only did this risk run-ins with snakes, but invariably I was found by a passer-by and in my obscure hiding place seemed an even more magnetic oddity. Every action taken or mouthful eaten was fascinating to the growing crowd, who I wished away as they muttered that damn word over and over like a mantra. The gaping crowds made me feel very alone. It's a strange and counterintuitive thing to wish for solitude as a cure for loneliness.

The heat rose for several days and the air's cloying steaminess thickened by the hour. The monsoon was fast approaching and occasional short outbursts of rain teased but did little to cool and clear the atmosphere. Finally, as I made my way into Fort Portal, a steely ceiling of darkening clouds spread from the west and began to thunder. Jagged flashes of angry light daggered downward and the streets cleared as people sought cover.

Ducking into a hostel in the nick of time I avoided the gutter-busting, six-hour downpour and caught up with the three Scottish motorcyclists. They had a birthday to celebrate and a crate of Nile Special Premium Lager with which to do so. After the rain relented we balanced all four of us on one motorbike and drove through rising steam to a questionable 'discotheque' playing ear-splitting Afropop.

I started to feel a building momentum as I cycled southwards across Queen Elizabeth National Park with its famous tree-climbing lions. A herd of buffalo grazed beside the road in the morning, each with a tense muscled mass that struck me as threatening, like an Aberdeen Angus on steroids. Baboons swaggered territorially back and forth across the tarmac, their inflamed bottoms wobbling. They watched me pass with dark, close-set eyes.

A mud track shortcut bore me through a vast banana plantation; a rolling sea of massive, drooping leaves that bowed and bobbed in the guttering breeze. I bought avocadoes and short, finger-lengthed *manzano* bananas, known locally as 'leetle fingas', from roadside village vendors who sat with me as I ate my fruit salad. The hills steepened and rose to thickly forested mountains of a million greens. Camped beside a high-perched nunnery, I sat out another great thunderstorm. In the chill dawn I stood beside a taciturn nun looking out over the forest mountains wallowing in languorous morning mist. She sighed contentedly and her eyes watered in the cool breeze.

That evening I climbed a steep and slippery mud track over a pass and down to Lake Bunyonyi. Sitting almost 2,000 metres above sea level, the lake is 900 metres deep and home to numerous inlets and islands. It's a startlingly beautiful spot and attracts most of the overland truck tours that ply the route to Cape Town. While camped near some of these group tours I noticed something new. In the past, when people learned what I was doing, I was normally greeted with enthusiastic disbelief. But now I had been on the road for over three years and was still facing yet another year, the response had changed. It was no longer, 'That's exciting … sounds like fun … I wish I could do something like that.' It had become, 'What did you say? How many years now? Why on earth? Don't you have any friends?'

But I'd gone too far and invested too much of myself to consider quitting again. My stubbornness propped me up and on I went in the morning, past the 30,000-mile mark and into The Country of a Thousand Hills.

TWENTY-SEVEN

A THOUSAND HILLS

All of us must bitterly regret that we did not do more to prevent it …
On behalf of the United Nations, I acknowledge this failure
and express my deep remorse.
- Kofi Annan, 1999

At first glance Rwanda, or *Le Pays des Mille Collines*, seemed not dissimilar to Uganda. People drove on the right-hand side rather than the left and things looked a little rougher round the edges. The villagers wore slightly more ragged clothes and shouted at me slightly less. But the Francophone nation I first visited seven years earlier had somehow turned Anglophone. French was no longer taught in schools and the road signs and shop fronts had all switched too.

A long, winding climb though a steep-sided valley with tea fields at its floor carried me to a pass and then briskly down to the capital, Kigali. I met with Robert and Jane, Ugandan friends of my uncle, who had flown over to officiate at their wedding five years earlier. They drove me to their suburban home where I met their young children, two of whom were named after my cousins in Britain. Rupert, Lavinia, and Akhive seemed like bright happy kids being brought up in a loving environment. I couldn't help thinking that Robert and Jane would have been children themselves when the 1994 genocide unfolded with indescribable brutality while the world watched, appalled but passive.

In the morning I steeled myself and made the journey into a haunted past. The first thing I saw at the Genocide Memorial Centre was an innocuous-looking concrete slab in the garden, about five by ten metres and only ankle high. A small sign informed me that it was a mass grave. Within it, and seven others like it, were the remains of 250,000 people. I walked inside a small whitewashed building and began working my way around the exhibition. With sickening photos and blunt text it detailed the causes, the genocide itself, and the aftermath.

The history of Rwanda is largely unrecorded, except by oral tradition, so there are many contesting stories. In the museum I read that there had been numerous tribes in Rwanda when the Belgians took the colony from the Germans during the First World War. At that time the Tutsi and the Hutu weren't ethnicities or even clans, although it's true that they had been once. Historically, both the predominantly agriculturalist Hutu and the pastoralist Tutsi were Bantu migrants who are thought to have arrived several hundred years ago and pushed out the pre-existing hunter-gatherer pigmies known as the Twa. The terms 'Hutu' and 'Tutsi' grew into a system of social class that had been largely forgotten by the time the white men arrived. Perhaps as a divide-and-conquer strategy, the colonialists resurrected the obsolete hierarchy and made the minority Tutsi the ruling class: an administrative elite, subordinate only to the *mzungu* Belgians, similar to the Brahmins in British India.

To formally codify the groups it was decided that every family with ten or more cows, about 15 per cent of the population, was Tutsi. Identity cards were issued and a tear was rent through the heart of Rwandan society. The colonial rulers also ham-handedly configured ethnicity into the equation, measuring cranial circumferences and nose widths to lend a pseudo-scientific authority to the project. The population was split and the rift only grew from there. The Tutsi received preferential treatment over the ensuing four decades and many came to think of themselves as superior and deserving of their privileged status. Simmering Hutu resentment was understandable and inevitable.

When Rwanda gained independence in 1962 the now-despised Tutsis faced heavy persecution from the majority former underclass. There were several smaller-scale massacres of Tutsi after independence, especially during the civil war which ran from 1990 to 1994 as the Hutu-led government fought the rebel Rwandan Patriotic Front (RPF), a Uganda-nurtured collection of Tutsi refugees who had crossed the border, fleeing extremist Hutu groups.

The final violence, as many international observers had foreseen, was beyond terrible. Juvénal Habyarimana, the Hutu president of two decades, was travelling in his private jet accompanied by the president of neighbouring Burundi. Most believe that the young leader of the RPF ordered the strike that downed the plane. Others speculate it was a Hutu conspiracy to provide the flashpoint for a 'final solution' to the Tutsis. Either way, the predictable outcome followed.

The aim, as publicly stated on national radio at the outbreak of the massacre, was to entirely exterminate the Tutsis. An estimated one million of the country's seven million people were killed, mostly with machetes but often with blunt implements, in an orgy of slaughter that lasted 100 days. Perhaps most disturbing is that the vast majority of murders were not committed by the Hutu militias. They were carried out by ordinary Hutu civilians whipped into a frenzy of bloodletting. Their victims were not vilified bogeymen from a distant land or of a differing faith. They were neighbours, school peers, teachers, and colleagues. The dead comprised three-quarters of the Tutsi minority as well as tens of thousands of sympathetic Hutus who refused to partake in the carnage.[36]

Before being murdered, many victims were tortured. Their Achilles tendons were often cut first so they couldn't run away. Some were thrown down pit latrines and showered with rocks until their cries fell silent. Many Tutsis sought refuge in village churches. Dozens of reports later emerged of these churches, some with over 1,000 people crammed inside, being locked and set alight or bulldozed. Hutu men known to be HIV positive were encouraged, or even forced at gunpoint, to rape Tutsi women. Upper estimates of the number of women raped nudge the half million mark.

In most areas, the massacre only ceased once all Tutsis

---

[36] The pygmy Twa are an often-overlooked victim of the genocide. An estimated 10,000 of the remaining 30,000 Rwandan Twa were killed as the Hutus strove for complete demographic dominance.

had either fled or been killed. Hundreds of thousands of people fled to neighbouring countries. Among them were both Tutsi refugees and Hutu *génocidaires* fleeing retribution after the RPF fought their way to the capital and seized power, bringing an end to the genocide. The escaped *génocidaires*, also known as the Interahamwe, crossed to Zaire (now known as the Democratic Republic of the Congo) in particular, where their unsettling presence contributed significantly to the decade of Congolese civil war that followed.

One of the big questions will remain forever unsettled: Who is to blame for the genocide? Rwanda today blames the international community. The UN did not send an intervening force, or mobilise their peacekeeping presence already stationed in the country. A French military unit on the ground at the time evacuated expatriates but refused to take Tutsis out of the country, allowing them to be dragged from lorries at Hutu checkpoints and killed before their eyes.

The genocide is widely acknowledged as an atrocity that could and should have been prevented. It is, however, near impossible to ignore the fact that it was the people of Rwanda, soldiers and villagers alike, who picked up machetes and hacked at their countrymen until the streets literally ran with blood. Foreign negligence cannot be blamed entirely for the astounding tidal wave of murderous hate that gushed exultantly and terribly forth when the floodgates opened. It is also all too easy to compare this horror story to the relative peace and tolerance of countries closer to home. But four-fifths of the Rwandan population were living in extreme poverty at the time of the genocide, the overwhelming majority of them Hutu, and scant few received secondary education. Hatred is much more easily incited among those who struggle to put food on the table and keenly feel the injustice that others are more fortunate. Late-eighteenth-century Frenchmen and early-twentieth-century Russians would probably attest to this.

I returned outside and walked along a wall with a dizzyingly long list of victims' names in inch-high lettering;

several hundred thousand appellations with the distinct combination of Franco-Christian first names and melodically African surnames. The jumbled and incomplete remains of many of their owners lay under the nearby concrete slabs. The list is still being added to but the true number of names will never be known.

Before I left Kigali, Robert took me on a quick tour of the city. A small 'tip' was paid to gain access to the eighteenth-floor rooftop of the country's tallest building. Rwanda is often cited as a modern economic miracle with a GDP that has grown by at least 120 per cent (in real terms) over the two decades since the genocide. It has become a regional hub for technological innovation and gender equality with women comprising 56 per cent of legislative body members. Reconciliation in the wake of the genocide has also been a staggering success story with convicted perpetrators released from prison if they ask for and receive forgiveness from the surviving family members of their victims.

We looked out over the many hills of a rapidly expanding and modernising city. The familiar orange-red mud roads, so redolent of Africa, were being tarmacked over and Robert pointed out several swathes of slum-cleared land being prepared for development. The president and former RPF rebel leader Paul Kagame had taken to ordering poorer residents out to make way for lucrative building projects. Mud-built houses were marked for demolition with crude paint crosses where high-rise apartments would be built, affordable only to the ruling elite.

After the genocide Kagame became vice president under a Hutu leader. However, he was also Minister of Defence and controlled the army, which was simply the repackaged military wing of the RPF. As such he was effectively ruler of the country and nobody was surprised when he acceded to the presidency in 2000. He quickly set about absorbing the other political parties into the RPF, making the country a de-facto one-party state.

Kagame changed the constitution in 2017, allowing

himself to run for a third term, which he won with a suspicious 99 per cent of the vote. Under his tight control stability has reigned and the economy has flourished, albeit with much international assistance. Comparison to China is hard to avoid. There is vocal opposition to Kagame's regime but, as in China, many of these voices disappear and most Rwandans are, for now, willing to swallow the pill of autocracy if it means peace and prosperity after such a painful past. However, China's endangered dissidents have been waking up over the past decade and the same is coming to pass in Rwanda. Dissatisfied refugees in neighbouring countries have been forming various armed groups intent on unseating the regime. The echoes of the early 1990s are hard to ignore.

TWENTY-EIGHT

MEN IN LYCRA

If we don't offer ourselves to the unknown, our senses dull ...
we wake up one day and find that we have lost our dreams
in order to protect our days.
- Kent Nerburn, *Letters To My Son*

Uphill and downhill, uphill and downhill. Demoralisingly slow climb followed by dangerously fast descent, again and again and again. Rwanda can be trying on a bicycle. The pacifying views of verdant and vertiginous landscapes unfolding around every bend only compensate so much for the exhaustion and sweat rash.

I clung to the back of a lorry for a couple of miles on one climb and was joined by two village men who deftly switched to side saddle and perched on their cross bars. One of them soon fell backwards and clattered to the tarmac when the lorry jerked into a lower gear. His friend laughed so hard that he soon lost his grip and went down too.

Droves of schoolchildren wandered along the road in their khaki shorts and shirts. Half of the population of 12 million is under the age of eighteen. The bolder boys reached out to touch my skin as I passed. I'm not sure what they were expecting but they often retracted their hands as if they'd received an electric shock. Dark white magic. Besides '*mzungu*', some shouted the familiar refrain of 'Jesus! Jesus!'

A storm gathered late one afternoon and I began looking for somewhere flat to pitch my tent. Following a footpath to a small village, I found a church and started pitching on the grass next to it as the first drops fell. Two kindly old men unlocked the building, led me inside and left me, padlocking the door for my safety. They said they would be back at dawn to let me out. I looked around at the cold room of dark concrete, ribbed with the close-packed slabs of low concrete pews. My sleeping mat was thin foam and the cold floor didn't appeal so I made my bed on an old wooden table at the back of the room, stripped down to my pants, and got into my sleeping bag. The resounding clatter of downpour on the metal roof ensued for several hours. Lightening strobed behind the small, barred windows and a chill wind whistled in.

Eventually the storm passed, it grew warmer, and I half kicked off my sleeping bag. A couple of hours before dawn I woke to the sound of tinkling keys and a latch being lifted. A clutch of the candle-bearing devout drifted in for prayer. They approached me and, embarrassed, I feigned sleep. Drawing closer they found a skeletally thin, long-haired white man dressed in only small shorts draped across what turned out to be their altar. There were gasps. Someone shrieked 'Jesus!' and ran out. The others knelt and began a strange, mournful chant in an unfamiliar language liberally strewn with the word 'Jesus'. After a couple of minutes of mortification, I pretended to wake up and explained who I was. They seemed more disappointed than angry.

At sunrise I mounted Old Geoff and glided down towards a valley floor, plunging into soupy morning mist. Women emerged from the whiteness balancing the day's supply of foraged firewood on their heads, only to be enveloped again shortly after I passed them. That evening, after bobbing and weaving southward over ridges of painstakingly terraced hills, I camped with the chief's permission on a grassy slope outside his village's 'administrative office'. An hour after I disappeared into my tent I was finally rid of the excited mass of children running around, shouting that I was a foreigner, and tripping on my guy ropes. Not long after, a crowd of adults gathered outside the office. Voices were raised and pronouncements were repeated, each time more vehemently. From my listening post ten metres away I eventually realised it was some sort of trial.

The lashes soon began. There were well over a hundred strokes before I stopped counting, each sounding a vicious swish and sickening crack as the cane tore into bare flesh.

The accused howled with each strike but eventually emitted only a continuous and pathetic moan; the individual strokes no longer registering above the general pain. The crowd chattered and laughed throughout. I didn't know if the man was guilty, or even what he was accused of. It was not my business and I was a stranger in that strange land. Even so, I struggled not to intervene.

The chocolate-brown Kanyaru river marked the border with Burundi. I had been rejected for a tourist visa at the embassy in Kigali and so paid the border guards for a three-day transit visa. The time press to cross the country and reach Tanzania was on. That afternoon I met some lycra-clad Burundian cyclists out for a Saturday ride. They insisted I tag along, so I followed Emmerie, Jean, Jean-Paul, Sylvestre and 'Le Docteur' towards the capital, Bujumbura. My legs burned as I forced my heavily laden bike to keep up with their sleek aluminium models. We pedalled past the dense forest of Kibira National Park. Emmerie told me it had been home to a thriving colony of mountain gorillas but that they were all poached when the country plunged into conflict in the nineties.[37]

Like their Rwandan counterparts, Burundian village cyclists often clung, side saddle, to the back of lorries for steep climbs. However, I was surprised to note that Burundians did so even when the lorry was speeding downhill. According to my new friends, holding onto lorries was illegal in Burundi. I saw a policeman give chase on foot behind a slowly climbing lorry and bodily knock the accompanying cyclist to the floor. The panting policeman then picked up the old one-speed bicycle and threw it down a

---

[37] The Burundian Civil War was another Tutsi–Hutu based conflict, inextricably linked with Rwanda's troubles, that ran from 1993 to 2005. Hutu militias (bolstered by fleeing Rwandan *génocidaires*) fought a Tutsi military regime that had controlled the country for a quarter of a century. Burundi had eight presidents in twelve years, two of whom were assassinated in a six-month period. Thousands of child soldiers were forcibly recruited, some as young as seven, and the estimated toll of the conflict is 300,000 lives.

rocky slope. The offender, with blood trickling down his face and shins, hobbled down to collect it while the policeman limped back to his post.

Finally, having ridden much further than I intended that day, we joined the rest of the Burundian Cycling Federation in a ramshackle village bar. I hadn't seen so many men in lycra since Europe. They were a friendly bunch and welcomed me into their fraternity. Fresh bottles of cold beer with irresistible beads of condensation kept appearing in front of me and we feasted on plates of spiced *nyama choma* (roast meat). The Burundian Minister for Sport arrived and the group gravitated towards him as he began holding court. The sycophancy the cyclists displayed towards this surly, bald man was impressively theatrical as they bowed and scraped, competing to fetch his next drink from the bar.

Darkness was fast approaching. We all mounted our bikes and I soon discovered why the rest of the cyclists had not got beyond this village. It was only another twenty miles to Bujumbura, but for that distance we sped lethally down 1,300 metres in altitude. Sweeping views of the city lumbering around the northern tip of Lake Tanganyika threatened to distract but I managed, just barely, to keep my eyes on the steep road and not hurtle off the tarmac.

The adrenalin-flooded descent was one of those moments completely antithetical to the downbeat exhaustion I often felt from being a foreigner in Africa, constantly shouted at and scrutinised. It had been a physically gruelling day but I made new friends, drank numerous refreshing beers, and then had that magical feeling of going somewhere unplanned and unknown with people I hardly knew but liked; the nervy excitement of uncertainty followed by the exhilarating surrender to life. It felt like giving up swimming against a current and letting the river sweep me away to an unforeseen adventure. That was why I travelled.

We swept euphorically into the low, humid city in failing light and set up camp at another bar for more beer and meat. A big storm was once again brewing, electricity was palpable in the dense air, and we sat outdoors in our sweat-stiffened clothes waiting for the clouds to burst. When they did we were drenched clean before retreating indoors.

A man called Kunta set me up in his guestroom late that night. Having covered almost 100 hilly miles, I felt I had earned the luxury of a late start in the morning. However, three of the group, Christophe, Charte and Bosco, arrived on bicycles at sunrise and hijacked me. We rode along the lakeside first, and then west to the Congolese border post. Men pushed bicycles back and forth unchecked, their rides stacked high with branches of bananas. Just across the border was arguably Africa's most troubled nation. The Democratic Republic of the Congo's (DRC) enormity stretched 1,200 miles from where we stood all the way to the Atlantic. I knew that when I eventually reached the southern cape of Africa and turned to cycle homeward, there would be no way around it.

After a lunch back in town I wearily cycled south along the shore of Tanganyika, alone again and racing towards the border of Tanzania against my visa's expiry. After ten miles I dismounted beside the Mugere river and pushed Old Geoff up a hill overlooking the lake. A three-metre high rock stood there alone. Carved into the stone, simple but neat lettering read:

LIVINGSTONE
STANLEY
25 – XI – 1871

TWENTY-NINE

TWO WHITE MEN

I will go anywhere so long as it is forward.
- David Livingstone

On 10 November 1871 Henry Morton Stanley walked into Ujiji, an Arab slave-trading hub on the eastern shore of Lake Tanganyika in present-day Tanzania. For the previous seven months he had been marching west from Bagamoyo, on the coast near Zanzibar, at the head of an expedition of over 100 African porters, guides, and guards. He was on assignment for the *New York Herald*, searching for possibly the world's most famous man at that time. The Scottish missionary-cum-explorer Dr David Livingstone had been missing for six years and was feared dead.[38]

In the Victorian era explorers were equivalent to Hollywood stars today. Celebrity status came from their books, newspaper dispatches, and speaking tours of the geographical societies of Europe and America. They engaged in daring quests to fill in blanks on maps and answer pressing geographical questions. Livingstone was the latest in a long line of men to venture into Central Africa in search of the source of the Nile. No news of him had reached Europe for several years and the western world yearned to learn his fate. Was he still alive? Had he found the source? What new discoveries had he made? What new calamities might he have survived?[39]

---

[38] Despite being unarguably the most famous European missionary to Africa, Livingstone made just one conversion during his thirty years of travels and that individual was soon regarded by him as a backslider. However, the Bakwena tribal chief he baptised, named Sechele, went on to become a pioneer of early African Christianity.

[39] In 1843 he was mauled by a lion in Southern Africa and set his broken humerus himself. While charting the Zambezi in 1855, he was the first European to visit the world's most voluminous waterfall, which he named Victoria Falls in honour of the British monarch.

Livingstone was still alive but in a deplorable, desperate state, ravaged by repeated illnesses and out of funds. In desperation he had thrown himself on the mercy of Arab slavers, whose occupation in Africa was the very trade that he had campaigned for years to end.

With the huge retinue of soldiers, flag bearers, camp attendants, and guides, Stanley's unexpected arrival represented salvation. Stanley's pithy address at their meeting under a mango tree has been immortalised. Since his commission by the *New York Herald* he had spent two years entirely focused on that one moment. He later wrote:

> *I would have run to him, only I was a coward in the presence of such a mob – would have embraced him, but, he being an Englishman, I did not know how he would receive me; so I did what cowardice and false pride suggested was the best thing – walked deliberately to him, took off my hat, and said: 'Dr Livingstone, I presume?'*

Today the sleepy village of Ujiji lazes on the lakeside. It's a peaceful place with a comfortable fishing industry, its outskirts increasingly blurred with the spreading nearby hub, Kigoma. The rich red mud roads had deeply scored tyre tracks in which occasional sunken cobblestones jutted out at jaunty angles.

I lingered a long while on the spot of the historic meeting. A grand old mango tree spread its shading arms overhead and, I was told by the caretaker, was grafted from the original tree that presided over the 1871 meeting. Within a chain link fence was a simple marble memorial to Livingstone depicting a relief of the African continent with a crucifix scored through its heart. As hard as I tried, I simply couldn't imagine the state of utter hopelessness that Livingstone must have been in. The length and hardship of his travels in an unmapped and often hostile land put into perspective my own ramblings, largely along smooth ribbons of tarmac through lands not only mapped but satellite imaged and dotted with telecom pylons.

After the two explorers met they passed four months together mapping the northern extent of Lake Tanganyika and verifying that it was not connected to the Nile. During this time they carved their names on the rock I had visited south of Bujumbura. Stanley then marched back to the coast and the ailing Livingstone, almost sixty years old, continued his explorations, finally succumbing to malaria and dysentery a year later in present-day Zambia. His long-serving guides and companions, Chuma and Susi,[40] buried his heart at the foot of a tree on which they carved his name.[41] They then carried his body over 1,000 miles back to Bagamoyo from where it was shipped to London and eventually interred in Westminster Abbey.

I relished visiting both the rock in Burundi and the meeting spot in Ujiji. Their physical links with the past was tangible. Those characters that I had read so much about stood on the exact same spots as me, consigning their names to legend. I recalled a similar feeling nine months earlier upon finding Stanley's name graffitied on the ancient stonework at Persepolis in Iran.

A more controversial figure than Livingstone, Stanley went on to explore more of Central Africa in a series of daring journeys that bordered on conquest. He was a complicated character with a shrouded past that he guarded closely.[42] His exploits in Africa won him renown and riches but his methods and motivations were less than admirable. Besides being an explorer, he was an intrepid vandal and a gun for hire. He laid the groundwork for his paymaster, King

[40] Chuma had been enslaved as a boy on the Mozambique coast but was freed by Livingstone in 1861. Susi was first employed by Livingstone as a woodcutter during the same six-year expedition (1858–64), the aim of which was to chart the Zambezi River.

[41] The tree, a mobola plum, was cut down in 1899 by a Royal Geographical Society expedition. The inscribed section of trunk today sits on the floor of a corridor in the society's London headquarters.

[42] Stanley's real name was John Rowlands and he was born in Denbigh in Wales in 1841 to an eighteen-year-old unmarried mother. He was abandoned first to relatives and eventually to the workhouse. Ashamed of his humble origins, when he was eighteen he stowed away on a ship to New Orleans, changed his name, and started a new life.

Leopold II of Belgium, to turn the Congo into a private fiefdom, thus creating one of the most brutal and exploitative colonies in world history. Although an American citizen, Stanley retired to London where he became a member of parliament and was knighted by Queen Victoria. He lived a few years into the twentieth century and is buried in Surrey. However, if he has a tormented ghost, it surely lurks somewhere deep in the Congo.

From Ujiji an immaculate new road swept east for sixty miles to a ramshackle little town called Uvinza, where salt has been extracted from some brine springs for several centuries. My route then abruptly became a swerving, rutted tangle of hard red mud. A solemn-faced shopkeeper warned me that the 130 miles to the next town, Mpanda, was stalked by lions who don't fear humans. Feeling uneasy, I put up my tent in the bush that night miles from the nearest habitation and a stone's throw from the jolting mud path I would be following for the next 400 miles. My tent was the same sweaty, tatty, bundle of worn fabric that I had been living in for three years. To a big cat, with its dense concentration of highly honed olfactory glands perfected through 25 million years of natural selection, I would be detectable hundreds of yards away. If a lion wanted me, I would be in its mouth before I awoke.

The few villages I passed all had both a mosque and a church of equal size and prominence. In the clutches of neatly uniformed children walking to school, roughly a third of the boys wore *taqiyahs*, the rounded skullcaps common in Islam. Tanzania is an impressively secular country that suffers little religious tension. The population is split evenly three ways between Islam, Christianity, and Animism. Religion is unpoliticised. The first post-independence leader, Julius Nyerere, was a socialist whose greatest achievement was *ujamaa*. The Swahili word translates to 'familyhood' and was used to engender a culture of collectivisation in which the nation and the village are more important than the individual. It was Nyerere's effort to combat the problems of 'tribalisation' that was plaguing many other newly independent African nations. Ethiopians had proudly told me that their country was home to eighty separate tribes. Kenyans spoke of forty-two tribal identities and Ugandans of fifty-six. Anthropologists write that Tanzania is home to 125 ethnic groups speaking as many different languages. However, when I asked Tanzanians how many tribes and languages their country had, the most common response was: 'One. We are all Tanzanian and we all speak Kiswahili.'

Economically, *ujamaa* was widely viewed as a failure. The collectivisation of village production led to a drastic drop in productivity and the initiative was halted when Nyerere conceded the presidency in 1985. However, even if Tanzania has never thrived financially, Nyerere left in his wake one of the most peaceful and cohesive societies on the continent, united by one language and a strong sense of nationhood. Perhaps for this reason, he is commonly referred to as *Mwalimu*, the Swahili word for 'teacher'.

The days were long and tiring, covering up to eighty off-road miles, and the nights were a blissful nine-hours of dreamless oblivion. The corrugated trail bounced and jolted me through dense bush with very few people and only one or two vehicles a day. Besides the creak of my pedals and the soft susurration of dry grass and breeze-tickled leaves, all was silent.

Occasionally I came across little clusters of basic grass huts where the inhabitants unfailingly scattered at the sight of me. The few antelope I encountered flew from me too. The weather was hot and humid. Little wind made it below tree level and the occasional streams where I washed and filled water bottles were toe-deep and murky.

Whenever I stopped for rest I was swarmed by flying ants that targeted my ears, eyes and nostrils. They hurled themselves at me, often getting trapped in body hair and wriggling until being removed by me or dying of exhaustion. I soon learned to put bits of tissue in my ears and nostrils.

I relished the few times when the track crested a rise and I could stand in a cooling breeze, gazing across the treetops. From these vantage points the endless bush of browns and lime greens stretched away in all directions to the steam-obscured horizon, buzzing and clicking and rustling as uncountable thousands of insects and animals, predators and prey, co-existed in their eternal fight for life.

After dark, nature's chorus unnerved me. Strange primal shrieks and rasping leopard coughs accompanied cacophonous birdcalls. When eating rice one evening, sitting on the dirt wearing only pants, I heard a twig snap and found myself in a staring competition with a black-backed jackal. The vulpine dog stood ten metres away, rooted to the spot, its big, bat-like white-haired ears twitching slightly. We remained still for a minute, searching each other's eyes without threat, before I slapped my thigh and sent him scarpering.

I reached the village of Nkondwe. It was a drab backwater of a place, forgotten by the capital and little more than a clutch of huts inhabited by alcoholic men and their long-suffering women. It was mid-morning when I arrived but already the men were bleary-eyed and slurring. Emptied plastic sachets of *konyagi* were strewn across the dust. The labels ominously declared the liquor to be 'Tears of the Lion'. Konyagi is a strong and strange substance. It's not quite gin, or vodka, or rum. It's somewhere between the three and yet impossibly far from all of them.

I'd been plagued by punctures during the previous two days and had run out of patches so I paid an inebriate to repair a tube with rubber and superglue. The whole village pressed close to gape at me while the man fumbled with his tools, twice gluing his fingers together. His associate, in a moment of surprising insight, noticed I was uncomfortable with the boozed huddle edging ever closer. He plucked a fistful of straws from the hut's thatch and lit it. Swinging this burning baton like a club, he forced the crowd back.

The next obstacle was Katavi National Park. There was no gate or guard so I rode on in, hoping it was safe. A swampy pool in a river near the entrance was home to fifty wallowing hippos. Their tiny black eyes and pinkish-grey backs bobbed above the waterline while tubular ears flicked away flies. I watched as two males fought a slow but violent duel. They disappeared underwater for minutes at a time before surfacing, both trying to bite the other's gaping mouth. Five minutes on I stumbled upon a dozen grazing giraffes. For a while they gazed at me impassively, still chewing. When I remounted they cantered away in a manner simultaneously knock-kneed and graceful.

The road through the park was thirty miles and I covered twenty of those in a stressful sprint as a swarm of tsetse flies followed me. The tsetse is similar to a horsefly but larger and considerably more aggressive. With their long serrated proboscis, they can deliver a painful bite, even through denim. The tsetse also carries sleeping sickness, which kills a few thousand people each year.

Most of my escort seemed content to sit on my saddle bags and wait their turn to fly forward and bite me. When I stopped cycling they all attacked at once so I hurried on, not knowing what to do. It was in this distress that I was pulled over by horrified park rangers. When they had finished slapping the flies on my back and legs, they informed me bicycles weren't allowed in the park. I asked why.

'If the lions do not eat you, then the buffalo will squash you into juice.'

After Katavi, the bush gave way to savannah and the tracks were a little better. I made quicker progress and reached the next town, Sumbawanga. Perhaps my favourite place name in Africa. It rolls off the tongue with a pleasing rhythm: *Sumbaa-waangaaaaa*. The town was little to speak of but it provided a decent meal, a cold drink, and the news that only twenty-five more miles lay between me and a freshly laid road. The effortlessness of asphalt after days on mud is hard to describe. It seemed the bicycle was powering itself and my legs were spinning more as a gesture than a driving force. I shot onwards sensing rest was just a few days ahead.

In the city of Mbeya I found myself suddenly retching. My eyes streamed and my throat burned while sirens blared just ahead of me. The police had used water cannons and tear gas to disperse traders rioting about a new tax law and the wind had spread the noxious air; many pedestrians were slumped against walls, vomiting. I washed my eyes with water and covered my face with a wet cloth until the air cleared. The stinging stayed with me for a day afterwards.

Before the Malawian border there was a climb to 2,000 metres and a region of mist-shrouded potato farms and sweet-smelling pine groves. The descent was steep and fast, with signs warning drivers of fatal loss of control. The previous day a lorry had smashed through railings on the bridge at the bottom and plunged into a river. Both driver and passenger died instantly, I was told. It felt wrong filling my water bottles beside the smashed lorry carcass, but the river was fresh and cool, and I was thirsty.

THIRTY

CHUCK NORRIS

*In a town like Mbeya I understood the sense of futility. Perhaps that
was why I liked rural Africa so much, and avoided towns, because in
villages I saw self-sufficiency and sustainable agriculture. In the towns
and cities of Africa, not the villages, I felt the full weight of all the
broken promises and thwarted hope and cynicism.*
- Paul Theroux, *Dark Star Safari*

The road had been pot-holed and repaired so often that it
resembled the patchwork trouser knees of the smiling
village children living along it. The buildings were decades-
old crumbles of concrete and the ancient road signs were
sun-faded to illegibility. It seemed nothing had been built or
done in many years.

Small, dog-eared, friendly Malawi: a landlocked, densely
populated, mineral-poor country that rarely leaves the list of
ten poorest nations in the world. And yet, Malawi has been
dubbed 'the warm heart of Africa' for its peaceful history and
friendly people. In the first town I saw a poster of the current
president next to a faded and peeling portrait of the founding
father.

After Africa's great rush to independence in the 1960s,
there ensued a period of chaos. Across the continent, men
with no training in governance, and often with a recent
background in guerrilla warfare, suddenly found themselves
in charge of huge nations with the fate of many millions in
their hands. However, the figure that came to the helm of
Malawi was a man more English than African.

Hastings Banda had been born to a peasant farmer but
had spent the previous thirty-three years as a practising
doctor in America and Britain, forgetting his native language.
Banda became Africa's most rigidly totalitarian leader,
banning all opposition and micro-managing every aspect of
the country's administration. By the standards of the time, his

three decades of rule were remarkably peaceful, stable, and even economically productive given Malawi's limited potential. He was perhaps the closest Africa has had to a benign dictator, but a dictator nonetheless. When he submitted to growing pressure and allowed free elections in 1994, he stepped down leaving the country in a poor condition but without civil divisions. Malawi is never going to be a powerhouse, but it has never been a slaughterhouse.

I followed the buckled road along the lake and down through the country. Fishermen repaired nets on the beaches and African fish eagles wheeled above the water. Lake Malawi makes up a quarter of the nation's surface area and is the world's fourth-largest lake by volume. It is half a mile at its deepest and home to more species of freshwater fish than any other body of water in the world. Livingstone reached the lakeshore in 1859 and allegedly asked a native what they called the lake.[43] The local man pointed at the water and said, 'Nyasa.' Livingstone duly named it Lake Nyasa, and this was used for over a hundred years. It is still used by Tanzania and Mozambique, the other two countries situated on the lakeshore. Livingstone wasn't to know that *nyasa* is simply the local word for 'lake' and he had just coined the name 'Lake Lake'. Similarly, the word *sahara* is simply Arabic for 'desert.'

While climbing a gentle incline one morning, standing out of the saddle, shoulders hunched, brow furrowed, and eyes narrowed into a tedious headwind, my left pedal snapped off. The sudden loss of balance sent me plunging down a slope and into an acacia bush. Once I had extricated myself from the needling branches I sat down and bit on my lower lip while pulling a thorn from my heel. It had entered the back of the sole, narrowly missed the heel bone, and embedded itself more than an inch deep in my flesh. Limping, I pushed Old Geoff for a mile in the company of a jolly pig farmer called Steve, who helped me find a new pair of pedals for £2 in the next village.

---

[43] Livingstone was the second European to reach Lake Malawi. A Portuguese traveller called Candido José da Costa Cardoso visited in 1846.

I stopped one lunchtime under a collapsing thatched structure hidden in the bush. A teenage boy walking past spotted me and froze on the spot, clearly startled. He stared in terror for several moments then ran a frantic few yards and scrambled out of sight up a tree. Ten minutes later he shimmied quietly down with a pawpaw fruit. He spotted me again and gasped then stood stock still, mid-stride, in the hot midday sun, staring at me and clutching his fruit. He remained rooted to the spot for half an hour until I left. It seemed he wasn't sure if I was real or not: a white ghost with dark, white magic.

Finally I reached Nkhata Bay and prescribed myself rest. In eleven days I had covered a gruelling 800 miles of mostly unsealed roads, and I was at the end of my tether, lapsing into sleep within a minute or two whenever I sat down. I found my way to Mayoka Village lodge, a lakeside sanctuary that I had fond memories of from seven years earlier. I had also caught up with the Scottish motorcyclists. Together we pitched tents on an idyllic terraced hill by the lake and fetched some beers. I let the exhaustion overtake me for a few days, plunging me into helpless indolence.

The final night in the lodge was riotous and sleepless, my last encounter with the African tourist trail for a long time. I had allowed myself to bend to parental pressure and booked flights out of Cape Town to visit home for Christmas week. This presented me with over 3,000 miles to cover in under two months. I had also arranged to meet a friend nearby in Zambia on a particular date and had left a day late. I began the sprint still drunk and facing an eighty-five-mile ride through steamy rubber plantations and past a vast tobacco farm. Malawi is the world's leading producer of a low-grade, high-nicotine strain of tobacco found in many ubiquitous cigarette brands.

For four days and 370 miles I was in the saddle before sunrise and collapsed out of it after sunset, too tired even to brush my teeth. I disliked rushing because it went against the intended purpose of the journey. I had no breaks but for hurried meals and regular puncture repairs. When rushing on a bicycle all there is to look forward to is food and sleep and an end to the rushing.

One night I unwittingly camped on a nest of inch-long ants. I woke in the dark to a strange sound and turned on my torch. A few thousand ants were marching busily back and forth on the tent fabric, inside and out. It was the soft, sticky flicking of their legion footfall that I had heard.

I reached Katete in Zambia and spent two days with Tori, a friend from university I had not seen for four years. She had recently qualified as a surgeon and was undertaking six months of voluntary work in St Francis Hospital. Primitive equipment and people with horrendous conditions made up her daily work. On the day I arrived she had just removed a section of intestine and sewn the loose ends together. The following day she bored through a living man's skull with a hand drill. Word had got out and patients came from far and wide, even across borders, to present themselves to the rolling contingent of foreign doctors at St Francis in the little junction town of Katete.

Two hundred miles of parched, brown bush was my first taste of Mozambique. The road dipped and bobbed across a hilly landscape punctuated by bulbous, freestanding rock formations. It was grotesquely hot and too dry for mosquitos so I slept in the open, despite again being warned of lions in the area. The fierce southerly wind blew into my squinting eyes throughout the day but cooled me as I lay under the stars each night.

Villages were few and far between, and very basic: rude mud buildings with grass-thatched roofs and simple decorative shapes roughly daubed on walls with a darker shade of mud. Maputo, the capital, is so far south it feels like a different country. Development funds rarely reach far into the remote northwest, which is geographically closer to the capitals of Malawi, Zambia, Zimbabwe, Tanzania, and Burundi.

Consequently, foreigners are seldom seen in those northern reaches and I was once again a terrifying oddity. In the mornings I would ride past numerous people walking along the road fetching water from the nearest borehole. Most were woman with twenty-litre containers balanced easily on their heads. Wearing sun-faded but colourfully patterned wraparound skirts, they stepped with a long-practised, smooth gait, their muscular necks comfortably rigid and backs perfectly straight. Usually a small sleeping baby lolled loosely on their backs in a simple sheet tied as a papoose. Often one or two small children also plodded along behind, each with a five-litre container on their head.

When I was spotted, usually by the children, there was always a fraught shout to alert the mother. Bicycles were common but were more usually laden with bundles of wood or a tightly bound goat. The weird, white-skinned, long-haired, bandanna-ed apparition bearing down on them was enough to terrify most Mozambican villagers. All would scramble into the dry, yellowing bush, abandoning their water containers on the roadside. Dark faces and wide eyes peered out as I passed on the broken tarmac, off which the soaring heat shimmered and danced. The whispered word 'Jesus' was sometimes audible. More often voices chanted 'Chuck Norris' whose output did a roaring trade in bootlegged DVDs in Mozambique.

My first night in the country was presided over by a clear sky housing a riotously bright full moon, which rose before me as the wobbling red sun was setting over my shoulder. Deep into the moonlit night, faint drumming floated through the bush from some unseen village.

I breakfasted in the silver-orange stereo lighting cast by the setting moon and climbing sun. After six months of Mozambican heat and drought, the rains were due any day but seemed reluctant. By 8 a.m. the temperature soared to the high thirties and fiery headwinds continued to heckle each pedal stroke. I stopped at every borehole water pump to top up my bottles. The few women that didn't run either eyed me suspiciously or laughed nervously. Several times water was kindly pumped for me one-handed by muscular women who were simultaneously breastfeeding.

Occasional groves of mango trees, massive and fecund, lined the road and were oases to me. I would crawl under their thigh-high lower branches to rest unseen in the dark shade that locked in cooler air. I read and dozed through the worst of scorching afternoons, eating as many of the wind-felled fruits as I could manage.

In the first city I reached, Tete, the temperature hit 46°C. The streets were empty and quiet but for the fiercely roaring fans of air-conditioned Land Cruisers belonging to mining companies. I didn't linger but crossed the 500-metre suspension bridge over the Zambezi and continued south.

For three days the heat hovered in the mid-forties. I rose early and watched from the saddle as the sun hefted itself over a quavering horizon. The wind licked with a dry, rasping tongue, mercilessly devouring any moisture. My tyres' friction on the baking tarmac melted the glue on past puncture repairs and I found myself wheeling Old Geoff off the road for surgery on an almost hourly basis.

Few people spoke English and I spoke no Portuguese so conversed little. I seldom saw people anyway. The shadowy shapes of human figures in various attitudes of torpid recline melded into the shade of roadside trees.

On the third night out of Tete the heat-blasting wind rose to a crescendo. I lay atop my sleeping bag on a patch of parched, deeply cracked earth and tried to sleep, but a field mouse had other ideas, silently and repeatedly creeping close to me, scuffling noisily around, and scurrying away. I spent half an hour trying to capture the pest with a trap of cooking pan, twig and string laid over some biscuit crumbs. Thwarted, I gave up on hunting and resorted to pitching my tent. Once in the tent I was too hot and the mouse chewed its way inside anyway. The wind flapped the tent violently and soon snapped the only pole. Defeated and exhausted, I struggled out of the collapsed tent and lay on top of it to prevent it being blown away. At this point the long-anticipated rains finally began. Utterly deflated, I wrapped myself in the remains of the tent and slept fitfully while the rain soaked though me. The mouse likely retreated into a warm, sheltered hole in the ground.

The rain continued through the morning when I rose to discover both my tyres were flat and my stove wasn't working. Sitting in the rain, wet through and trying to patch the punctures, I was as close to the end of my tether as I had been in many months. Thankfully I reached a town mid-morning and was revived in a café, where a friendly Eritrean called Aman talked about his secretive home country and gave me cup after cup of sweet, milky tea.

Mentally restored, I wheeled back into the rain and resigned myself to an afternoon, night, and following day of general sogginess. Wind drove chilly water down my neck and through my panniers. However, once accepted, discomfort is less of a problem. The rain drizzled to a halt during a night spent in the cooking hut of a sympathetic family. A mangy cat cuddled up to my side and a couple of chickens roosted on a bar overhead. It was a good night's sleep.

THIRTY-ONE

TEARING UP THE TRUCE

*If danger was involved it would be as a consequence
rather than a prerequisite.*
- Nick Danziger, *Danziger's Travels*

I rode into Chimoio late morning and followed directions
to the offices of The HALO Trust. A mutual friend had
put me in touch with Olly, who had been working for the
mine-clearing charity in Mozambique for a couple of years.
Olly showed me samples of the various mines they dealt
with, explaining how they detect them before safely
detonating. HALO had been operating in the country for
almost twenty years, since shortly after the civil war ended in
1992.[44]

Mozambique's civil war began in 1977, two years after
independence from Portugal, and was a classic Cold War
proxy conflict. Having fought the Portuguese powers with a
nationalist movement for over a decade, the Front of
Mozambique (Frelimo) declared independence and came to
power in 1975. They quickly set up a one-party Marxist–
Leninist state supported by the USSR. In response to this,
the Mozambique National Resistance (Renamo) formed and
launched an anti-communist guerrilla insurgency. Renamo
had the backing of both South Africa and Rhodesia, while
the United States uncharacteristically watched the situation
unfold from a distance.

It was a dirty war with atrocities committed all round.
Both sides used child soldiers and peppered the land with an
estimated 200,000 mines that rendered vital food-producing

---

[44] On 17 September 2015 the Mozambican government declared the
country mine-free after HALO removed the last known mine. Over two
decades they removed 171,000 mines in Mozambique, roughly 80 per cent
of the total. HALO operates in numerous other nations with unexploded
ordinance. In 2008 the UN estimated it would take 1,100 years to clear all
the world's current mines.

land unworkable. By the close of hostilities, over one million had succumbed to fighting or starvation. Peace was finally struck in 1992 when Frelimo acceded to Renamo's demand for multi-party elections, which Frelimo narrowly won.

Olly kindly put me up for a couple of days and I started riding again feeling rested. My stove was fixed and a welding rod was stuffed inside my tent pole as a makeshift repair. South of Chimoio lay 800 miles to Maputo. The bumpy tarmac simply unfurled through indistinguishable bush. The only breaks in the monotony were a few blackened areas of sad-looking, charred tree stumps with unattended bags of charcoal on sale in front of them.

Traversing this flat, repetitive scenery, time splayed strangely. There was nothing to note the passage of miles except the sun's movement and my increasing fatigue as each day wore on. Three hours could pass in an instant but then ten minutes might last an eternity. I stopped looking at my mocking clock.

I'd heard from Olly of trouble stirring along my route before the Rio Save. Ten days earlier the government had seized Renamo's military base near Mount Gorongosa, forcing their leader of four decades, Afonso Dhlakama, into hiding. In response, the former rebels declared their withdrawal from the peace accord that had held for twenty years. Before dawn on 22 October 2013, Renamo forces crept up on a police station in the village of Muxungue and opened fire. The police fled and the guerrillas began attacking vehicles crossing the seventy miles of road to the riverside village of Save.

When I arrived in Muxungue a week later, the village had been retaken but the government had closed the road. Vehicles were being allowed through once daily in heavily armed and fast-moving military convoys. A long queue of lorries and cars was already lined up waiting for the convoy to depart. Strangely, the soldiers manning the barricade of concrete-filled barrels simply waved me through. A little confused, I pedalled on and found myself in a completely forsaken land. Everyone had fled into the bush; it was eerie. Empty huts dotted the roadside, evacuated in a hurry with valued possessions abandoned. Shoes and cooking pots and water containers were left on unswept dirt clearings. In an entirely deserted village, the doors of a new health centre banged in the wind. I filled my bottles from the nearby borehole. It was the only time in Africa that I had a water pump to myself.

For several hours I saw not a soul. What was left of a flatbed lorry sprawled in the middle of the road. Long skid marks spoke of an abrupt stop and dozens of bullet casings on the tarmac and holes in the metal work told of the struggle. The windows were smashed, the fuel tank had exploded, and the cargo had been looted. The burned-out husk of the vehicle sat in a puddle of its own debris and the melted rubber of the tyres still smouldered, turning the air acrid.

I hurriedly rode on. The daily convoy soon shot past me at a frantic pace. There were roughly 100 vehicles in close formation, most with soldiers perched on the back clutching automatic rifles, eyes nervously scanning the bush for guerrillas. The rearguard and vanguard were armoured personnel carriers, each with half a dozen soldiers on top manning artillery pieces. There seemed no question of them stopping and I was soon left in unnatural silence once more.

I started to feel uneasy. When I got a puncture I dragged Old Geoff behind a bush to repair it and a convoy going the opposite direction sped past. I threw myself flat on the ground and lay still, hoping I wouldn't be spotted and shot at. That night I camped far from the road, surrounded by the most aggressive looking thorn bushes available. I lay awake with ears pricked deep into the darkness hours. The slightest rustle of leaves or snapping of a twig lurched me into fretful wakefulness. Long before daylight I was back on the road rushing silently southward. Shortly after dawn I crossed a bridge over the Save River and reached the safety of another roadblock, where another northbound convoy was forming.

The troops manning the barrier were shocked to see me

and asked incredulously what I was doing. I sat a couple of hours in a café with two special forces soldiers. Lewis and Miquel told me of their imminent deployment into the bush to hunt the rebels. While anesthetising themselves with sachets of cheap liquor they told me quietly of their inner turmoil. As with many from the central belt of the country, their sympathies lay with Renamo but their pay came from the Frelimo-led government. I watched as the two young men drained sachet after sachet, drugging themselves into acceptance of their mercenary status on the eve of battle.

I neared the coast and even sniffed salt in the air, but the route remained largely inland. The dry bush gradually gave way to tall palms and lush, tropical jungle. Groups of boys stood under mango trees hurling unripe fruit into the higher branches to dislodge the juicier prizes. The glade-like areas underneath the palm canopy harboured tidy huts with frond-woven walls. I'd reached the coast on my bicycle for the first time since the Red Sea in Egypt five months earlier.

As the land was dotted with homes and garden plots, hidden camping spots became harder to find. One night was passed in an empty, grass-roofed hut belonging to Vasco, a Mozambican who worked in Johannesburg for five years but was recently detained for having no work permit. After a month behind bars he was deported. Many of his friends had undergone the same process. Another night was spent in a mud church with half a roof remaining. Word got around that a white man was sleeping in the old church and I had half a dozen visitors, all insistent on holding my hands and reciting Catholic prayers in Portuguese.

Maputo was a shock to the system: a sprawling modern city with few well-hidden traces of the neat, colonial town that once was. The small, thickset Portuguese fort still had its rusting cannon pointed out to sea and the ornate, century-old train station still stood proud. I rested a day before a brisk, sweaty morning carried me to the border of Swaziland.[45] I

---

[45] In April 2018 the king of Swaziland, Mswati III, renamed his kingdom eSwatini to mark the fiftieth anniversary of Swazi independence. Among

climbed over the diminutive Lebombo range and onto the Lowveld, where endless panoramas of forested hills were separated by rolling emerald farmland. I had been put in touch with Lee and Rowan, who live on a cattle ranch at the heart of the country and kindly hosted me for a couple of days.

Sandwiched between Mozambique and South Africa, the tiny mountain kingdom of Swaziland is easily overlooked. Smaller than Fiji and with just over a million inhabitants, it is one of the world's last absolute monarchies. The king personally picks his prime minister, the cabinet, and the senate. This makes Swaziland a member of a fairly unattractive club along with Brunei, Saudi Arabia, Qatar and the United Arab Emirates. The country also holds the unfortunate record for the highest HIV prevalence in the world (currently 27.4 per cent), a low life expectancy of fifty-seven years, 63 per cent of the population living below the poverty line, and a rigorously state-controlled media.

However, Mswati III seems genuinely popular. He rules from any of his numerous palaces that house his fifteen wives and countless children.[46] Swaziland seemed a happy place, and the people I encountered on the road were friendly and enthusiastically welcoming. As a British protectorate until full independence in 1968, Swaziland avoided both colonisation and absorption into its southern neighbour with its race-related tensions.

The atmosphere changed tangibly the moment I crossed into South Africa. Suddenly I was no longer a visitor or a tourist. I was 'a white'. That was how South Africans, both white and black, formed their first attitudes towards me. Gone were the African-accented shouts from the roadside of 'My friend! How are you? Come here, sit down, let us talk.'

---

his rationale was the fact that Swaziland, which is often referred to as 'The Switzerland of Africa', was apparently regularly mistaken for Switzerland at international summits.

[46] Mswati III's father was less restrained in his polygamy. Sobhuza II had 120 official wives by the end of his 82-year rule, which he began aged five months. It is still the longest recorded reign of a monarch.

Race was evidently still a huge and divisive factor in South African society. The history of the nation is a catalogue of inter-ethnic conflict as first the Dutch and then the English established settlements in the Western Cape and started to probe inland. Over the course of three weeks I encountered many Afrikaners (modern-day descendants of the seventeenth-century Dutch settlers, or Boers) and all were incredibly kind and welcoming to me, a white man, one of their own. Cycling is a popular leisure activity among white South Africans and many showed a deeper than usual interest in my journey. However, when conversation turned to race, as it invariably did despite my best efforts to steer clear of the topic, I was continually shocked by the opinions held and generalisations made. Frequent fragments of conversation included:

'This will *sound* racist but …'

'The *blecks* resent us but look what they've done to *our* country …'

'I hear you've got big problems with *blecks* in your country too, eh?'

During the 1,400-mile ride to Cape Town I had startlingly few conversations with black people, despite them comprising three-quarters of the population. I wasn't approached in public and interactions in shops were usually curt. There was simply a gulf between the races. Half a century of *apartheid* had left indelible marks. Despite an end to white minority rule and racial segregation in 1994, the divide still exists across most of the country in the form of economics. According to the World Bank, South Africa has the world's highest Gini coefficient, or income inequality. The white 8 per cent of the population have an income average six times higher than the black citizens.[47]

Black people tended to warm a little when they learned

---

[47] The disparity is particularly jarring as South Africa is a rich country by the standards of the continent, second only to Nigeria by economy. Indeed, South Africa's 2017 GDP was larger than those of Sudan, Ethiopia, Kenya, Uganda, Tanzania, Rwanda, Burundi, Malawi, Mozambique, and Swaziland combined.

that I was not South African but I rarely had time to slip that into the curt conversations or sufficiently overemphasise my British accent.

THIRTY-TWO

CAPE

No one is born hating another person because of the colour of his
skin ... People must learn to hate, and if they can
learn to hate, they can be taught to love.
- Nelson Mandela, *Long Walk to Freedom*

Having descended from Swaziland's plateau, I joined a dirt road and crossed a vast, hilly patchwork of farmland broken by neat pine copses. The land was drenched alternately by stabbing sun and penetrating rain. The downpours worked themselves up to riotous thunderstorms with jagged symphonies of lightning strobing at furious-paced intervals across the yawning spaces of tamed former bush.

One of my early afternoons in the country was darkened by yet another bout of intensely brooding skies. The storm would soon begin and the buffeting winds had slowed me to a crawl. I heaved my bike over the barbed-wire fence lining the road and hurriedly pitched my tired old tent. The rain soon thrummelled exultantly on the fly sheet and the wind began twisting and bending the poorly repaired pole. After two hours the pole snapped in three places simultaneously, and for the rest of the night I cowered, windswept, waterlogged, and wrapped in the soggy skin of my shattered shelter.

Not many miles through the following morning's chill drizzle brought me to Wakkerstroom. The small, picturesque town, founded in 1859, loomed out of the melting mist: first just a tall steeple, then the well-spaced roofs of handsome cottages, punctuated by rich green trees and watered lawns. Finally the township appeared; a claustrophobic sprawl of low-budget housing for black people set apart from the prettier buildings where the whites lived. Piles of rubbish surrounded it, visible from half a mile, and no cars plied the narrow roads.

I dried my feet by the fire in a quirky gallery-cum-restaurant. A young ornithologist and her elderly friends said the rain was forecast until nightfall and that I should share their bottle of wine. A blurry afternoon followed, culminating with drinks in a bar at the defunct train station, where the owners kindly unlocked the old guard's hut for me to sleep in.

Forty miles and only two passing vehicles later I was spilled back onto tarmac lined by an electric fence enclosing herds of springbok, oryx, kudu, bushbuck, and waterbuck. They grazed nonchalantly by the road, unfazed by the swish and roar of traffic. South Africa often felt like a tamed and sanitised version of the Africa I had come to know.

I passed into the Free State, a former Boer Republic until it was annexed by the British in 1902. In 1880 the white Boers made up 45 per cent of the population of the 'Orange Free State' but that figure had dropped to under 8 per cent and racial tensions ran high, with the minority white Afrikaners still owning the majority of the land.

In a gaping valley another tall, blackening storm front raced towards me. Just as the first heavy drops began to fall I spotted a small, lonely building and veered off the road to partially shelter in its lee. The black inhabitants peeped around the wall at me. I waved meekly and they wordlessly returned inside. As the rain hardened into marble-sized hailstones that clattered deafeningly on the metal roof, I realised that nowhere else in Africa, or, indeed, the world, had I been left out in the rain when there was somewhere to be invited into. I had been treated to many a warm welcome by white Afrikaners. This was the starkest example of indifference I experienced from black South Africans. I watched the ricocheting balls of ice bounce off my white forearms. Skin is a funny thing.

Approaching the outskirts of a town called Bethlehem I was contemplating where to shelter from another fast-approaching storm when a car pulled over.

'Where do you think you're going, young man?' said the grinning white lady in a strong Afrikaans accent.

'Cape Town,' I replied.

'And would you like a warm bath and a bed before you get there? Follow me.'

Without waiting for a reply, Alda drove on while I rushed along behind. Soon I was showered, dressed in borrowed clothes, and deeply ensconced in a leather armchair. Alda was horrified to hear that I had cycled all the way from Egypt. I encountered this reaction often. To white South Africans their continent was an unspeakably dangerous place full of wild people.

While he barbecued beef steaks I spoke at length with Alda's husband, Johann. He was frank with his account of history.

'When we Dutch arrived and spread into the interior of the country, there was largely empty land and zero cultivation. There were a few bushmen folks here and there who soon wandered onwards with their livestock. Our ancestors, the Boers, laboriously cut farms out of the tough bush, turned the earth, irrigated, and cultivated the land. Through very hard work they prospered. Soon though, they found themselves competing for the land with African tribes migrating from the north, and British coming from the south.

'Apartheid came and the tensions mounted. After apartheid went, bitterness remained … on both sides. But individual, ordinary folks like us did not make the legislation. We simply lived by the rules.

'Now that white minority rule is history, there is *positive* discrimination in our country. I swear it. Land disputes are decided on colour, not on who was actually there first. I'm sorry, but the *blecks* do feel a sense of entitlement. They expect to grow rich from the land as they saw us whites do. But they *don't* want to put in the work. The *bleck* people in this country are different to others. This is why so many folks from other African countries can find jobs here so easily. Because they are willing to work, and to work *hard*. We whites are resented for our hard-earned success.'

It was interesting to hear Johann's angle, however subjective, and I wondered if this was the history he had been taught. Either way, I was relieved to move on from that intractable topic when he started talking about an upcoming rugby fixture between England and South Africa.

The following day I approached Lesotho. The mountain wall on the horizon loomed higher as I neared the independent kingdom that is an enclave within South Africa. Almost twice the size of Swaziland, Lesotho is ringed by high mountains and no point of the country is lower than 1,400 metres in altitude. The road wound up to a pass in the rock fortress and then swept down to sloping fields of wheat and maize.

The country was visibly poorer than its neighbour. Men drove patient oxen pulling wooden ploughs, and barefoot herders wore tatty blankets for clothes. Naked toddlers chased chickens with delighted abandon and old women, who I suspected were not very old, sat listlessly in the sun. Lesotho has 8 per cent infant mortality and an HIV rate almost as high as Swaziland's. The doctors, at approximately one per 20,000 people, struggle to keep up.

However, crossing into Lesotho was to instantly feel a different atmosphere from South Africa's race-based reticence.

'Hello! Hello! How are you?' shouted the children.

'Good afternoon, mister!' shouted the men with a cheery wave.

'Hahahahaha! Eeeeeeeeeeeh!' cackled the old women with broad smiles.

I was back in the jovial Africa I'd left behind at the Swaziland–South Africa border. Everyone wanted to talk, to question, to touch, to shake hands. A century (1868–1966) as a British protectorate meant no white settlers moved onto the land and there was no interracial tension. The country, although poor, has independence, a well-liked constitutional monarchy, and a population with one unifying language and tribal ethnicity: Basotho.

I only spent two days crossing the northern reaches of the small, scenic country. Grand storms were always brewing in different darkened corners of the neck-achingly vast sky. I loved the ride, the friendly shouts and the positivity despite the poverty. All too soon I had passed through the capital of Maseru, crossed a bridge, and was back in the quiet, sparsely populated farmlands of South Africa.

Small windmills endlessly spun, drawing up water from deep boreholes and spilling it into troughs for livestock. Packs of rock hyraxes scuffled for cover at my approach and huge scrub hares leapt clean over fences, bouncing towards the horizon. Gradually my road descended from the agricultural Highveld onto the Great Karoo, a vast, semi-desert that stretches west for hundreds of miles, almost all the way to Namibia. There were few trees, many ostrich farms and countless bowl-like valleys carpeted with stiff, brown grass. I could picture terrified redcoats facing massed ranks of nearly naked Xhosa warriors in those timeless landscapes. I also imagined those spear-brandishing fighters wondering who on earth were the strange, sweaty pinkish-red men in so much stifling clothing.

An evangelical white couple in a small town gave me coffee and cake and explained how their respective spouses had run away together. They had made the best of a bad situation and moved in together themselves.

'Father saw fit to provide me with a new woman. Father above always comes through,' preached the kindly man.

A passing motorist stopped one morning to tell me that Nelson Mandela had died. South Africa launched into a period of national mourning for the loss of 'Madiba', the republic's first president. Flags flew at half mast, phone networks texted condolences to their customers, and television stations ran round-the-clock features about the great man, his twenty-seven-year incarceration, and his magnanimous policy of reconciliation after apartheid. The wildly unpopular current president, Jacob Zuma, did his best to politicise the passing of his party's greatest figurehead.

Mandela had been in an 'irretrievable vegetative state' for

six months, his life eked out on dialysis and life-support machines. Rather than switch the machines off and humanely let the body die along with its already deceased mind, the decision had been made to keep the once-great heart artificially and pointlessly pumping. It was rumoured that the incumbent African National Congress party (ANC) had aimed to keep Mandela alive through the upcoming election campaign. He was the ultimate unifying and rallying poster boy for the increasingly out-of-favour party. Mandela's large family and ANC royalty were already publicly feuding over his legacy and estate.

Zuma's presence drew boos from the crowd at the funeral in the country's largest stadium. The event was attended by 173 other current heads of state, sixty-nine former leaders, and a further audience of 90,000 in the largest memorial service the world had ever seen. After the allotted ten days of national mourning a newspaper headline read: 'ANC encourages people to continue mourning.'

Sitting in a café one afternoon in Aberdeen, gazing at the uneasy tilt of the southern hemisphere's tallest spire, I was approached by a British woman in her mid-sixties. She bought me lunch and told me that her father had cycled from London to Nairobi in the 1950s. She had several drinks and suddenly told me that she lived in a nearby house.

'You know, you don't have to cycle away today. Stay with me! There's plenty of room for you in my big bed, and I'll cook you breakfast afterwards …'

Thirty seconds later, after a polite '*thankyougoodbye*', I was pedalling quickly westwards, happy to disappear in the setting sun.

Leaving the Karoo behind, I turned west at Uniondale and followed a fertile valley. On my left, thick mist spilled ominously over the valley wall from the Garden Route on the coast beyond. In the evening I climbed up and into the dense cloud headed to a pass in the Outeniqua Mountains. Visibility dropped to ten metres by the time I began the 800-metre descent to the fruit plantations of the Garden Route.

I was onto the final stretch to the Cape and forged on across stubbly farmland dotted with stacked hay bales. After a great flat expanse I reached Struis Bay, which could have passed for an idyllic coastal town in southern England. Braced by stiff, salt-laden breezes, thatched holiday cottages with whitewashed walls and colourful window frames dotted the rugged coast. It was 8 a.m. when I pushed my bike to the end of a footpath at Cape Agulhas. A strong easterly wind whipped and slapped at my ragged clothes. It was otherwise peaceful. Nobody was there to watch as I scrambled over the rocks and dipped my feet in the chilly meeting point of the Indian and Atlantic oceans. It was the third and final of the three goals I had set myself when I cycled out of my childhood village three and a half years earlier. I cried briefly at the end of the African continent.

Eight months had passed since I disembarked at midnight on Egypt's Mediterranean coast. In that time I had cycled 9,000 miles through fourteen countries. I had been sunburned, stung by a scorpion, shouted at, pelted with stones, attacked by a mob, and soaked by storms, and was constantly saddle sore. I had mostly been physically exhausted and emotionally vulnerable. However, more than all of the above, I had been cared for, welcomed in, fed, looked after, and smiled at. Africa, its history, and its questionable future may at times have broken my heart. But Africa as a home to a billion predominantly friendly individuals gave me hope. I turned and wheeled my bike the first few metres of the 10,000-mile homeward journey.

Outside a supermarket back in Struis Bay a burly, brown-toothed Afrikaner confronted me while I was loading food into my panniers.

'Where you cycling to, boy?'

'I'm riding home to Britain,' I said.

'You British are all fucking crazy,' he spat, apparently angry, and walked away without another word.

THIRTY-THREE

NORTH

*I never knew of a morning in Africa when I woke up
and was not happy.*
- Ernest Hemingway, *Green Hills of Africa*

After a fleeting Christmas visit to Britain, the temptations of summer, friends, food, wine, and relative normality held me captive in Cape Town for a few weeks. I first stayed with friends Brian and June then took a room for a month in a house with Archie the Scottish motorcyclist, who had set up there at the end of his ride. I found bar work in a nightclub to provide a meagre income during this extended 'holiday'. The job was minimum wage, paying 80p an hour and forcing me to charm hard for tips. In the daytime I read unsolicited manuscripts for a publisher, sorting the wheat from the chaff.

In early February Old Geoff, hardy veteran of 34,000 miles, was stolen. I was upset and irritated but tried hard to focus on a solution and not to despair. My dwindled funds already promised to make the journey home threadbare at best and certainly wouldn't allow for a new bike. At a loss for what to do, I was invited on a radio show to talk about my journey. I mentioned the theft and half a dozen proud Capetonians called the station offering replacement bicycles. I walked back and forth across the city, working my way down the list of addresses, at each of which was a hopelessly unrideable bike. One was a child's bicycle, two were antiques, and the rest were damaged beyond repair.

However, I was also put in touch with the Bicycle Empowerment Network, who salvage donated bikes from Europe and place them in poor communities along with bicycle maintenance training. Solly, the jovial mechanic of thirty years, gave me the rusted frame of an old Schwinn from a pile of other twisted metal spectres. Judging from the rust, Solly reckoned it had been found in a river or canal. I was offered three other ruined bikes to salvage parts from and eventually managed to build one small but serviceable mount.

I took the as-yet-unnamed bicycle on a 100-mile test ride to the Cape of Good Hope. Loaded on it were a new tent and sleeping mat, my first inflatable one in over a year. The night was a pleasure, sleeping on a comfy mat rather than hard ground. There was no chance of rain so I pitched only the tent's mesh interior layer, which was wind-cooled and allowed stargazing. The final stretch to the Cape was treeless and windswept, with roving flocks of ostriches and troops of baboons. The bicycle was undersized and unfamiliar but, I thought, might just about carry me home.

*   *   *

Table Mountain receded over my shoulder. My legs spun sluggishly as I hugged the coast and headed north in the soaring mid-February heat. My body ached from my lack of fitness and the unfamiliar position on the stunted bike. I was breaking in a hard new leather saddle, and within two days had angry blue bruises on my sitting bones and sores in the tender plot where my legs met.

The road soon stretched across scrub desert with little traffic. While taking a dirt road alongside rail tracks, I passed a farmstead where two men were beating hell out of each other. Locked in combat, they rolled across the dusty road with limbs flailing and shirts ripping. Ten or so other farm workers looked on silently.

Near the small town of Eland's Bay I camped in the neglected garden of a lorry driver who proclaimed himself a 'proper Boer'. We sat on the floor drinking strong brandy and cokes in the late sun while sausages cooked on the *braai*. A shockingly blue-eyed son slept on his lap, having swigged a few times from the father's glass.

I climbed through low, dry hills into the Cederberg mountains. There I found the Fynbos ecoregion, where the sandy, seemingly sterile earth produces all of the world's rooibos (red bush) tea. The Bergh family took me in for a day and showed me the tea planting, harvesting, and processing. We waterskied on the Clanwilliam dam in the evening and drank home-brewed ale with dinner.

The road led me further north into yet more parched regions where gnarled scrub plants dotted the red-dust ground. Occasional mongooses lurched for cover beside the road and comically chubby rock dassies trundled to their nearest hiding place. Small herds of springboks leapt and bounded across the arid landscape, a pure celebration of nimbleness and grace.

Afternoon temperatures reached 47°C and headwinds dried my mouth in seconds if opened. Water in my bottles soon grew as hot as tea and left me feeling nauseous. Towns become few and far between and, without exception, they had a collection of ragged, loitering men draped along the main street, delirious with drink and sun.

My daily highlight came at night. The joy of finally lying back after bolting a bland rice dinner was compounded by the magnificence of the infinitely speckled sky twinkling through the tent mesh. When I switched off my head torch the stars doted and faded in and out of focus as my pupils dilated to see in the dark.

I was soon descending over plains of amber dust, dropping down to the Orange River and across into Namibia. Beside the river were tidy, green vineyards, incongruous in their desert surrounds. A district of threadbare straw huts slumped across the rocky landscape behind, awaiting their harvest-time inhabitants. All around was a daunting, roomy barrenness without a trace of humans in sight.

Namibia is vast and very empty; not a place suited to crowds. The eastern bulk of the country is the Kalahari Desert. The western strip is the ancient Namib desert, the oldest in the world, that has thirsted relentlessly for 80 million years, making the Sahara's three million look infantile. Namibia is four times the size of the UK but has only 2.5

million inhabitants. For low population density, only Mongolia beats it.

The tarmac ceased and I launched onto several hundred miles of corrugated desert tracks with very few vehicles and little available shade. The routes connect the scattered tourist attractions of southern Namibia. Citizens have very little reason to travel to them and the scant passing traffic carried tourists almost exclusively.

The fences lining either side of the road protected the wildlife from vehicles but equally trapped animals that managed to get over one fence. A distraught young leopard fled before me for ten minutes one morning before hiding badly behind a small bush. I passed as fast as the corrugated path would allow me, watching over my shoulder for a killer's approach.

On days when no withered bush appeared to shelter and doze under in the afternoons, I skipped lunch and sweated on through the cruellest hours. The heat was almost unbearable, but the breeze generated by cycling, however slight, was preferable to sitting exposed to the sun in the still and sweltering air.

A side road deposited me on the lofty precipice of Fish River Canyon. I peered over the ravine and down 550 vertical metres to where the silver ribbon of water slipped silently past, the only vein of life in an otherwise desolate land. I wasn't spotted when passing through the gate to the national park and so illicitly camped next to the canyon. My tent stood spitting distance from the edge of the darkening abyssal depths. At dawn I watched, mesmerised, as light bled back into the world. Coffee cupped in my hands, I was a lonely, illegal voyeur. The chasm beside me yawned ever wider and deeper as it had done every daybreak for 650 million years.

The next day, while I lazed away the afternoon swelter at a lonely petrol station, an Ovambo girl called Inaccessia spoke wistfully of her desert home in Northern Namibia and the semi-spherical thatched hut she was born in.

I regularly shared the road with oryx, ostriches, and stocky mountain zebras. Meerkats stood in lines to watch me pass and one night I drifted off to the chattering and calling of rare spotted hyenas. I wondered how all these animals found enough water. A village marked on my map turned out to be just one listing building, roofless and abandoned. My water ran out soon after and had me fretting for several hours until I stumbled upon another abandoned building. This one had a rusted tap that trickle-filled three of my bottles with smelly water before drying up; brackish, brown but drinkable. I resolved to ration the little I had. I camped two metres from the road that night, feeling too weak and desiccated to bother hiding. No vehicles disturbed me and the stars were majestic that new moon night.

After a few hours riding in the morning, I was snoozing in a thorn bush when a passing roadwork gang asked for a sip of water. I handed over a bottle and watched with alarm as they drained two litres of my precious, briny water. Thankfully I soon found squatters in the ruins of another abandoned village who replenished my supply.

Hills appeared and bore me to 1,800 metres, where recent rain had rendered the valleys green. Many of the trees in the area played host to vast weavers' nests. They looked like haystacks hefted thoughtlessly among the branches but had actually been built one dry blade of grass at a time by thousands of tiny, finch-like birds. The nests are a favourite haunt of the egg-eating yellow cobra so sitting under them was not advisable.

I stopped into a farm to ask for water and was soon enjoying my third beer with David, Penny, and Leslie. The decision to stay the night was made on my behalf and we feasted on barbecued oryx steaks for dinner. At that altitude it was gloriously chilly after dark. Although surrounded by harsh desert, the little island of hills even received snowfall each winter. At first light I braced myself and descended to the heat once more.

THIRTY-FOUR

THE WILDMAN OF DEADVLEI

When the spirits are low, when the day appears dark, when work becomes monotonous, when hope hardly seems worth having, just mount a bicycle and go out for a spin down the road, without thought on anything but the ride you are taking.

- Arthur Conan Doyle

At Sesriem I guiltily sped through the gates of Namib-Naukluft National Park, once more unnoticed and without paying the entrance fee. Tourists converge there to visit some of the world's tallest sand dunes and the otherworldly Deadvlei. I pedalled forty miles to the end of a rare tarmacked road, beyond which there was only soft, deep sand. Beside the small car park full of 4x4s I ate lunch and snoozed a under a tree. When I woke all the cars had gone. I abandoned my bike and after an hour of laboured trudging found myself in the midst of grand, towering dunes. I spent a while scrabbling up and charging down the baking sand slopes, getting thoroughly lost, before continuing to Deadvlei.

Nestled between vast marmalade-orange walls of sand, Deadvlei is a large, flat pan of bleached-white clay. A marsh originally formed there when an occasional river, the Tsauchab, periodically flooded, allowing acacia trees to grow. However, the climate grew drier, the ephemeral river stopped flooding, and the marsh slowly withered. Roughly 700 years ago the trees died. However, there was no moisture to allow decomposition so their ghostly dried skeletons remain, baked black by centuries of sun.

With the place entirely to myself, I decided on a whim to strip down for a naked photo. My clothes were the only signs of human modernity in the primordial place so it seemed fitting to remove them and wander away from where they were stashed. Just as I was standing in a coquettish pose, waiting for the timed shutter to click, a light aircraft flew overhead, evidently carrying tourists on a scenic sundowner flight. At first I ran for cover, but there was none aside from the fragile trees. The plane wheeled around to make another pass. Defeated, I embraced the absurdity of the situation, danced around, waved, and turned a few cartwheels. After the third flyby, the plane departed and I retrieved my clothes.

I climbed 325 metres to the top of 'Big Daddy' dune and watched the sinking sun ignite the sands to a furious red while the sky's unblemished blue grew deeper and richer. The scene had such absolute majesty that all the thirst and the hundreds of miles of hard roads were suddenly, unquestionably worthwhile.

Under cover of darkness, I once again illicitly camped in a national park, pitching my tent at the foot of 'Dune 45'. The morning saw me packed up and sitting 100 metres high on the dune an hour before sunrise. It was cool, windless, and utterly silent. I could hear my steady pulse whooshing in my ears. As dawn approached, warm colours seeped into the variously grey world of sand and sky.

The stillness was broken when headlights flickered in the distance and the tour trucks approached. Sleepy groups spilled out of their vehicles and began climbing the dune.

Back on the northward road I took a lunch rest at one of the strategically spaced petrol stations that overcharge tourists in their tiny cafés and shops. Dirty and dust-bearded, I sat inside with the cheapest drink available watching a steady stream of tourists climb out of their vehicles in crisp safari suits. Many photographed my laden bicycle with its tatty panniers and a pair of pants drying on the handlebars. When readying to leave, I overhead a conversation at the next table.

'Did you hear about the Wild Man of Deadvlei?'

'What's that?'

'Some people on a sunset flight spotted a sort of feral, naked, white bushman running around Deadvlei last night. It's a mystery who it was but the park rangers are searching for him.'

'That's seriously weird!'

I quietly finished my drink, slipped past them, and rode out into the desert. That night I was woken by a noise at 3 a.m. The waxing moon shone brightly through my mosquito mesh. I had been too tired to lift my bike over the fence so was once again camped on the roadside. A zebra stood five metres from me, its white stripes glowing in the moonlight. The creature was stuck between the two fences lining the road. It wandered off along the fence, snorting occasionally, only to reappear five minutes later and pass at arm's length from me. After a couple more catwalk passes, the zebra began testing fence posts with its head, butting them hard. Soon it found a weak one, knocked it over, and was free again. At daybreak a scrawny black-backed jackal slipped through the fence and came to scavenge breakfast from me. Besides proffering a bowl of water which it drank nervously by my feet, I had nothing to share.

Glorious clouds rolled across the land as I crossed the Tropic of Capricorn. In this cooler air I made a small pass through some barren hills and was approaching the coast again when my rear axle snapped. The bicycle was unrideable. I pushed for a couple of hours before an Afrikaner couple drove me the last thirty miles to the German colonial harbour town of Swakopmund.

With a new axle, freshly grease-packed ball bearings, and several broken spokes replaced, I headed north and camped on the coast. A salty haze hung heavy over the beach when I woke but the sun soon fizzed through. I turned inland once again and began climbing towards the narrow strip of coarse vegetation that separates the Namib and Kalahari deserts. The grey pall over the sea shrank behind me and the sun bleached the sky to a dizzying white. Having reached an altitude of 1700 metres, I joined an arterial highway for the 150 miles to the capital, Windhoek.

The highway was narrow, busy, and frightening. Often I was forced abruptly off the road by inconsiderate drivers. One car's wing mirror clipped my handlebar, sending me careering into the dust. The jagged edge of the tarmac surface tore a gash as long as my hand in the tyre's side wall. It was evening, so I pitched my tent and stitched up the tyre as best I could with a hotel sewing kit.

It was dark by the time I went to fit it to the wheel. I felt an itch on my foot and looked down to see a couple of hundred ants streaming up my legs. Some sort of signal must have been given because they all bit at the same time. While hopping around in my pants trying to brush them off, I narrowly avoided stepping on a large scorpion. It turned to face me for a while, tail-poised and pincers snapping pugnaciously, before backing away.

It was now autumn and the cannibalistic armoured bush crickets were in peak season. Thousands of them strove to cross the road, each as big as my thumb. When one is flattened by a vehicle, another scuttles over to feed on the yellowish mess. This interloper is inevitably crushed in turn and a third hungry cricket wanders into the line of tyre. Hundreds of thousands of these splodges dotted the road, as well as the odd foot-long millipede. The shiny black shells and countless orange legs were just about discernable among the general mess of exoskeleton and entrails.

The tyre repair held up and I reached Windhoek having patched four punctures that afternoon. The rear axle was making ominous sounds and more spokes had broken. In the last good bicycle shop for 1,000 miles, the kindly mechanic asked if I had a name for the bicycle. I looked at the thing for a few seconds.

'Little Bastard,' I said.

*　　*　　*

'To Zambia?' asked the Botswanan border guard, incredulous.

'Yes,' I replied
'By the cycle?'
'Yes.'
'No!'
'Yes.'

'I do not believe you!'

'It's true.'

'Eh! You mad man! Beware of the lions … they will eat you all up!'

His warm smile and energetic wave acted as partial salve for the alarming warning as I pedalled away from the border. However, the journey across northern Botswana was largely boring. The long ribbon of tarmac ran through flat, unremarkable bush, each mile identical to what came before and after. There was a town every few hundred miles and almost no villages between. Some days I met nobody and didn't utter a word except occasional curses in the mornings when I discovered armoured crickets nibbling my leather handlebar grips.

The headwind was constant and exhausting. Each day I started early, rode a steady thirty miles, slept and lunched under a tree, rode another thirty miles, put up my tent, cooked, ate, and slept. I was left with little choice but to observe the abundant insect life and force my mind to wander.

The insects were prolific: big grasshoppers, small grasshoppers, ground crickets, giant beetles, winged beetles, dung beetles, millipedes, white butterflies, yellow butterflies, oh-so-prettily patterned butterflies, stick insects, praying mantises, hornets, hoverflies, horseflies, flying ants, red ants, safari ants, huntsmen spiders, golden orb spiders, six-eyed sand spiders, scorpions, caterpillars, and, of course, regular old, irritating black buzzing houseflies.

Each rare village I passed was a portrait of African gender roles. Women washed clothes, pounded maize, cooked over fires, swept the dirt yards, and kept an eye on the children. The men were little more than hard-to-spot collections of horizontal shapes grouped under trees; long, thin limbs splayed carelessly across the dust in the tiring act of falling asleep.

So sparse were the brushstrokes of habitation that I took little care of where I camped. One night I woke in the small hours to the sound of some men passing. One strummed loosely on a guitar, singing Bob Marley's 'Redemption Song' in a scratchy but beautiful voice. The noise faded into the night's soft cicada rasp. I felt lonely.

In the town of Ghanzi I met a group of missionaries driving from Cape Town to Cairo. They were stopping to play Christian music in orphanages along the way. On the side of their minibus was a crude map of the continent with 'Africa4Jesus' scored across it in thick black capitals. To my mind they spoke about 'saving souls' with a sense of spiritual acquisitiveness rather than charity.

The bush was dotted with huge baobab trees, the largest of which were estimated to be 2,500 years old. These trees, sometimes called the upside-down tree, have trunks with circumferences up to fifteen metres and are topped with short, stubby branches that look like roots. They are common in Africa, surviving because their trunks are high enough in water content to be useless as timber or firewood.

The final three days were along the 'Elephant Highway', which is a stretch of unfenced land roamed by large herds of elephants and plentiful lions. Thirty miles along this stretch I stopped to relieve myself. A hefty bull elephant wandered out of the bush not fifteen metres from me, briefly stared at my frozen form, and strode across the road before plunging into bush again.

That evening I camped in a clearing among thorn bushes, pulling fallen branches across the narrow ingress to seal me in. I woke several times in the night to the deep groaning of lions. However, a year of camping in Africa had rendered me fatalistic, and it didn't take much to fall asleep again each time.

I passed hundreds of elephants over the following two days. They were usually in small herds of mothers and young, always with a watchful, baggy-skinned matriarch standing guard. I stopped pausing for photos after one lone bull elephant reared to his intimidating double-decker bus height, trumpeted, and then charged me, cavernous ears flapping wildly. I was lucky to get away.

After a short ferry ride across the Zambezi, I was in

Zambia. After barren Namibia and empty Botswana, Zambia was refreshingly lived-in. Neat little villages punctuated the roadside and groups of women sat behind little piles of homegrown vegetables for sale. Men slashed at grass on the verges with little scythes and children played with homemade kites or wire toy cars.

Near the town of Livingstone I gaped at the mighty *Mosi oa Tunya*, 'The Smoke that Thunders', better known as Victoria Falls. There the entire ponderous power of the deep-flowing Zambezi is funnelled over a shallow precipice and into a tight gorge. Every second two million pints of water plunged over its lip and down 108 metres to a broiling pool at the head of a deep, winding chasm. An eternal mist plume is kicked up 200 metres above the entire scene. This frothing and frolicking cloud hung like an amorphous crown and could be seen from thirty miles away. After half an hour of hiking in the surrounding area I was wet through and invigorated.

In a campsite bar that evening I saw a story on the news about an outbreak of something called Ebola in a small southern Guinean city. Apparently the virus was one of the most horrific known with roughly half of those infected dying within a fortnight. It could be transmitted by a simple handshake and symptoms included vomiting, diarrhoea, and bleeding from every orifice until death from dehydration. The outbreak had only been detected three weeks earlier but had already spread to neighbouring Liberia and Sierra Leone, killing several hundred.

The route to the capital was a main road but wasn't busy, and it largely passed through untouched woods. Small adobe huts with grass-thatched roofs and fragile smokestacks stood beside subsistence plots of maize crops, fecund fruit trees and neatly planted vegetable gardens.

I stopped for a roadside chat with a British cyclist headed south. Ed was ten months into a round-the-world ride and told me enthusiastically about the anticipated highlights of his journey ahead. It was invigorating to listen to him. I saw in Ed the fresh-faced enthusiasm of myself four years earlier: the energy, the absence of cynicism, and the seemingly inexhaustible excitement. My ebullience had dried and hardened, along with the leathery, deep-tanned skin on the backs of my hands. I felt weary, relieved to be on my homeward leg, and unsure if I would ever again have the mental energy to begin such an undertaking.

For three years I had lived an unpredictable existence – always on the move, seeing new places, new faces, sleeping rough, wondering where I'd find food or water, and grappling with unfamiliar tongues. This abnormality had become my normal and no longer surprised me. I needed to fight to recapture and harness a sense of novelty. I remembered wistfully the simple things that pleased me so long ago when I hurtled wide-eyed through Northern Europe, brimful of heady expectation. Not for the first time, I wondered if I had been on the road too long.

After five days and another broken axle, the peaceful forest gave way to a steadily rising cacophony. I joined the honking, chugging traffic vying for space as the pockmarked road sucked us all into pleasant but pricey Lusaka.

THIRTY-FIVE

DIEU DE L'ARGENT

The Congo war had no one cause, no clear conceptual essence that can be easily distilled in a couple of paragraphs. Like an ancient Greek epic, it is a mess of different narrative strands – some heroic, some venal, all combined in a narrative that is not straightforward but layered, shifting, and incomplete. It is not a war of great mechanical precision but of ragged human edges.
- Jason K. Stearns, *Dancing in the Glory of Monsters*

Archie flew in on Easter Day. During our flatshare in Cape Town we had drunkenly pored over a map of the Congo one evening. The evocative, fun-to-say place names were the first things that struck us: Kabongo, Bosobolo, Kafakumba, Bulungu, Kibombo, Mobayi-Mbongo, Popokabaka, Kongolo, Songololo, Katako-Kombe.

We also noticed that the massive country was awash with rivers all funnelling into the mighty Congo, which then flowed through the capital, Kinshasa, on its way to the Atlantic. The Congo may only be the world's ninth-longest river, but it is the deepest, and it has a formidable discharge volume second only to the Amazon. During the rainy season 50,000 cubic metres pour into the Atlantic every second, enough to fill twenty Olympic swimming pools. The 2,900-mile-long river drains a 1.5-million-square-mile basin: an area larger than India. Such is the force of this river its outflow has carved a canyon into the seabed almost a mile deep and reaching well over 100 miles into the Atlantic. The first Portuguese mariners probing down the west coast of Africa in the fifteenth century were roughly a hundred miles from land when they noticed the water they were sailing through had turned brown. They tasted it and were amazed to find it was fresh water, still undiluted after a hundred miles of surging through the salty ocean. They sailed east into the river mouth and were the first Europeans to set foot on

Congolese land.

Over many drinks Archie and I devised a vague plan to cover the 1,100 miles as the crow flies from the Zambian border crossing to the capital. The Democratic Republic of the Congo (DRC) is vast. It is larger than Greenland and bigger by far than it appears on traditional world maps, where equatorial lands are distorted and shrunken. The DRC's westernmost to easternmost points are roughly the same distance apart as London and Moscow. The northernmost and southernmost points are equally distant.

Maps said that there were roads crossing the country and that it would be a 1,600-mile cycle journey. However, we had been told of the deplorable route conditions, where roads wash away during the rains and sometimes never existed in the first place. Apparently the road across the south of the country was in a relatively good state as it connected the mines of the mineral rich 'Copperbelt', which straddles the Congo–Zambia border and is where copper has been mined for over 1,000 years. After 500 miles this road crossed into Angola, for which we wouldn't have visas. However, on the map was marked a slim river, the Lulua, close to the Angolan border, which ran north many hundreds of miles until it joined the Kasai which in turn joined the Congo river 100 miles upstream from Kinshasa.

Our idea was to cycle to the Lulua and then buy a dugout canoe to paddle to the capital, or as far as we could get within the timeframe of our visas. The route seemed exciting and dangerous and daring, but the first big obstacle was simply to get a visa. To that end we headed to the DRC embassy in Lusaka in our best clothes. I sported a travel-worn collared shirt, jeans patched in the crotch, a neat-ish ponytail and trimmed beard, and a jacket I borrowed from a Zambian man. We both wore sandals as we had nothing else, but Archie wore black socks underneath to hide his bare skin. We looked like bizarre, aspiring gangsters as we walked into the embassy. The apathetic woman at the front desk instantly said 'no tourist visas'. We persevered and eventually she accepted our applications and told us to return in the afternoon. We did so, looking equally daft, and were informed our applications had been rejected as we were not Zambia residents.

And so began three weeks of wrestling with various authorities and agents to secure our visas. The DRC didn't really get tourists, especially not ones entering by land borders on bicycles. It soon became clear we would have to send our passports to a company in London who would expensively lodge our applications there.

We set about gathering the numerous pointless documents we would require: proof of employment (forged), police records check (forged), official letter of invitation (cost £100), proof of return flights (forged), daily itinerary (fabricated), proof of sufficient funds of £100 per day for a ninety-day visit (most definitely forged), permission documents from nine different high officials, a hotel booking, and proof of a guide meeting us on arrival.

While waiting for various documents to come in, and to escape our sweaty Lusaka campsite, we hitchhiked to the South Luangwa valley for a few days. My cousin and a friend of Archie's were working there for a safari company. On the first evening we stood by the slow-moving Luangwa with sundowner drinks and watched as a single-file herd of elephants crossed the river, the mothers nudging and shepherding the calves. The smallest of the elephants were completely submerged with just their trunks clearing the surface like snorkels. We camped by the river that night and Archie woke just as a hippo was waddling through the tight space between our tents, emptying its bowels as it did so. Archie didn't sleep for the rest of the night.

Back in Lusaka, we sent off our applications, each with fifteen accompanying documents and a fat stack of bills. The process had cost almost half of my remaining funds and the journey home was sure to flirt with penury later on.

We started riding slowly north, killing time until our passports would be sent to a town near the border. Starting his first ever bike tour, Archie was on a shiny new bike found in Lusaka. I was on Little Bastard who I had come to resent, having by then replaced six broken axles.

The rainy season had petered out, giving way to warm, dry, cloudless days with cool, breezy nights. There was no rush. We made late starts in the mornings and took long breaks. After one lunch we lay back in the forest to doze awhile. A large, plump cobra chanced upon our clearing, coming within a metre of my head before rearing up, turning tail and slipping away.

At Kabwe we left the main road and took dusty back tracks. We found idyllic camp spots and made fires beneath the bright Milky Way in our nests of flattened vegetation surrounded by walls of head-high grass. We drank from wells and washed in river pools. Boiled eggs on wood-smoked toast for breakfast started each day and spiced, slow-stewed vegetables finished it. Friendly house-proud villagers waved from homes with old tyres placed around the doorway as improvised pots for plants and herbs. Stumbling, beer-swilling men shouted greetings from rough-and-tumble village shebeens where Afropop blared from oversized speakers.

Most Zambians we spoke to told us that they would never dare cross the Congolese border because of the country's reign of lawlessness. For many years the DRC had both attracted and terrified me in equal measure. During the last year of pedalling through Africa, it had weighed heavy on my mental horizon as the biggest obstacle remaining. There was no way up the west coast of Africa without crossing the Congo, but it had become the African country most closely associated with civil war, corruption, and societal decay. The Congolese unarguably had the most brutalising experience of colonisation at the hands of the Belgians, and their homeland has been in a state of perpetual deterioration since independence in 1960. Every change of government since Belgian withdrawal was brought about by coup or assassination.

Monikers such as 'the Dark Heart of Africa' and the 'Heart of Darkness' nurtured my unease. But they also drew me in helplessly, like a moth to the flame. I decided to cycle through Africa precisely *because* it would be challenging. I often grumbled to myself about the hardship and sense of alienation, but really I relished the difficulty. And where would be more difficult than the eternally troubled DRC?

With these twin senses of trepidation and fascination, Archie and I collected our passports in Kitwe and cycled the last sixty miles, camping just short of the border. Despite our hard-won ninety-day visas, we fully expected difficulties at the border and demands for covertly palmed dollars. However, to our surprise we were in and out of the immigration building in fifteen minutes having met nothing but welcoming, smiling officials wishing us *bon courage* for the journey ahead. The money changers offering Congolese francs for our Zambian kwacha, shook our hands, and didn't try particularly hard to cheat us. Patrice, the guide paid to meet us at the border, was nowhere to be seen but someone called him for us and he set a place for us to meet in Lubumbashi that evening.

We cycled sixty miles to Lubumbashi, the capital of Katanga province and the DRC's second city.[48] Besides the villages being more basic and the people marginally more tattily clad than their Zambian neighbours, nothing seemed wildly different. During that day in the saddle we gradually relaxed, our apprehensions melting further with each cheery Congolese that waved and shouted enthusiastic greetings. As when entering other ill-famed countries, I soon came to the obvious realisation that, regardless of politics and conflict, the DRC was a place predominantly populated by normal people doing their best to live normal lives.

Patrice showed us to the miserable, overpriced hotel we'd been obliged to book and emptied a whole can of bug spray inside before wishing us *bon chance* and leaving. Ironically, we were then forced to wait outside for several hours, being bitten all the while, until the toxic fumes had subsided.

In the morning we took a walk through the city, first passing an industrial area on the outskirts. A 100-metre-high

[48] In 2015 Katanga was split into four smaller provinces: Tanganyika, Haut-Lomami, Lualaba, and Haut-Katanga.

volcano-shaped slag heap centred the scene, the accumulated tailings from seventy years of copper processing. Since the 1920s most of Katanga's copper ore had been trucked to Lubumbashi for refinement before being driven through Zambia and to a coast for shipment to wealthier parts of the world. Since some new technology had emerged to salvage further mineral value from the pile it was being reprocessed, and hundreds of men scrabbled over its surfaces in haphazard lines like ants breaking down a discarded cake.

On the outskirts of the industrial district was a stream of black, sewage-rich water through which ragged children chased a ball. Coiled piles of human faeces were visible beside it among the spread of plastic waste. Young boys with filthy sacks picked through the toxic mess in search of recyclable materials. A number of areas had been neatly cleared and planted with rows of vegetables but remained surrounded by rubbish and shit.

A little later we were wandering down a narrow back alley when we heard what sounded like a rally. We followed our ears towards the chanting and found a simple church; iron girders, breeze blocks and corrugated metal roof. A woman lay in the dirt by the open door, retching. Curious, we slipped past her and joined the fracas of faith within.

The dense eyebrows of the minister danced furiously in accompaniment to the rapid French and Swahili spat from his mouth. Sweat poured from his wide, bald pate, and from the bodies of the 1,000-strong congregation folded into the small *Église Evangélique*. The microphone clutched in the minister's hand was backed up by an extensive speaker system and a well-equipped sound desk manned by two technicians. A junior minister, also armed with a microphone, howled *Amen!* every third or fourth second in a ceaseless call-and-response with his colleague. The assembled faithful stood with their shaking hands held aloft. They chorused every Amen, simultaneously thrusting palms skyward as if shunting each prayer to heaven.

The lead minister was also followed by a camera crew with the live feed projected above the altar and displayed on flat screen monitors around the room. Men stalked through the crowd with containers into which the mesmerised audience stuffed handfuls of banknotes. The minister began simply chanting *'Dieu … l'argent … Dieu … l'argent'*, each word followed by the inevitable *Amen!*

On the stage was a choir and band with drumkit, guitars, and a keyboard set to 'organ' mode. They stood calmly in smart clothes, playing with smartphones and utterly unaffected by the proceedings. Facing them across a two-metre gap stood the closely packed, yammering front row of poorer, shabbily dressed Congolese, fiercely competing with one another in their displays of zealousness.

The floor between the frenzied congregation and the business-like people on stage was a writhing confusion of bodies. When the proximity to God's might became too much to bear, various female congregants started flapping their arms, ululating, and doing their best to make it obvious that they were nearing breakdown from religious ecstasy. The throng parted and the shaking, jerking, god-struck supplicants were carried to the front to scream, collapse, speak in tongues, pound the floor, or attempt to vomit. A couple of men were on hand to aggressively splash holy water in their faces: blessed bottles of Dasani mineral water bottled by the Coca Cola Company.

We sidled outside after half an hour and noticed CDs and DVDs on sale by the door with the minister's face and signature on them. A man shouted over the din that there would be twelve more of these services during the following two days, each two hours long, each with sales and collections. In Kenya there is a common joke: if you want to get rich start a bank, but if you want to get mega-rich start a church.

We cycled west among laden lorries going to and from the region's many mines. Katanga province provides almost half the world's cobalt as well as copper, diamonds, gold, silver, uranium, tin, rare earth metals and coltan, which is essential for the manufacture of laptops and mobile phones. It is largely due to this mineral wealth that a Katangan secession movement sprang up in the wake of the Congo's independence. Katanga declared itself an independent state but this was opposed by Patrice Lumumba, the prime minister in Kinshasa. Belgium and the USA backed Katanga's separation as it was considered easier to maintain mining interests in a smaller country. It was also the height of the Cold War and Lumumba was suspected of being a communist in league with the Soviets. The CIA conspired with Belgian agents and Congolese officials to have him arrested and flown to Lubumbashi in January 1961. Under the supervision of four Belgian officers, Lumumba was taken deep into the forest, shot, dismembered and dissolved in sulphuric acid.

At the end of the ensuing five years of political turmoil, a thirty-five-year-old former military officer named Mobutu Sese Seko, seized power in a coup. Mobutu held power for over three decades, during which he slowly dismantled the state apparatus and siphoned off untold billions of dollars of the Congo's natural wealth.[49] His overthrow by *coup d'état* in 1997 came at the head of six years of fierce and complicated warfare in the Congo. At least twenty roving militias, loitering Rwandan *génocidaires*, government loyalists, guerrilla fighters imported from other regional conflicts, and military forces from nine other countries all clashed in some of the most brutal fighting the modern world has seen. Supported by other Tutsi-aligned forces, a Rwandan–Burundian–Ugandan coalition invaded and occupied the DRC, plundering resources for as long as possible. Under the control of Laurent-Désiré Kabila, an aged Marxist guerrilla, the Congolese government fought back as best they could, but the territory was simply too large and disconnected to control. After Kabila was assassinated by a bodyguard his son

---

[49] The DRC is one of the most resource-rich nations on earth. A 2009 estimate of the country's untapped mineral deposits by *African Business Magazine* came to $24 trillion.

Joseph took up the mantle of power and was still in office.[50]

The conflict was the inevitable culmination of over a century of exploitation and mismanagement. The death toll is estimated in the low millions but is hard to pin down as the overwhelming majority of those who perished did so undramatically, not killed by guns and blades but by the ensuing wave of poverty and starvation that engulfs societies when all order and structure breaks down.

Unfortunately for DRC's people, its wars and their causes have been too complex and tangled for the world to easily understand and so international efforts have focused on more graspable catastrophes: Rwanda, Kosovo, Cambodia. The DRC remains an untreated victim of its alluring natural assets.

---

[50] Joseph Kabila served his two constitutionally permitted terms and delayed the 2016 election for two years, finally stepping down in January 2019.

THIRTY-SIX

LIKE A THIEF IN THE NIGHT

In this project there is no question of granting the slightest political power to the negroes. That would be absurd.
- King Leopold II of Belgium

We passed dozens of local cyclists transporting huge sacks of charcoal who rode alongside and nattered with us in a mixture of French and Swahili. We camped in the bush each evening and usually heard drums from nearby villages pounding unchanging rhythms throughout the night. Outside the city of Likasi we passed the turning to Shinkolobwe mine, which had supplied the uranium used in the Manhattan Project to produce the first nuclear weapons in the 1940s.

Likasi itself was known as Jadotville during the Belgian colonial era. After Katanga declared independence in 1960, Katangan forces besieged a United Nations peacekeeping detachment from Ireland. The 158 lightly armed Irish troops were attacked by a force of over 3,000 men that included Belgian, French, and Rhodesian mercenaries with heavy arms and the air support of a jet. The Irish held out without loss of life for six days under heavy bombardment and repeated waves of attack. Finally they were forced to surrender and were taken prisoners of war for a month before being traded for Katangan captives.

In the town of Fungurumu we watched as a fight broke out by the water pump. A couple of shouts were enough to instantly gather a crowd of several hundred, which encircled the two pugilists and cheered gleefully when one picked up length of wood and started threatening the other.

After Kolwezi the tarmac ended and we rode into an orgy of orange dust swished skyward every time a laden lorry ploughed past. The mining traffic thinned and we continued down a quiet, narrow road through spacious forest. In the mission village of Kanzene we found a colonial Catholic church. Half the windowpanes were missing and the brickwork was very worn but the inside was a cool, peaceful haven of wooden pews and plastic flowers. A short row of graves alongside the church accommodated several Belgian missionaries, a couple born as early as the 1860s.

The Belgian colonial thrust into the Congo was spearheaded by that redoubtable rogue Stanley. Three years after finding Livingstone he returned to Africa and crossed the continent from east to west, navigating and mapping hundreds of miles of the Congo river. Off the back of this widely celebrated achievement he was contracted by King Leopold II to stake out a new colony. Belgium was a new nation and Leopold yearned for an empire to compete with his European neighbours.

Stanley spent five years building roads, establishing trading stations, and forcing tribal chiefs who had never seen writing to sign over in perpetuity the rights to their lands and the labour of their people. To achieve his ends Stanley distributed gin and cheap trinkets and employed various tricks to convince chiefs he had dangerous supernatural powers. These included lighting fires with a magnifying glass and using an electrified wire to give shocks when shaking hands. The prize was initially ivory, but increasingly became raw rubber to supply the pneumatic tyre boom in Europe and America.

During the first forty years of ruthlessly extractive Belgian rule, implemented by a sadistic cast of hired desperadoes, the population of the Congo halved to ten million. The country has never truly recovered.

The track continued through increasingly dense forest and narrowed until it was threading a picturesque tunnel through trees interwoven overhead. The formerly paved road disintegrated into soft sand punctuated by loose rubble and we began long stints of pushing our bicycles.

A grand avenue of poplars lined our entrance to the forlorn ruins that remain of Mutshatsha, once an important stop on the train line to Angola. In the early twentieth century the Belgian colonists constructed an extensive network of railways, roads, and steamboats plying the rivers. This web, built at the expense of countless thousands of Congolese labourers' lives, made the colossal country of tropical forest an easy matter to cross. Had Archie and I arrived in Lubumbashi sometime in the 1950s we would have had a smooth and speedy journey to Kinshasa by train and boat. The colony's 70,000 miles of road was maintained with the *cantonage* system. The roads were divided into thousand-metre sections, each with a villager on a monthly retainer responsible for its upkeep. However, the breakdown of civil institutions saw the railways and roads neglected. The jungle slowly reclaimed its ancient possessions and the Congo approached impenetrability once more.

Time-stained colonial bungalows sagged behind Mutshatsha's poplars. The deserted railway station had a neighbouring train maintenance warehouse where cobweb-cloaked machinery bore the imprints 'Made in Ohio, 1920' and 'Sheffield Steel, 1919'. Through a missing windowpane we viewed the office: a dusty clutter of sepia files, age-crinkled ledgers, and an archaic telephone. Outside, a couple of rusted steam engines wallowed in long grass, the tops of their wheels just visible but the tracks they once stood on long lost to the inexorable creep of nature. A teenage tree had sprouted through one engine's broad chimney.

The town's market was the most dismal I had ever seen. Twenty or so women were each hunched over a tiny bundle of produce spread on the ground on a dirty scrap of fabric. Most had only a cassava root or two and a pile of cassava leaves, which are bitter and contain trace cyanide but are a reasonable protein source. One woman offered a prized pile of four marble-sized tomatoes and ten similarly small onions. They looked appetising but were absurdly expensive so instead we bought all seven of the market's potatoes from four separate women.

Being white strangers it was assumed we were missionaries as no other foreigners visit. We were led by an excitable boy to the crumbling Catholic mission. Père Sylvan and *L'abbé* welcomed us in and showed us each to a bare cell in the spartan concrete building. That evening we ate *foufou*, the national staple of cassava flour pounded with water and topped with boiled cassava leaves. The *abbé* apologised for the terrible road conditions, saying he had been charged by the government with reintroducing the *cantonage* system but given no funds to get started.

Fighting our way through deep sand the following day, we passed the scuttled remains of a 1930s armoured vehicle. However, we had no way of knowing if it was used during the Second World War or if it was a relic from one of the numerous conflicts that have convulsed Congo in the intervening decades.

One or two vehicles passed each day, and the only other road users were the men who push loads of up to 100 kg stacked on decrepit, unrideable bicycles, most without even a chain. There are so few vehicles and such poor roads that the majority of cargo in the DRC is moved in this fashion. The small, wiry men travelled roughly twenty miles a day, sometimes for several hundred miles. When they reached their destination they would sell their goods, pocket a pittance of profit, and start the return journey. They were always cheerful and friendly, joking and laughing with us when we fell in step behind them to push our bikes in their deep tracks through the sand.

The few villages were simple and filled with waist-high children who quickly flocked around us when we stopped. The average Congolese family has six children and in rural areas it is closer to eight. The countless young were dressed in ragged clothing, repeatedly patched, that would take considerable care to don or remove without further tearing. Many of the boys' buttocks showed through the webs of rags that were once pairs of shorts. The children seemed largely happy but the telltale distended belly of malnutrition was widespread. This was hardly surprising given that the country had almost no agriculture, despite its abundantly fertile land. An elderly man told me cassava was grown in village plots instead of the more nourishing maize as it comes to harvest quicker. People dislike taking longer term gambles on time until harvest, as they are never sure when the next wave of instability will flood across the region, sweeping them into the forest for refuge. According to USAID, 43 per cent of the DRC's children under five years old have stunted growth due to malnutrition.

One lunchtime we were sprawled under a tree in the bush, messily devouring a pineapple, when a man walked past carrying an ember. He rattled off several sentences in Swahili and we nodded, smiled, and generally showed our approval as we tended to do when in utter incomprehension. He happily wondered into the bush and padded back past us a few minutes later with a thumbs up which we returned. It wasn't long before we heard the approaching crackle of flames. We hurriedly packed up and left the growing 'slash-and-burn' fire. Over the previous week we had seen numerous large swathes of charred land with mournful charcoal tree stumps. Earlier that year the DRC's government had requested $1 billion from the international community as payment to preserve its extensive oxygen-producing forests. If the money is ever given I doubt the cheerfully jabbering individual we met will see any of it or alter his practices.

In one village we were talking to a schoolteacher when a leery looking man approached and demanded our documents. There was avarice in his eyes.

'*Qui es-tu?*' I asked.

'*Je suis un gendarme. Police! Policier!*' he shot back. He wasn't wearing a uniform.

'*Avez-vous identification?*' I tried.

'*Attends deux minutes,*' he ordered, pointing at the ground we stood on, before hurrying away to fetch his ID.

'*Homme dangereux,*' the teacher whispered under his breath. We shook his hand and hurriedly rode away.

On the last evening of our ride to the Lulua river, we crested a hill and stopped to watch the reddening sun sink into the orange-hazed spread of trees before us. The dust created an arresting sunset panorama and we watched the bike-cargo boys we had been chatting to descend into the scene. When the road was empty we ducked into the trees and pushed our bikes until we found a suitably distant clearing. With tents up, we wandered off in different directions and returned, arms laden with firewood, to find five men waiting. Someone must have seen us sneaking off the road and these men had got wind.

The self-proclaimed chief wore a torn ice hockey shirt. He had bloodstained eyes, strong body odour, and alcohol on his breath. He said in fast pidgin French that his village was a mile down the road and we were on his land. He demanded our documents. We showed our passports, likely the first he had ever seen, and watched him wrestle with the first page's impossibly pompous proclamation: *Her Britannic Majesty's Secretary of State requests and requires in the name of Her Majesty all those whom it may concern to allow the bearer to pass freely without let or hindrance …*

He couldn't read English and soon became frustrated, demanding more papers. We produced our trump card: written permission, in French, to travel freely by bicycle in the DRC. The document was signed by the directors of both the Ministry of the Interior and Security, and the National Intelligence Agency. The man seemed to understand that the papers had bureaucratic heft but his cupidity still saw opportunity. He decided $30 was reasonable tribute to pay him in return for camping in the forest near his village – roughly a fortnight's wages to a government clerk in a town. We said we had no money but he countered that we must go to the village to 'pay our respects' and sleep there. Archie and I didn't need to confer to agree that this was not an attractive option.

The discussions had already gone on a while and a heavy gibbous moon had risen. After a long day's exertion we were yet to eat and the men were clearly in no rush, sitting down to await our next move. We decided to pack up, ride past the village and camp further on.

Without lights, the ride down the hill to the village was frightening. The dark track was comprised of bumps, loose rocks, and sandy patches. It was peaceful, with most villagers sitting outside their huts, chatting around small fires set back a little way from the road. Unexpectedly, the village ran on about two miles, much longer than most. We kept quiet and glided stealthily through, not wanting to draw attention. Night can be menacing and people act differently in the dark.

All went smoothly until, in the centre of the village, someone shouted something in an angry tone. I turned and saw a dark shape, vaguely silhouetted by a fire, hurtling towards me. I hit my brakes just in time and the man shot past in front of me, tripping as he went.

'Go, go, GO!' I hissed to Archie.

We hurried on, but the alarm had been raised and our silence deemed suspicious. In a country reeling from eight decades of horrific colonial exploitation followed by another five of brutal internecine conflict and constant foreign meddling, strangers creeping around in the darkness automatically drew mistrust. My pulse rocketed and my breath became a gasping, groaning tremble. In Ethiopia I had experienced the insanity of anonymity and overexcitement that can seize a mob in the dark. *Not again,* I thought, *please not this again …*

A chain of shouts was spreading through the dark village and soon there was uproar. Maddened dogs bayed in concert with the maddened humans. More barely visible shapes began charging towards the road, trying to thump us or knock us from our bikes. The track became firmer. It was still uneven but with hard-packed earth instead of sand. We rode faster, dodging and weaving with white knuckles gripping handlebars. Hitting a pothole and falling could spell disaster. Some men swung thick sticks that bounced off our wheels and clattered off our bike frames. A couple struck my back and hands grabbed at our vests. A stick was thrust side-on at my spokes but stabbed my panniers instead. A man I never even saw managed to land a punch on my face. I spotted a couple of figures sprinting in our wake brandishing burning logs snatched from fires.

Archie and I were unable to communicate over the noise but we both knew instinctively that we had passed a point of no return. If caught, we might not have time to explain that we were simply tourists – and not spies, rebels, or mineral thieves – before something regrettable happened

I rode just behind Archie, yelling to reassure him that I was still there and that we should keep going as fast as possible. If he discovered that I had been caught then he would be faced with an impossible decision, like a climber with still-living deadweight at the bottom of his rope. Would he turn back and help me, or save himself? Our instinctual actions in such situations are primal and are things we hope never to discover.

Thankfully confusion and darkness were on our side. After a few fraught minutes we made it to the end of the village and hurtled onwards. We gained ground and the pounding chase of footfall receded from just a few metres behind to a stone's throw and then further still. The rusty-chained croak of single speed bikes were also in pursuit but we were faster, spurred by the adrenalin of terror. The sound dropped away further. My ears strained over the deafening thump of my heart, listening for the ominous splutter of a motorbike kickstarting

'Keep going, Arch. It's OK. We'll be OK. Just keep going …'

The whole incident cannot have lasted more than ten minutes before we gained enough ground to leave the road and plunge unseen into the forest. We tore through the trees for a couple of minutes before finding a space hidden by thick bush and a toppled tree. We erected our tents for the second time that night, but this time with shaking hands. The hue and cry in the village was still audible and sounded uncomfortably close. Dogs still barked, men still shouted, and motorbikes began driving up and down the road.

Would there be search parties? How long would they bother to look? Would their hunting dogs stalk our scent? Not daring to speak, we chewed stale bread in silence and then retired to our sleeping bags for several hours of fretful wakefulness.

The sunrise, when it came, was sanity-bearing and eagerly welcomed. The daylight relaxed us and we warmed our hands over a fire, trying to rationalise what had happened, desperately scratching around for explanation and consolation. But we found little. The Congo had finally cowed us.

THIRTY-SEVEN

PIROGUE

The Congo stands as a totem for the failed continent of Africa. It has more potential than any other African nation, more diamonds, more gold, more navigable rivers, more fellable timber, more rich agricultural land. But it is exactly this sense of what might be that makes the Congo's failure all the more acute.
- Tim Butcher, *Blood River*

After two weeks we caught our first glimpse of the Lulua River in Sandoa, another rotting colonial outpost. First we followed a fallen signpost to the Salvatorian Catholic Mission, a quaint and ramshackle square of farmstead-type buildings around a picturesquely overgrown courtyard. The senior father rented us a room and we walked into the slowly re-wilding town centre beside the river.

Archie and I sat on the riverbank and shared an almost-cold Simba beer. The Lulua was only forty metres wide and invitingly placid. Dusk's dying light reflected silver on the water as the last few fishermen unloaded their catch nearby. This was the river we had spotted on a map, half a year earlier when tipsy in Cape Town. If we followed the water for long enough it would carry us all the way to Kinshasa. We had no idea if we would have time or if it was even possible, given the potential obstacles rivers can produce.

The mosquitos rose and we retreated to the mission. We had found our river, but still needed to find our rivercraft.

In the morning we cycled down to the colonial iron bridge that spanned the river. There were no more bridges downstream until Kananga, many hundreds of miles away. We approached the two policemen manning the bridge and introduced ourselves. A small crowd soon formed and tuts echoed around the group of men when we explained our intention. Their responses were intimidating.

'C'est impassable! C'est impossible!'

'Les crocodiles will get you! *Les hippopotames* will break you!'

'Les rapides will swallow you! *Les cascades* will kill you! The waterfalls are *très grandes!'*

'You will be drowned!'

'You will be eaten!'

'You will be drowned first and *then* eaten…'

Our research on the river was limited by the sheer paucity of information available. The upper Lulua was apparently unnavigable due to several sets of dangerous rapids and the odd waterfall. But besides grainy satellite images we could only guess at where they were. To our knowledge, nobody had tried to descend it before and the people of Sandoa seemed to corroborate this. However, it seemed plausible that a dugout canoe, or *pirogue*, literally a hollowed-out tree trunk, could be roped through rapids and carried around waterfalls.

There was one pirogue landed beside the bridge, which we took a quick look at. It was about five metres long and half a metre at its widest. Apart from its obviously venerable age, a few poorly repaired holes, and a worryingly long crack, it seemed serviceable. However, we knew not to buy the first canoe we saw. We also had a plan to fix two smaller pirogues together in a catamaran-style structure for more stability in turbulent waters.

We pedalled across the bridge to the village of Mbako and let it be known what we were after. A man led us to cluster of huts where we sat with a bald and jumpy man who pronounced himself chief. He may have been chief of that particular collection of huts, but he was certainly not the chief of Mbako. Congolese village structure is farcically hierarchical and there is a series of petty chiefs deferring to section chiefs who, in turn, defer to the actual chief. The village chief is subordinate to the regional chief who answers to the local tribal king or queen. This structure exists across the DRC's 200 tribes in uncomfortable parallel with government-appointed officials.

'Bald and jumpy' wore a fake leather jacket with a print of

Tutankhamun's sarcophagus on the back. He had the face-scratching, nose-brushing, eye-darting mannerisms of a drug addict with an itch. He was also very drunk. Eventually we all walked down to the river, followed by fifty jostling children.

We were keen to lose our twitchy new guide and soon jumped into a small pirogue with two large, leaking holes, piloted by a reserved young man called Christophe. He punted us upstream, where we saw many pirogues of various shapes and sizes but none that fitted our requirements. Christophe landed us back in Mbako where we gave him some money and said we would return in the morning. He seemed on the ball and said he would have some more boats for us to view. Before we left the 'chief' slipped on wet mud and fell comically over a pirogue and into the water. The assembled crowd of children joyously roared with laughter.

The next day we returned to Christophe's but he was sheepish, not looking us in the eyes. He offered his leaky little pirogue for an outrageous price. He was also hungover and smelled strongly of spirits. He must have spent the money we gave him on drink.

Disappointed, we cycled five miles further to a village called Sakanono. A local teacher called Molière led us another couple of miles, first down a footpath and then wading across a calf-deep bog. We arrived at three pirogues, all of similar size and shape and in good condition. They were exactly what we had in mind and any two of them would do for our catamaran.

Back in the village we met Monsieur Msweka, who owned the first pirogue. A sulky, uncharismatic character, Msweka mumbled something about £150. We knew the correct approximate price to be £50 and said this. He looked at his feet and said he might sell it in three days for £70. He wanted to go fishing in the meantime.

The second owner was Monsieur Mbaza, who we warmed to immediately. He sat us down on bamboo chairs in palm-shade beside his hut and explained that he had no plans to sell his pirogue. He reckoned he could make £100 on a good day's fishing. This begged the question why he didn't fish more often but he was kind and gentle and we didn't question him.

The third pirogue belonged to Mbaza's brother, who was in nearby Angola but returning 'maybe tomorrow' and might be keen to sell. We gave Molière some cash for his help and cycled back to the mission in twilight.

We passed Molière on the way back to Sakanono the next day and said we would drop by his home in the tiny hamlet of Namwan on our way back. However, we hoped we would be returning by river. Msweka was out but Madame Msweka seemed angry with us for some reason. Mbaza was still resistant, saying he would sell us his pirogue for as little as £30 if it weren't for his 'plans'. We couldn't help but notice that, once again, he was not fishing but enjoying a sedate day in his bamboo armchair. He was kind, though, and seemed genuinely keen to help us. He led us by bicycle down several miles of footpaths and through a couple of desolate-looking villages with elderly, wasting inhabitants. We abandoned bikes, left the paths, and walked barefoot through dense, swampy jungle.

In a tight clearing was a new, nearly completed pirogue. The rest of the tree lay, felled and discarded, at either end of the rough-hewn canoe. The sweet, sappy smell of fresh, raw wood swilled around us in the clammy air. The owner, who we had collected in a village on our way, said it had taken a week so far, would be ready in two more days, and we could have it for £20. Sadly, it was too small.

Back at the bridge in Sandoa a man was waiting for us. Crispin asked if we were interested in the nearby pirogue, the first one we spotted. Now prepared to abandon our catamaran scheme, we haggled him down from £400 to £100. Then it transpired it wasn't his pirogue and he wanted to act as an intermediary for the owner, who was called Mungenu.

It was getting late so we arranged to meet Crispin again the following morning. We waited two hours at the bridge but he never arrived. The pirogue had gone too. He sent us word in the evening claiming he had been in church all day and that Mungenu had taken his canoe fishing for an indeterminate number of days. Besides, he wouldn't sell for under £200. We arranged to meet again the following day but felt like we were back to square one.

The following morning there was once more no sign of Crispin. After an hour I left Archie at the bridge and cycled back to Sakanono. Msweka was out again. Apparently he had been hauled into the police station for unpaid debts.

Mbaza said his brother had still not returned but I watched as he dug a fire pit and began smoking yesterday's catch on a grill woven from saplings. He had 120 fat, foot-long fish after just one day of casting his nets. I later saw these fish on sale in the market for almost £1 each. It seemed Mbaza's plans were not so fanciful after all. For three days running I had found him lounging in the shade outside his house talking about the riches available. To the contented Monsieur Mbaza, there was an abundant resource of fish in the river, but he seemed to have all he needed and didn't feel compelled to graft unnecessarily on the river day in day out.

Back at the bridge Archie, who didn't speak French, was confused. Crispin had arrived several hours late without Mungenu but two new prospective sellers. They claimed their canoes were of similar size and condition to Mungenu's, which was still nowhere to be seen. Patrick wanted £125 and Gaspar was after £180. I told them to return early in the morning with their boats.

We asked Crispin when Mungenu would be back from fishing. He seemed surprised and said he'd been back since yesterday and lived nearby. We were led to a hut on the outskirts of Sandoa and met the diminutive Mungenu. After exchanging pleasantries for an appropriate length of time we began negotiating. Mungenu soon shook hands on £100 including two paddles. We returned to the mission feeling triumphant.

It took a further day to prepare the pirogue for our journey. First we patched a couple of leaks and nailed plastic patches on the underside to protect the repairs. We then attached a couple of wooden cross beams with empty twenty-litre water drums on either side for buoyancy and stability. We loaded our bags and bikes and a week's supply of food. It had been a full week since we reached Sandoa, but the *Lady Lulua* was finally ready to cast off.

With all the dire warnings about the dangers and the unfeasibility of descending the river it was perhaps hubristic to even set out. But we were stubborn and finally we were about to paddle our very own canoe into unknown lands. Feeling like the explorers of old, we launched our forty-year-old hollowed-out tree trunk with almost no idea of what lay ahead. We didn't know where the rapids were, how far we would get, how many crocodiles and hippos there would be, and if we would survive the journey. Shaking their heads and tutting, the onlookers waving from the bridge seemed sure we wouldn't.

THIRTY-EIGHT

BOATMEN

An empty stream, a great silence, an impenetrable forest. The air was warm, thick, heavy, sluggish. There was no joy in the brilliance of sunshine.
- Joseph Conrad, *Heart of Darkness*

We paddled downstream in the unfamiliar vessel, struggling to keep straight, to balance, and to synchronise our strokes. Similar to the pirogue, the paddles were heavy and clumsy, carved from single chunks of hardwood. Like stabilisers on a child's bicycle the water drums kept us safely level, but they created a lot of drag so we soon flipped them up, saving them for choppy waters. With our training wheels off, the slightest ill-advised lean to the left or right tipped the pirogue alarmingly and threatened to let water over the rim.

We saw no villages but passed several fishermen who we greeted in Swahili. After an hour, someone from the bank shouted a warning about rapids close at hand. As we rounded a corner, hurriedly flipping the stabilisers down, we saw a tiny break of ripples no more than fifteen centimetres high, which we sailed over happily. Were those the kind of rapids the people of Sandoa had worried about? We felt heartened. Maybe they exaggerated. Perhaps they overstated the threat of crocodiles and hippos too.

As evening approached, we steered into a little space on the east bank, tied the *Lady Lulua* to a tree, and lugged our kit up to a clearing. We cooked over a campfire and ate with our backs nestled in the bough of a papaya tree. With feet warmed by the fire and shoulders slightly aching, we felt satisfied. Pasta, potatoes, tomato paste and avocado was to be our staple meal that gradually simplified as we ran out of various ingredients. We cooked double what we needed and saved the remainder for lunch the next day. A chill rose from the river after dark and we lay in our cosy tents listening for the grunting honk of a hippo but hearing none.

The river slowly shed its dramatic mist shroud in the morning. As the fog fell and melted into the cool water, a pinky-orange spread softly from the east until it suffused the whole scene and finally melted in turn. After a quick coffee and a light breakfast we launched. We paddled hard and established a routine that was to see us through our river journey: two-hour stints, switching positions after each.

The helmsman sat at the back on a wooden seat projecting from the canoe's rear rim. To steer he switched his paddle from side to side as required. The other sat in the middle behind the bicycles and most of the bags. He had the better of the two paddles, pulling away consistently on one side and providing most of the power. After each stint we stopped for a quick biscuit and scanned the water for crocodiles before taking a cooling swim. We then awkwardly hauled ourselves back into our switched seats and paddled on. We usually stopped for our lunch of leftovers perched on the grand and twisting tree roots that often lined the bank.

The meandering Lulua repeatedly turned back on itself like the ubiquitous aerial footage of the snaking, jungle-pressed Amazon river. The pirogue was sluggish and hard to steer. It sat low in the river with only a handspan above the water. Neither Archie nor I could lift it alone, even unladen. Very unscientifically, we tried to measure our average speed. We guessed the distance to the next corner several times, recorded the time it took to reach it, and then averaged them out. We landed on four miles per hour – roughly the speed travelled on foot when slightly late for work but not quite enough so to bother running.

Towards the end of the second day we approached some islands. The water quickened and, before we could choose otherwise, we were committed to running a small set of rapids. The waves were only thirty centimetres high but this was enough to lap generously over the pirogue's sides at the rear and slowly start to sink us. Archie was up front and began to jubilantly cheer that we had come safely through. Seconds later the canoe was underwater.

It held near the surface due to the buoyant water drums but our bags started floating off in all directions. We began a frantic collection process, fetching the bags and dragging them back to the submerged pirogue.

'Quick! The camera bag is getting away. Go, go!'

'Look! That one behind you … it's got the money and the passports. Hurry!'

We struggled to shepherd the boat and bags to land while the swift current bore us on. Finally we gained the bank and hauled out our soaking kit. We refloated the canoe and busied ourselves with wood collecting, fire lighting, and putting up drying lines. Some of the bags were relatively watertight, but none were entirely dry. We cooked all the water-contaminated food and ate an uncomfortably large dinner while considering the incident. It hadn't been too serious: we weren't hurt and had lost nothing. However, it was a wake-up call. A short stretch of mildly lively water had managed to sink us. There would certainly be bigger challenges ahead. We would also have to ration our remaining food.

Before setting off in the morning we tied all the bags to the canoe so they couldn't float away. We also fixed all four water drums near the back of the pirogue, which sat lower in the water. Several fishermen told us that a big set of rapids were not far ahead and that we couldn't pass them. We rounded a dozen bends and then heard an intimidating roar growing in the distance and saw spray rising from the river. Figures were visible on the rocky right bank so we headed that way and landed a stone's throw from the start of the rapids.

The men were busy installing a fish nursery. It was a large, open-topped, circular basket balanced atop two pirogues and was being ferried into position before lowering into the water. Tightly woven from vines, the nursery was chest-high and three metres across with branches placed inside as habitat. A man explained to us that when small fish are caught they are placed inside the nursery until large enough to be worth eating.

We scouted ahead on land and quickly realised that paddling down the rapids would be suicide. The obstacle before us was half a mile long and consisted of various aggressive gauntlets of steeply cascading water divided by banks of jagged rock. There were a few waterfalls too but none more than two metres high.

We enlisted eight men to haul our pirogue over a smooth rock bank and steeply down to a sedate channel of water weaving through the forest. We paddled along with two passengers while the other men chased excitedly through the trees. Then the *Lady Lulua* was again yanked out of the water and dragged for 100 metres. I gritted my teeth at the sound of the hull scraping over rock.

When we reached the end of the rapids payment was demanded and we handed some money to the chief. I explained that he should distribute it among the eight men who helped. The banknotes were quickly deposited in the chief's pocket and more money was demanded.

'I, the chief, have received my tribute. But what about those who helped you?'

We doubled what had already been a generous sum but this too landed straight into the unsmiling chief's pocket. More was demanded. Seeing that the game of feigned indignation could be endless, we apologised, thanked them, and boarded our canoe. The disappointed crowd melted into the trees before we had even started paddling.

We camped that night on a large, flat boulder in the centre of the river and fretted that it would be an attractive haunt for crocodiles. It had been a long and physically draining day, yet we were sleeping only a few miles from our last campsite.

We were warned of more rapids ahead and set off in the morning expecting a bubbling cauldron of white water around every corner. The first challenge soon became audible as the river widened and a mess of small islands and rushing water came into view. A young boy in a miniature pirogue calmly pointed out an apparently passable route and we had little choice but to trust him. Braced for the battle we picked our line, each with a saucepan handy for bailing out water. Thrillingly we glided unharmed through the waves, slid over a flat rock shelf and shot safely into the calm water beyond.

There was a boulder garden shortly afterwards. We landed on the bank and walked ahead, scouting for a route. Tying a six-metre rope to the back of the pirogue and a long stick to the front, we managed to slowly guide her through the worst of the danger, hopping from rock to rock as we did so. We boarded and successfully ran the less hazardous final section. Chuffed with our teamwork, we bore onwards to yet another challenge.

Trying to circumnavigate these bigger rapids we followed an errant waterway that seemed to take a safer long way round. However, the channel soon narrowed and the quick, clear water ran through a thickening tangle of forest. We often snagged on low branches blocking our route as the strengthening current pushed us inexorably forward. It was gloomy in the forest, with a thick canopy overhead: the darkest of greens. A couple of times I had to jump in, out of my depth, and hack at vines with a machete while also clinging on to avoid being swept away.

Archie manned the pirogue and fended off branches with the paddles. It was frantic and it was frightening. The pirogue frequently wheeled side-on to the current and threatened to capsize. We were torn between excitement at the drama and dismay at the dangerous situation we had rushed into. Nobody knew where we were, so an accident could mean our fate would never be discovered. And all the while, images of crocodiles snapping at ankles played across my mind's eye.

When I forced the machete through the last blocking vines, our lumbering pirogue suddenly surged into the daylight. We were scratched, soaked, and wielding two damaged paddles. I looked up. We were in trouble; we were midstream and speeding into a deep field of rapids and rocks.

Archie shouted something but it was lost in the water's roar. Heaving on the paddles, we dodged a few boulders while the river spumed over and around us. We raced onwards as the water quickened and the rocks proliferated. An underwater boulder spun us and we tilted. Water poured in and we both leapt overboard. The river mercilessly tumbled and dunked us, and all the while we feared being hurled over a waterfall.

Finally it was over. Shivering and shaken, we gained the bank and pitched camp. Sitting by the fire that night, finally warmed and fed, we were both quiet. My back was bruised and bleeding, and Archie's ankle was swollen. The painkilling adrenalin had drained from our overworked systems and we were both in considerable discomfort. My hands were a mess of cuts, with three knuckle caps torn roughly off. Simple tasks like brushing my teeth were becoming a painful nuisance. It was only our fourth day on the Lulua and we still had a long way to go.

We ate our remaining food for breakfast: a quarter of a worse-for-wear pineapple and a couple of biscuits. A hairy, hand-sized tarantula sidled out of a hollow log on the fire and sauntered into the trees. After making a temporary repair job on the growing crack in the front of the pirogue, we took to the river once more. There were two sets of smaller rapids that morning. We rope-relayed down the first and took our chances paddling the second on the instructions of two old men. Their advice proved sage and we gladly reached the landing place for the village of Tshibamba at midday.

A vast pirogue, fifteen metres long, was ferrying pedestrians, bicycles, and a couple of motorbikes across the water. The village was two miles away, and by the time we unloaded a bike and played rock-paper-scissors for who would make the supplies run, the chief and his elders had arrived by bicycle to check our papers. They were friendly and gave us their idea of what lay ahead on the river. Archie went with them and returned with what meagre supplies could be found, as well as a new wooden paddle.

We slept that night on a charming riverbank made grotto-like by ancient trees and their intricate web of roots spread across the ground. A full breakfast and another dramatic sunrise had us boarding our embattled *Lady Lulua* in high spirits. The Tshibamba elders told us to expect several smaller rapids leading up to Tchala Falls which were *vraiment impassable.*

We made light work of the first rapid by simply steering through the flattest-looking section. We had created a vocabulary of curt, shouted instructions and, mixed with hand signals, were increasingly able to act as one. We were then helped down the second rapid by two young fishermen, Jean-Baptiste and Benny. They had been casting nets in the strong, waist-deep water before the rapids. Often losing footing on the fast river's rocky bed, the four of us waded through the 100-metre gauntlet, nursing the pirogue down to safer water.

We pulled hard on the paddles and covered long miles through the afternoon until arriving late in the day at what was unmistakably Tchala Falls. The river accelerated again and splayed into a maze of small, thickly forested islands with countless narrow waterways coursing between them. Battling currents tugged us this way and that on approach but we managed to land on a rock midstream.

Half an hour of rock-hopping and wading revealed a set of small waterfalls that looked like they might not destroy the *Lady Lulua* entirely. Having successfully rope-relayed down the first 200 metres we stopped before a larger drop, roughly head-high, and unloaded our kit. Without allowing time for reflection, we launched the pirogue at the cascade and miraculously managed to lower her unharmed. Tchala Falls was behind us.

Perched high on a bank a few hundred metres downriver was a ring of tiny thatched huts around a smoke stack. It was the first riverside dwelling we had seen since Sandoa. We scrambled up the bank and dumbfounded the small man we found there. He did a double take and froze on the spot for several seconds, deciding whether or not to run. He had heard of stories of the *mzungu* but had never seen one in the pale flesh. Eventually he relaxed and responded to our greetings, walking forward to shake our hands. Like all the people we had met along the Lulua, he was under five foot in height. At six-foot-four, Archie towered over our new acquaintance, M'baz, who welcomed us to sit by his fire. We brewed three cups of sweet tea while he puffed on the cigarettes we gave him. He told us his village was a day's walk from the river but he regularly came to the camp with two friends to fish.

Nobody else was around and M'baz showed us to one of the five huts where we could spend the night. The circular domed shelters were two metres across and only shoulder-high inside, with an entrance we had to crawl through. They were made from dry grass hung over a sturdy frame of woven sticks. One of the huts was billowing smoke, from fish drying over a fire inside.

It was after dark when Willie and Baraka returned. They dumped their basket of small fish, peeled off their soaking rags and joined us by the fire. They understood our basic Swahili but spoke a different Bantu dialect that we struggled to make sense of. Conversation was laboured but also unnecessary. We shared our dinner with them and they shared their catch with us. Fish constitutes most of the river peoples' diet and, at certain seasons, all of it.

In the warm confines of our hut that night I had the first of what became regular anxiety dreams; a night terror in which we helplessly careered down the river towards rapids or impenetrable trees. I woke in a confused panic, flailing my limbs and shouting frantically at Archie to steer left, back-paddle, and dodge the rocks. He patiently talked me down until I plunged back into fitful sleep.

THIRTY-NINE

PUSHING LUCK

I was at that flush of youth which never doubts self-survival, that idiot belief in luck and a uniquely charmed life, without which illusion few wars would be possible.
- Laurie Lee, *A Moment of War*

Willie and Baraka returned from checking their lines early in the morning. Each carried a catfish as long as my arm and they posed proudly while the gills gulped and flapped for water. We thanked our hosts and enjoyed our first full day of tranquil water; ten hours of leaning heavily on our rough-hewn oars and playing word games to pass time.

We camped on a high, sandy bank and were joined at our fire by a French-speaking fisherman called Joseph who explained the local system of fishing rights. The river was split into zones, each owned by the hereditary chief of the nearest village. Anyone can fish anywhere but must first visit the chief to pay tribute, which is usually a small sum of money. After fishing he must visit the chief again and give a portion of his catch – roughly a fifth.

After two more sets of rapids we arrived at the landing spot for Kapanga; an actual town with a road of sorts. It was a major milestone for us – only 100 miles from Sandoa as the crow flies, but we had already covered several hundred river miles. The pirogue was quickly emptied and the bikes loaded up for the short ride to the centre. We left our sorry-looking pirogue by the river, trusting it wouldn't disappear, then spent an hour fending off questions in the office of the district administrator.

'We don't have tourism. Why are you here? What minerals are you looking for?'

'We're not looking for minerals, sir.'

'Then tell us, which church do you represent?'

We tried to explain what we were doing but he remained

confused. We were then led a couple of miles to N'tita Catholic mission. Word of the two strange *mzungu* had preceded us and we were warmly welcomed by the Catholics. We asked to stay one night but the kindly Père Guillaume said we looked terrible and insisted we stay two nights and rest for a day. The seventy-year-old mission was built entirely without cement and structured with a three-sided cloister. The fathers and their novices were friendly and interested, and as they had met foreigners before we were temporarily relieved of novelty status.

At breakfast we met Père Jacques, a jovial, rotund man who came to Kapanga from Belgium in the early 1970s. With no formal technical training, he was approaching completion of his second EU-funded hydro-electric project on a Lulua tributary that would soon power the district. Father Jacques was an authority on the river and warned of many more rapids to come – bigger ones, as well as the certainty of hippos and a strong possibility of crocodiles. He also fed our egos with his strong belief that we were the first people stupid enough to descend the Lulua by pirogue. His Congolese colleagues said everyone knew it was impassable and that people only used pirogues to cross the river or to paddle up and down safe areas for fishing.

When we were driven into town in the afternoon to buy supplies, Père Guillaume greeted an ordinary-looking woman sitting beside the road. He explained that she was the local tribal queen and that the dilapidated colonial villa behind her was her 'palace', where people came to pay tribute. Had we walked past without one of the fathers, we would have been summoned in to make payment.

Before leaving Kapanga we made more repairs to the embattled *Lady Lulua*, who was taking on a lot of water through two growing cracks in the prow. We were watched by a mischievous gaggle of over 100 children that edged ever closer but were repeatedly beaten back by adults with sticks.

Over the next ten days we passed another twelve sets of large rapids and countless lesser ones. Our routine became slick and we confidently navigated the smaller challenges without fretting or having to scout ahead. As we descended and nudged slowly north, the climate became hotter and wetter and the forest grew thicker.

After landing each evening we efficiently set about making a fire, brewing tea, pitching tents, cooking dinner, and drying kit. Sometimes we had visits from curious river men, drawn to our camp by the fire. One evening, six men landed in the dark and asked us a few questions. The oldest man was introduced as a great chieftain and tribute was demanded. We were sceptical but Archie dug out a packet of cigarettes, opened the lid, and offered it first to the chief. Rather than taking one, he snatched the whole pack. He gave one cigarette to each of his men and pocketed the remaining fifteen.

'Je suis satisfait. Au revoir!' he said, and they left.

I was irritable and Archie tried to placate me; it was only a packet of fags and had cost us very little. Besides, neither of us smoked and they had been bought specifically to mollify potentially difficult men. However, it was more than that. It was a perfect analogy for one of Africa's biggest problems: the headman culture; the concept that a single man, born into his position, can take 75 per cent of what is given to a group. The uneven distribution that we witnessed repeatedly at village level was a microcosm of what was continually enacted at government level across the continent, and many places elsewhere. This feudalism had an insidious stranglehold on one billion people's potential for prosperity.

A day later we were treated to a much more positive experience when Moïse materialised out of the morning mist, paddling his ancient pirogue, his smile as broad as the river. He began an endless barrage of French-babbling positivity. He shook our hands repeatedly and expressed his amazement and delight to find two foreigners on his river *'dans une pirogue ... comme les Congolais!'*

He spoke nothing of the hardships of a fisherman's life and he asked nothing of us. When he released my hand for the final time and made to leave I gave him my spare pair of sunglasses. Wonder filled his face and he grasped my hand once more.

With no maps or GPS equipment we rarely knew where we were or how far we had travelled. Information from people on the riverbank was usually contradictory or wildly inaccurate. Occasional tracks intersected the river where huge pirogue's ferried people across. However, the people loitering at the crossings always disagreed about how far away key towns lay. I made a ten-mile round trip by bike along one track in search of supplies and was brought before a village official demanding to see papers. Chairs were fetched and I was placed under a mango tree before a semicircle of five officials. A tight ring of 200 incredulous villagers pressed close around us, straining necks to glimpse *le fantôme*: the ghost man.

As we scanned the banks for a camping spot that evening, four men crossing the river spotted us and gave chase. They had lean hunting dogs in their canoe and waved their machetes fiercely in the air, shouting aggressively as they did so. We waved politely and then paddled as hard and fast downriver as we could. For twenty minutes this fearful chase continued with us gaining and then losing distance. Eventually they gave up and turned back. We continued a safe distance around two more bends and camped without a fire, dragging our pirogue out of the water to be less visible.

The river often split into numerous channels winding their way around thickly jungled islands. Edging down an avenue of low-hanging branches with me sitting at the stern, I was suddenly grabbed by the hair and yanked backwards into the water. Archie wheeled around and beat the gentle current to return and free me. It turned out that an abandoned fishhook dangling from a tree had been perfectly placed to snag my hair's sartorially ill-advised topknot. Archie cut the line with a machete and I clambered back into the pirogue. When he went to pull out the hook he found that it had pinned a dried-out frog into my hair – the bait from the abandoned line.

One evening we rounded a bend in the river and were hit

by an unpleasant smell. A large crowd of men on the bank began shouting at us. Not sure what was going on, we quickly paddled past and slipped through a small rapid. When safely distant, we pulled over to ask a man advice for the river ahead. He told us the men up-river were celebrating because they had killed a five-metre crocodile. Apparently crocodiles and hippos were very common downriver, and so no fishermen worked the next stretch of river. He added that there were three large rapids not far away. '*Totalement impassable!*'

We cooked in an unusually cramped camping spot that night. The honking of hippos was audible close at hand and their tracks ran right past our tents, but there had been nowhere else. The fish-like whiff of slain crocodile was a living memory in our noses. Both feeling unnerved, we discussed our options: proceed with extreme caution, backtrack to the last crossing and try to reach a road, or abandon the pirogue and strike inland in search of paths leading to a road of sorts. We talked it back and forth for a long time but eventually settled on proceeding cautiously.

It only took an hour to reach the first rapid in the morning and we had, indeed, not seen a soul along the river. We steered to the left of the many islands and plunged into a dark channel but soon found it blocked and had to laboriously backtrack. The next route we attempted was clear and, bracing waist deep in the pummelling water, we relayed our pirogue past the problem. As we paddled on we looked back at where all of the other routes would have led us. The cataract was a bubbling theatre of spray and foam and thunderous noise.

Another hour of paddling had us standing on another rock staring down yet more white water. We picked a route and again began to relay. However, the water was too fast and too deep, and the rocks too far apart. The current's merciless drag was pulling the pirogue, ripping the ropes from our grips, faster than we could keep up with while hopping dangerously from rock to rock. I was at the back and was losing my grip. If the end of the rope slipped through my fingers the *Lady Lulua* would be carried away with all our belongings and we'd be in serious trouble. I made a decision and shouted to Archie.

'Jump in. I'm losing hold. We have to go!'

We leapt into the pirogue and, hearts in throats, tried to run the frenzied waves in our inflexible tree trunk. All went surprisingly well for 100 metres but then we struck a submerged rock dead on. The pirogue spun side-on to the current, tipped, and filled with water. Somehow it held on the rock and we clung to it, scrabbling for precarious footholds in the chest-deep water.

It was a dire situation – too far from any rock or bank to climb out, floundering in the fastest water we had yet encountered, and with very few options. The current was quickly tiring us. We watched with futility as a paddle and a sleeping mat rose out of the water-filled pirogue and sped away. After ten minutes of yelling and discarding various ideas over the clamour, we realised our only choice. We were weakening and wouldn't be able to hold our positions much longer. I had already lost my footing once and been swept under the pirogue, where I was pinned against the rock for a frightening few seconds before fighting my way to the surface. We looked at the rapids ahead. There was a jagged rock followed by a sizeable drop and then fifty metres of fast, flat water running past an island before the next rapid.

The pirogue started to shift and we knew what we had to do. One well-placed shove was enough to dislodge our canoe before throwing ourselves after her, feet first and face up. Miraculously we rode through the rapid unharmed and immediately began yanking the rope in the direction of the little island. It was frantic but we managed to grab tree branches and haul our way into the eddy at the end of the island. It was crawling with army ants.

Half an hour of swimming across channels and following jungle footpaths revealed several huge and utterly impassable rapids. There was, however, one narrow and potentially passable chute with some nasty falls. We would have to unload our bags and then launch the battle-worn *Lady Lulua* at the gauntlet, hoping she would survive.

On our way back to the island we wondered why there were footpaths and no people. There was even a deep hippo trap dug in the middle of one path with upturned wooden stakes planted in it.

We eventually met three tiny men, who were as shocked to see us as we were pleased to see them. They agreed to help us, and the unloaded pirogue was piloted towards the head of the channel. The strongest of the men aimed our delicate canoe into the thrashing current. Clutching the rope, he leapt from rock to rock, lethally and utterly out of control, as the poor pirogue pinballed down the gauntlet until she came to rest past the rapids, underwater and abused.

We surveyed the damage. The two cracks in the prow had met and the wedge between them was half detached. She floated but was no longer equal to more than fair-weather paddling. We paid our helpers generously and they gave us a poorly woven bamboo paddle to continue with. According to them, that was the last of the big rapids, but we had learned to be wary of advice.

An idyllic island provided us refuge that night. I hadn't felt so worn out in a long time. I was starting to feel weak and achy, with a dim but persistent headache. We were both near our physical limit, covered in cuts, bites, and bruises. But we had made it through another seemingly impossible challenge and felt contented. Noisy hippos surrounded our camp after dark but it was hard to care as we cooked a large dinner and warmed our feet by the fire.

An hour and a half down the misty, eerily quiet river in the morning and we heard the growing roar of rapids. None appeared after rounding several bends but the thundering rose further. Finally, the river cornered and accelerated. We pulled over just in time and rock-hopped around the corner. It became very obvious that our time on the Lulua was at an end; the panorama before us was explicit on that point. There were countless falls and angry explosions where various currents collided. The river splayed widely and dropped forty metres over the course of a ruinous half mile. I couldn't even begin to spot a way down and, truth be told, was too exhausted to care. We had pushed our luck far enough.

There were men nearby collecting an edible weed from the shallows. We offered our pirogue to them in exchange for help portering our belongings to some sort of track where we could load up and push our bicycles.

Before we ducked into the forest and plodded uphill with our column of helpers, Archie and I took one last look at what had been our world for hundreds of miles and almost a month. Together we turned away from the river.

FORTY

GETTING OUT

Oh Congo, what a wreck. It hurts to look and listen.
It hurts to turn away.
- Philip Gourevitch, *The New Yorker,* 2000

The sound of the river, our constant companion for many days, faded behind us. Carrying our bags, Archie and I followed the two men carrying our bicycles along the tight, jungle footpath. We ducked low branches and our clothes snagged on the thorns that sprouted from just about every plant. Two young boys with bamboo fishing rods walked behind us with another bag each. Their quiet chatter accompanied the calming ambience of monkey hoots, bird calls, and falling leaves.

We were unsure where we were, feeling like we had been airdropped in the Congo with battered bicycles and tasked with finding a way out. The accumulated exhaustion of the river's many challenges lapped at our frayed bodies. Like a swelling tide, it threatened to inundate us before we reached a resting place.

As we climbed away from the Lulua, the tall trees, broad palms, and hanging tangles of vines thinned and gave way to bush. Two sweaty hours had passed when the trail widened and we traipsed into a village. A jovial, rotund man placed bamboo chairs under a tree for us to rest. A crowd of children gathered to stare at the two ailing *mzungu.* Apparently it was 100 miles of tracks to the city of Kananga, but a Catholic mission lay at Bilomba, just twenty-five miles away.

We decided to push for Bilomba, where we could have peace and rest without a crowd. Movement was becoming painful. We both bore various cuts and insect bites on our feet, hands, and legs that seemed to be infected and gave us stabbing pains. After a clumsy fall on a slippery rock that morning my right hip had swollen and now throbbed whenever I moved.

We mounted our bicycles and wobbled down the sandy path for the next four hours, often having to push for long stints. Our power waned and the pace slowed. There were frequent villages along the track. Although still pitifully poor, the villagers seemed better off and healthier than the river people. They were taller and wore less-ragged clothes. They had occasional goat, chicken, and cassava in their diet. However, the village markets we passed had little more than a few bundles of cassava leaves on sale.

Arriving at the mission at dusk, we were shown to a damp concrete cell where I collapsed onto the sagging bed and spiralled into a fitful sleep of feverish dreams, including the recurring nightmare of barrelling helplessly down white water. In the dense, unshifting mist of the morning I could barely walk and it was obvious we were going nowhere that day.

We opened, drained, cleaned, and dressed our wounds. Then we hobbled to a bare-shelved shop in our dirty clothes, receiving quizzical looks from people walking to church in their Sunday best. Bilomba was an eerie clutch of poorly built homes and the people traipsing past us were ghostlike in the lingering fog. Doubtless they thought the same of us. From different quarters of the village came Catholic song, fire-and-brimstone evangelical preaching, and the incessant drumming of the more African-adapted churches.

In the afternoon we heard a commotion. A shirtless man ran past the mission shouting and with a wailing woman in close pursuit. The cry was gradually taken up across the village over the following minutes and more people ran past rending their clothes and hair. There rose a general, keening lament that warbled ominously in the air.

We fretted that news had reached the village of a coup, or war, or perhaps the president's death. If that were the case then we could be in trouble. However, one of the Catholic fathers finally informed us casually that an evangelical minister had died.

'*C'est la vie*,' he added and wandered off. The drumming, wailing, and singing of the funeral took place a stone's throw from our room and lasted until after dawn.

Still feeble, but keen to escape Bilomba, we paid the Catholics for the cell and climbed stiffly onto our bikes. We struggled forward for ten miles and reached a scene of wild destruction. The path we had followed abruptly ended in a crowd watching orange hydraulic diggers with Chinese operators tear aggressively at trees, flipping them to the ground like matchsticks. Roads were once again penetrating the depths of central Congo.

The passage in the wake of the diggers resembled a twenty-metre-wide stretch of freshly ploughed beach: soft sand with one thin groove dug by the many bicycles pushed along it. It was harder work than the previous path but we pushed on regardless. On a brief downhill my bicycle frame snapped by the seat post, rendering it unrideable. A few miles on, we came across a lorry headed for Kananga.

The 1970s French military vehicle had been stranded for two days but the oil-smeared men leaning over the engine felt sure it would be running shortly and that they would find space for us on the overloaded roof. I slumped to the floor under a tree and fell asleep instantly. By night the engine had not turned over so we bedded down under the stars. The morning was cold and my head throbbed, while my shivering body ached with fever. Archie and I sat watching the daily life of the surrounding village unfold. A woman racked by malaria sat stoically on the ground next to a fire. Her companion prepared a concoction with some apparently medicinal leaves that the Congolese have used for hundreds of years.

At midday a jeep approached and we flagged a lift to Kananga. Bikes were dumped on the roof and the driver lurched the car into action. He drove as if chased and nearly ran down numerous village children. When we reached Kananga and he deposited us outside the largest Greek Orthodox church in Africa, it was all I could do to not lie down in the dust and surrender to unconsciousness.

We had been instructed by a friend in Lubumbashi to go to the Greek mission and give his name. However, they had never heard of him and Archie was told there was no space for us. Phone calls were made and the senior priest, a charming Congolese man called Kallinique, arranged for his English-speaking brother, Stefan, to drive us to the Catholic mission. His car had a Greek icon dangling from the rear-view mirror.

Unwashed and racked by shooting pains, I lay on the bed that the Catholics led me to. I had two conflicting physical sensations: my leaden body weighed an inestimable amount and was immovable, and yet my legs had withered to sharp, bony appendages that grated teeth-grittingly against one another. As sleep and dreams came and went, blurring together, my fevered mind grappled vainly for reality. I had cold sweats and hot shivers. I couldn't eat. Archie sat beside my bed at mealtimes, torn between sympathy for me and delight at the mission kitchen's hearty and varied fare.

Stefan returned with a nurse called Martin and a malaria diagnostic kit. My finger was pricked and a drop of blood squeezed onto the test strip.

'You are malaria!' he exclaimed as the first indication bar showed red. After a few seconds he looked again.

'Eh! You are *very* malaria!' The second bar had coloured; I had *falciparum malaria*, also known as 'malignant malaria'. It is the deadliest parasite in humans, killing half a million every year, and can even develop into blood cancer.

A quinine drip was plugged into my arm by Martin, who didn't believe in swabbing skin or using a fresh needle for the next IV. He once even blew on the needle to remove dust. Four hours of drug infusion ensued while I lay breathing heavily in my sweaty cot, my ribs jutting through my sallow skin. Rolling over in bed left me breathless for minutes and visiting the toilet was a mammoth undertaking. Long-suffering Archie as good as carried me down the corridor.

After another quinine hit in the morning, Martin and Stefan said I should be up and about by evening.

'Malaria go away now! Don't rest. Don't sleep more. It is

finished!'

Indeed, I did feel stronger for a time and even ate some lunch, but by evening I was fading again. In the morning a different blood test returned a verdict of typhoid fever on top of the malaria. There followed five more days of Martin's Russian-roulette intravenous antibiotic drips.

Slowly my appetite and strength returned. I could walk outside to sit in the sunlight and could even read a book. The infected wounds were healing and the fading fever dreams even put an end to the night terrors of piloting pirogues through impossible waters. After the last drip we took Stefan and Martin out for beers to thank them. Their care and patience had meant a lot to me and I gave them each some money. They both got drunk and when they dropped us back at the mission Martin locked his lips onto mine for a second before I could push him away. I pitied him – he was due to be married a month later and revealing his sexuality would likely get him killed.

During my convalescence, we vaguely planned to take a train onwards and then a barge down the Congo river. However, we learned that it could take a month to reach Kinshasa this way and cycling would take a similar amount of time. I was in no condition to ride and our visas were running short. The only remaining option was to take lorries.

We climbed onto the roof of an impressively overloaded lorry along with fifty others at about 5 p.m. and it set off three hours later. Our crowded, six-metre-high perch was regularly raked by low tree branches and we clung to whatever we could to avoid being thrown off as the lorry pitched and lurched along the uneven track.

We held on in the moonlight for several hours until the engine coughed to a halt. It had grown cold and many of the passengers climbed down to light fires. We crawled into sleeping bags and slept in furrows dug by the wheels. Several hours later the lorry was moving again.

We broke down several more times. The sandy mud road was appalling and the driver, Charles, said the 700-mile journey to Kinshasa takes a month in the rainy season. At 2 a.m. on the second night, we stopped among a tiny group of huts and each found a patch of dirt to sleep on until sunrise.

When we pulled into Tshikapa, we paid passage on another lorry with no cargo and only people sitting in the open-air, metal-walled and -floored back. More and more people paid up and joined us but the lorry didn't start. The caged roof was increasingly covered over with water containers and other items of cargo. Darkness fell. More and more people clambered into our metallic prison. Space was at a premium and tempers flared. Men began arguing, and then fighting. More cargo, mostly heavy sacks, were hoisted blindly into the back. These heavy sacks were thrown back and forth across the human press onto the unsuspecting heads of men, women and children. We still hadn't set off and yet more people climbed in.

Our cattle cart eventually started on the road long after dark, with anger still boiling over. Everybody was uncomfortably squeezed but some had more space than others and wouldn't surrender it. There was a complete absence of cooperation to the detriment of all. The driver pushed the lorry's accelerator to its limit. With each violent lurch of the road, the unsettled human traffic was thrown into disarray. Sometimes we were all hefted into the air before crashing down in a jumble of bruised bodies. Spats resumed and fists flew. The only light came from occasionally flashing torches or phone screens. I saw a man thump an old woman's head and a small child was bodily thrown a couple of metres onto a tangle of knees, heads, and elbows.

The frequently urinating elderly woman next to me pinched and twisted the flesh on my leg that was pressed against her. I was unable to move as I had a woman and child jammed against my other side. A bald man with sharp-edged shoes butted the side of my head with the back of his own from time to time in a bid to win more space. That night of shouting and crying and punching and pissing and darkness ranks among the worst of my life. The total abandonment of human feeling hacked at my frayed heartstrings. In that lorry I pitied and hated all the passengers. I was disgusted.

We stopped in the small hours and a drunk policeman demanded $30 from Archie and me. In my rattled state I was aggressively forthright, demanding his name and badge number. We eventually got away without paying and snatched a couple of hours sleep in the glorious space outside the lorry. Most of the miserably huddled passengers remained in their crushed positions, reluctant to concede hard-won space. The smell of sweat, piss, and vomit was overwhelming to me but they endured.

For the second day Archie and I coughed up for one cramped spot in the cabin and took turns to escape the hellish back. We stopped often to take on yet more cargo and passengers. The road was the worst I had seen. In one place it was a five-metre deep canyon, sheer and narrow, carved through the mud hillside by lorries and undoubtedly impassable during the monsoon. At a river crossing another lorry got stuck in mud and a digger came to the rescue only to get stuck itself. It flailed its two hydraulic buckets, front and back, wildly like a fish caught in a net.

At length we reached tarmac, darkness fell, and we swept into Kikwit. We were too late for the onward night bus to Kinshasa so bedded down beside the road again. Our bicycles had been strapped to the roof cage and sat on for many bumpy hours, leaving wheels warped and frames bent. We whiled away the day until our evening departure on a tarmac road. The bus had narrow allocated spaces on hard wooden benches and windows that didn't close. It felt so luxurious that I didn't mind the frequent urine running down onto me from the goats tethered on the roof.

After twelve hours we reached the hubbub of Kinshasa, a world away from the Lulua. The wide streets were crowded with food vendors, music stalls, and commuting crowds of tall people wearing new clothes. We made our way to the empty apartment of a friend where we took hot showers and used shampoo for the first time in two months.

After gazing at our hollowed eyes and prominent ribs in the mirror, we switched on BBC World Service: Israel had invaded Gaza with thousands dead; the horror in Syria rumbled on relentlessly; Ebola showed no signs of slowing its rampage across West Africa; and the Commonwealth Games in Glasgow were about to begin. We both felt lost.

That evening we were taken out for a beer by a Red Cross worker. It happened to be Belgian National Day and we soon found ourselves smartly dressed in borrowed clothes attending an elegant soirée with a couple of hundred people at the Belgian ambassador's residence.

The following morning we stepped outside to find the city had shut down. Soldiers were patrolling the pavements and tanks rolled down the roads, restoring order after a failed coup attempt. The news channels informed us that twenty men armed with machetes had stormed the barracks of the presidential guard but had been overpowered.

FORTY-ONE

MUD PIT

Travelling – it leaves you speechless, then turns you into a storyteller.
- Ibn Battuta

Archie flew back to Cape Town and I recuperated for two weeks, eating and sleeping as much as possible. I found a welder to fix Little Bastard and obtained my next two visas. A ferry bore me across the two-mile-wide Congo river shortly above where it narrows and crashes down the furious 220-mile-long Livingstone Falls (so named by Stanley) to the Atlantic: probably the world's most formidable cataracts.

I disembarked in Brazzaville, the capital of the neighbouring Republic of Congo. It was much smaller than Kinshasa and less developed, likely because of the many well-funded NGOs working on the humanitarian crises in the DRC. However, it wasn't always the lesser neighbour and for two years after the Nazi invasion of France, Brazzaville was the capital of the Free France government in exile, although the leaders all remained in London.

During the one day I spent in the city I noticed the large number of Chinese people living there. I watched as a Chinese shopkeeper served his Chinese customer, who walked outside, climbed into his Chinese car, and drove away on the Chinese-built road. He was presumably heading to his job on one of the many Chinese construction projects in the area. The country was formerly known as The People's Republic of Congo, so China's interest *could* have been ideological. However, I suspected that the huge, timber-rich country, almost as large as Germany but with only 4 million people, had other attractions for savvy eastern investors. It is also said that many of the Chinese workers in Africa are convicts serving out their sentences in exile. Today's Africa is rumoured to be for China what yesterday's Australia was for England.

The road out of town followed the river east, leading me past a half-built stadium with colourful Chinese characters over the entrance. Then it turned north and away from the powerful, brown river towards rolling, open farmland. It was the 1,500th day since I left home and I felt sluggish. My legs were heavy as I fought to shake the swampy lethargy that settled over me while recovering from fever.

While watching a horizon glowing with slash-and-burn farming on the second evening, I decided *I* needed a baptism of fire to shake my bodily stupor – to forcibly toughen myself up and become road-hardened once more. I began waking before dawn to pull long days: 65 miles, 80 miles, 95 miles, 105 miles. My angry body resentfully rebooted each morning as I fuelled it with slurps of strong black coffee. It was filtered through a torn-off scrap of t-shirt and drunk with pragmatic joylessness. My two-week visa was tight and the 750 miles to Cameroon had to be covered one way or another.

Villages of concrete buildings with sheet metal roofs drifted through my periphery. The clusters of adobe, palm-thatched huts across the river in the DRC were nowhere to be seen and people wore newer, brighter clothing. Yet I also saw a woman selling little twists of torn up plastic bags, each holding six or seven pieces of penne pasta. Outside of the capital, the Republic of Congo may have seemed less destitute than its vast, self-mutilating neighbour, however, the two civil wars of the 1990s that flattened much of Brazzaville were still fresh in the memory and the country remained fragile.[51]

I crossed a cool, high plateau on a good road with light traffic. The steady stream of passing Chinese in 4x4s gawped

[51] A few years after independence from France in 1960, the country was rebranded the People's Republic of Congo and developed ties with the USSR, Maoist China, North Korea, and North Vietnam. Cuban troops trained the army well and the self-proclaimed Marxist–Leninist regime survived numerous attempted coups. After the break-up of the USSR, elections were held and the two ensuing civil wars were predictable power struggles between rival factions.

at my anomalous appearance. Chinese dominance was not complete, however. Village shops were nearly all owned and run by Mauritanian Arabs who sat on high stools behind their counters. They mostly sneered at my attempts at conversation until I mentioned that I had visited their country. They then soliloquised about the beauty of their land and the degradation of their adopted country; an expatriate pastime the world over.

After watching a mist-blurred moonset one morning, I descended from the plateau into dense rainforest choked by humidity. Across the Alima river I had expected to find a northern Congolese city, but on arrival in Oyo's centre I found myself in a replica of the homogenous county towns that I had come to know in China, with its familiar layout of government buildings with blue roofs and white-tiled walls surrounded by knee-high white metal fences. There was the familiar half-hearted topiary and needlessly wide streets with the same blue signs. Apart from the Africans milling around, I could have been in a freshly laid coal mining town in Hunan province.

A Congolese man I asked said that part of the town was indeed planned by Chinese architects and that the many Chinese men were either installing an electrical grid or exporting countless tonnes of immensely valuable timber to China. Many lorries had been passing me on the road, each with three or four vast trunks of mahogany or other hardwood ratcheted onto their extra-long flatbeds.

The Chinese are not the only ones investing in Congo. I chatted with the night watchman of a Malaysian-funded palm oil plantation. Regis said with surprising pride that there were tens of thousands of trees and the project had been running for over twenty-five years. He liked working for the Malaysians. He thought they made more effort to communicate on common grounds. The Chinese did not deign to learn French or Lingala, preferring instead to send a few bright Congolese to China to learn basic Mandarin.

I stopped at a road-building camp for water one day. The Chinese workers gave me a beer and chuckled at my misremembered Mandarin language. They were interested to see a European passport and when I showed them, one pointed out that it was my twenty-seventh birthday. I had forgotten. We drank another beer and they warned me about deteriorating road conditions ahead. I cycled on in a cheery mood. Despite the arguably neo-colonial policies of the Chinese government, the individuals shipped overseas, convicts or not, were just simple people and as friendly as any of the smiling villagers I met during my ride through China.

The dire tracks that I'd been warned of soon became reality. My progress slowed and I was forced to carefully extend my visa expiry date with a ballpoint pen. At some point I crossed the equator but there was no sign marking it. The path rolled and pitched onwards over short, tightly packed hills divided by small, fresh streams. Bridges were simply made from fallen tree trunks. I pressed along these mud tracks, only stopping briefly to eat or rest.

Boys with rudimentary hunting spears made mock-threatening gestures as I passed and then returned my broad grin with thumbs up. They were always accompanied by hunting dogs and often had a dead bush buck or duiker slung across their back.

I passed roadside Pygmy villages nestled in small, carefully maintained forest clearings. The short, jaunty people grinned at me while carrying cassava, bushmeat or firewood to and fro in small wicker backpacks. I never received the brusque shouts for attention in Pygmy villages that I'd become used to in most of Africa. There was an endearing quietness and gentleness about them.

On a couple of mornings I spotted fresh elephant prints plodding alongside me on the muddy track. The elusive forest elephants are much smaller than their savannah-dwelling cousins, but each footprint was still big enough for me to sit in. Apparently chimpanzees and lowland gorillas were common in the area too but kept well-hidden because of hunting.

In one village an old, mud-caked Peugeot stood with its open boot displaying a range of bushmeat on sale: knee-high antelopes, various monkeys, jungle cats, snakes, porcupines, and slender ferret-like creatures I didn't recognise. The smoked monkeys' flesh was burned back from grimacing teeth and looked shockingly similar to a human child. The charred gums and sinister, silent scream haunted my mind's eye for a couple of days.

The first heavy rain of the monsoon season caught me by surprise. I sat on the forest floor with my tent's flysheet draped over me for ninety minutes while the mud turned to sludge.

The daytime jungle had a pleasant, soothing soundscape but at night it rose to an unnerving cacophony of shrieks, hoots, screeches and grunts of every kind imaginable. Unseen nocturnal creatures were all around, their calls often accompanied by scuffling near my tent or thunderous crashes through the branches overhead. The sheer volume and density of life was as impressive as it was intimidating, and the frenzied calls in the darkness had an edge of insanity. I was often glad of the familiar, ordered confines of my tent. Camping spots were easy enough to find but large ants diligently found holes in the tent and trooped inside to bite me. Their mandibles remained resolutely locked in my skin when I yanked them off.

The second downpour of the season effectively wrote off the track, as a slippery course of deep, churned, red clay was all that was left. Two cars and the handful of motorbikes I encountered were utterly stuck, some having slipped off into the trees. It soon became impossible to even push Little Bastard, as clumps of sticky mud jammed the wheels. I began to porter my saddle bags on foot in two loads, two at a time, returning a third time to carry the bike. My bare feet plunged and squelched in the sucking, ankle-deep surface. For a whole day I walked back and forth, five miles for every one mile of progress, along the final stretch to the border post.

The Congolese immigration official giggled at my mud-smeared appearance. His dilapidated hut had no power and he logged my illicitly altered visa details in a dusty ledger using the light from his mobile phone. I carried my kit uphill a few hundred yards along the deserted jungle track, again in three loads, before pitching my tent on higher, drier ground at last.

Stateless pigmies lived in the handful of sylvan villages lining the twenty miles of no-man's land between the Republic of Congo and Cameroon. The free-roaming villagers hunted and gathered where they pleased, paying no heed to the white man's imposition of borders.

I was muddy and shirtless when I rounded a corner and arrived at the collapsing hut housing Cameroonian immigration. An immaculately dressed guard stepped out.

'How dare you arrive like that! What if there were women here? Go! Go away and dress,' he yelled in throaty French.

I wheeled Little Bastard back around the corner to dress. While doing so two women emerged from the bushes with water containers on their heads. They wandered past the guard's hut with bare breasts swinging freely.

At lunch I finished my little remaining food. I had no map, no food, and no idea where I would next find a shop. The sticky humidity was intensified by the close-pressed trees of the imposingly dense jungle.

I was experiencing hunger cramps when I arrived at a traffic jam. Ten or so lorries were backed up, each with formidable trunks of African hardwood strapped to their backs. Men with trousers rolled to the knees milled around wondering what to do. The path had again become a cloying pit of rich red mud. I watched as some of the lorries wiggled hopelessly halfway into the foliage in their attempts to escape. The twenty-tonne vehicles slid slowly, helplessly sideways while their wheels spun uselessly, spraying the assembled with mud.

Word got around that I was hungry and various biscuits and bananas were forced into my hands by smiling, insistent men. I struck up a conversation with Gilbert, who was driving a van with four-wheel drive that was managing better with the mud. He was a friendly man in his thirties from the small Anglophone area in Cameroon's west. Gilbert was on his way back to the capital, having delivered barrels of petrol to power generators in the remote region's various telecommunications towers.

It was clear that I couldn't cycle the track and reports of the next fifty miles were similar. I didn't fancy 250 miles of portage and so gladly accepted a space in Gilbert's empty vehicle. We skidded left and right across the path for three hours. When the track improved I got back on the bike and bought some smoked bushmeat in a village for my dinner. It looked like wild venison but I couldn't be sure.

The path climbed and the jungle thinned as I neared more populous parts of the country. On the outskirts of Sangmélima I was waved over by a Middle-Eastern man in a faded blue overall. Hamid was an Iranian sent by his government to construct the new road. He gave me a tight hug and the traditional Persian triple kiss when I produced a few Farsi pleasantries. He asked me where I was going and I told him Nigeria. Frowning, Hamid told me he heard something on the radio that morning. There had been a number of fatal cases of Ebola in Lagos and Cameroon had officially closed all borders with Nigeria.

Eager to get online, I pedalled fast towards the capital, wondering what other routes across West Africa might be open to me. There were frequent roadblocks on the way into Yaoundé. At each I was stopped and my passport was closely scrutinised by policemen. They treated me with high suspicion and many asked absurd questions about being a terrorist or carrying concealed weapons. The capital was on high security alert after recent cross-border raids made by the fundamentalist Islamic group Boko Haram. To the eyes of Cameroonian policemen my burned and bearded face looked Arabian. As I cycled through the suburbs, many people shouted 'Boko Haram' at me; some in jest, others less so.

Yaoundé's only campsite was deserted. The large, officious woman in charge chanted a catechism of rules at me and then suggested I pitch my tent as close to the building as possible because Boko Haram had recently made night-time attacks in the area.

In an internet café I assessed my options. I had reached a geopolitical cul de sac: Nigeria's border was closed due to Ebola, Chad's thanks to Boko Haram, and Central African Republic's because of civil war. I had no choice except to fly. But to where? Emails trickled in from family and friends suggesting I head to Morocco, to Spain, or straight to England. Five months after the disease first appeared, the Ebola panic had finally gone global. Many European airlines were cancelling all flights to the region, and some people in the UK thought that it wasn't safe to be anywhere on the entire continent of Africa.

I considered flying to Ghana and continuing through Burkina Faso and Mali. However, Mali was also gripped by an Islamist insurgency and countries across West Africa had closed their borders or were threatening to. If I became stranded again, my withered finances simply wouldn't stretch to a second flight. I eventually caved in to logic and booked a flight to Senegal from Douala in western Cameroon.

The two-day cycle to Douala was an exercise in self-justification. I busied my mind with laboured arguments to excuse the upcoming flight over West Africa. Somehow disease and war weren't sufficient reasons to me. I had been through plenty of dangerous areas on my journey and they had proved some of the most interesting and rewarding. Perhaps I was getting soft, or lazy, or was simply ready to go home after four years of homeless roaming.

By the time I had dismantled my bike and checked it in at the airport I was feeling low. I had somehow failed myself. Dakar to England seemed a cheat – a short hop across the Sahara, Spain, and France when I should be slogging through West Africa's diverse mosaic of places and peoples. It might have been my only option, but it was an easy option and I had taken it. I was irritable and fidgety in the departure gate, pacing back and forth.

The plane took off and I put my MP3 player onto

'shuffle' mode. We climbed into low, grey cloud. As the plane broke through to the serene world of blue and pillowy white above, *The Swan* by Camille Saint-Saëns struck up in my earphones. The tranquillity outside the window twinned fittingly with the beautifully mournful cello strains. I exhaled. What did it all matter? I was on the plane to Senegal and that was that. Better make the best of it. I slouched comfortably in my seat and fell asleep.

FORTY-TWO

DESERT RAIN

There are now more slaves on this planet than at any time in human history.
- Foreign Policy Magazine, 2008

Loic was waiting at the airport in Dakar. We had met briefly in Southwest China three years earlier and he'd slurred over the umpteenth watery beer that I should get in touch if I made it to Senegal. He was a short, bouncy Frenchman with an impish smile, a heavy-duty accent, and a wonderfully uneven mullet.

I assembled my bicycle on the roadside and followed him on his motorbike. Located on the fringe of the Sahara, Dakar was a world away from the tropical lushness of Central Africa. The sun-bleached streets were strewn with sand and plied by emaciated horses pulling makeshift carts. Many of the 95 per cent Muslim population wore longer, more conservative clothing.

We dumped my kit in Loic's home and headed to a reggae party with Rose, his friend visiting from Burkina Faso where he had lived for seven years. We spent the warm night dancing on an outdoor basketball court in a thick fug of sweat and cannabis smoke. We got home at 5 a.m., took sleeping mats onto the roof, and gazed blankly at the paling stars until the sun rose and forced our retreat to the cool of the floor tiles inside.

I spent a week with Loic getting to know and like him. We explored the city together, drank beer with his friends, and shared the stories of our lives with each other. One afternoon we picked our way through back streets to a run-down beach at the westernmost point of mainland Africa that was formerly owned by Club Med. When it was time to leave the city I hugged my new friend goodbye. I was excited to truly be on the home straight and he was looking forward to an upcoming visit from an Ethiopian woman with whom he had had a son. He felt optimistic that he would convince them to move to Dakar so he could be a part of his son's life. Loic said he intended to visit London soon so we parted with *à plus tard*.

The route out of the haphazard city was busy and confusing. I accidentally cycled onto a motorway and was stopped at a toll gate. The two guards said I'd broken the law and that the police were on their way. I was ordered to lean my bike against the wall and wait. Looking around, I saw that the men had no car. I couldn't afford to be fined so took a running start, jumped onto Little Bastard and pedalled as fast as possible. I raced onwards for half an hour before ducking into a mosque and chatting with the imam until I deemed it safe to rejoin the road.

A hot, vigorous headwind sprang up that I knew I would be battling for the next 2,000 miles. Making the most of the cooler evenings, I rode on through dusk and into the dark along rutted back roads. Northern Senegal became increasingly dry and barren; the temperature rose to 40°C and the landscape teetered on desert with short, tough trees and occasional patches of laboriously won cultivation. Pastoralists wearing beards, skullcaps, and long, striped robes ambled behind their skinny flocks. I was reminded of images of seventh-century Arabia from an illustrated children's Koran I once thumbed through.

I reached the border town of Rosso and paid a boatman £1 to ferry me across the Senegal River to Mauritania, the lesser known of the world's four Islamic Republics. The visa officer told me to wait and then slept in front of me for two hours. He then stood up, announced that his lunch hour had arrived, and wandered off. Ninety minutes later he greeted me as if we had never met and stamped a visa into my passport.

On the north side of the border were a lot of Arab men wearing pale blue *daraas*; baggy robes worn over baggy cotton trousers with billowing crotches. Large, patchwork tents and semi-permanent lean-tos dotted the sand dunes through which the road carved passage. Hardy, skinny goats bleated as they stood on their hind legs to reach the higher greenery on nearly bare bushes. The wind intensified, the bushes disappeared, and all was sand. The Sahara proper had begun.

The following afternoon a great black storm rose out of the north and began rolling towards me, growing taller every minute. With nowhere to shelter I sped towards it with rising excitement. There was a seductive sense of insanity about flying as fast as my adrenalin-spun legs would take me, hurtling pell-mell at a dark, towering horizon, strobed with lightning. I thrashed maniacally at the pedals with total abandon, primal stupidity driving me hard into a wind starting to fleck with the coming downpour's vanguard. Just as the horizontal raindrops swelled and began to explode on my face and chest, I spotted a nomadic tent and dragged my bike across the sand to it.

The veiled mother and her three young children inside were just finishing securing their canvas home against the coming tempest. They seemed utterly unsurprised at my arrival and welcomed me with a bowl of honey-sweetened camel milk. The wind flapped and whipped and snapped at the tent and thunder cracked overhead so loud it could be felt through the ground. The violence of the storm was thrilling. The children yelled *Allah u Akbar* jubilantly after each deafening peal of thunder. Their mother rocked back and forth on a three-legged stool, muttering invocations to her God and fingering her prayer beads.

Finally the fury waned. I thanked my hosts and rejoined a shimmering, rain-polished road. The deliciously cool aftermath coaxed me on and I neared the Atlantic. A salt tinged breeze buffeted my left side and, exhausted, I finally pitched my tent on a rare patch of baked dirt.

I slept deeply and woke early to a bewitching stillness; a rarity in the wind-raked Sahara. Sitting beside my tent, I drank coffee and chewed bread by moonlight before sensing an electricity in the air. The stillness grew ominous and I turned to look over my shoulder. Another vertiginous storm stack was racing out of the horizon and soon blotted out the moon. I pegged my flysheet over the tent and crawled inside to await more madness.

The early pitter-patter lasted just moments before escalating to a deafening drumming. I sat upright bracing against the bending windward side of my tired tent. Soon the ground water began to rise and before long I was hunched in a whirlwind of spray with my camera and MP3 player perched on my knees. The water rose to 20 centimetres before the torrent abated. I emerged into the dawn to find dry land just ten metres away. I had camped in a puddle in which goat droppings were bobbing about.

Later that day I reached the ugly outskirts of Nouakchott. The loose-knit buildings were strewn on the sand like toy building blocks. The centre was no prettier. Dusty, baking, and beige, the capital is inexplicably built three miles from the coast, where the desert's heat blast is untempered by Atlantic airstreams.

I had disliked Nouakchott on my previous visit and disliked it again. The sense of social and racial hierarchy was still apparent and painful. Mauritania forms the western extent of the large and blurred border between black sub-Saharan Africa and Arab North Africa. There is a long and culturally ingrained history of slavery in the country, with slave status inherited from generation to generation.

Unsurprisingly it is the black African population that has traditionally been enslaved. The lighter skinned *Beydan,* ethnic Berbers or mixed-race Berber-Arabs, were the slave masters. The slaves were darker-skinned *Haratin*, or 'black Moors', who were descended from sub-Saharan Africans captured on slaving raids over the centuries. In 1981 Mauritania became the last country in the world to abolish slavery, but the abolition was nominal and slave-owning was only criminalised in 2007. In 2012 it was estimated that between 10 and 20 per cent of the population, possibly as many as 680,000 people, were still living in slavery.[52]

---

[52] Estimate by the UN's special rapporteur on contemporary slavery. In 2018 Global Slavery Index updated this to 2 per cent, or roughly 90,000

Beyond the city limits there were no more buildings or nomadic tents. Occasional checkpoints were manned by friendly policemen who tried to insist I camp near them for security reasons. But I was more drawn to the desolate emptiness of the open desert. I started rising at 3 a.m. to utilise the cooler, less wind-blighted night hours. There were no more rainstorms but the winds remained fierce.

One afternoon a windstorm caught me in the open while cycling along a dirt track. Dust and sand whipped violently off the ground and I felt abused by the time I reached shelter in a tiny hut attending a telecoms mast. I took refuge with two men who seemed to be living there. They welcomed me in and I managed a cup of tea before collapsing into several hours of sleep on the floor. We had to dig our way out through a waist-deep drift after the storm.

Another day brought me to the border where I crossed the three miles of roadless no-man's land, keeping as close to the tyre tracks as possible. The area was an active minefield after a 1970s conflict with Morocco, and a number of twisted, burned-out vehicle husks lay abandoned on their sides.

Just past the border post the first kilometre marker of a long road announced the distance to Tangiers as 2,337 kilometres (1,452 miles). From there I could finally board a ferry to Europe.

---

people. The government's official line is that there is no longer any slavery in the country. However, to date more anti-slavery activists have been jailed than slave owners.

FORTY-THREE

ALL ROADS END

The whole object of travel is not to set foot on foreign land; it is at last to set foot in one's own country as a foreign land.
- Gilbert K. Chesterton

The next day I fell into a punishing routine that I maintained for two weeks across the Sahara. An alarm woke me at midnight. The wind that had blasted out of the north for eons had completed its nightly ritual of softening to a stiff breeze. I had slept in the open as dust and sand always found ways into the tent anyway.

Breakfast was a triangle of processed cheese scraped over a dry, stiff hunk of bread. I forced it down with frugal sips of water. Excepting the wind's eternal whoosh, there was no sound. After eating I allowed myself a few minutes of lying back to star gaze. There probably wasn't a cloud or electric light for 100 miles and it was tempting to stay and stare and snooze again. But I didn't. I packed up and mounted my cumbersome bicycle.

With the moon over my shoulder I slowly chased my soft shadow into the wind. The pace was frustrating but better than during the windier daytime. The surrounding landscape was a muddle of eerie shapes in the darkness, all sculpted linearly north to south by the eternal gales.

At 6 a.m. I watched the east lighten and spun onwards through the dawn as the rest of the sky faded into focus. The heat was rising and the wind rearing up. The east was no longer a shifting transfusion of rich reds and oranges; there remained only the pale, heat-singed hue of a bleached desert horizon. I forced my complaining legs to complete the last of the day's sixty miles while the whitewashed kilometre stones gave an agonisingly slow countdown to the Mediterranean.

At 8 a.m. I wheeled Little Bastard off the road to shelter behind a rock. I scraped more plastic cheese over more stale bread and ate it before dozing on the dust until the afternoon heat woke me. The sun set and the land cooled: I set my midnight alarm and slept again.

There were very few people in Western Sahara, the southern half of Morocco. Larger than the United Kingdom, it is home to only half a million people. The territory is a disputed breakaway state partially controlled by the self-proclaimed Sahrawi Arab Democratic Republic. The Sahrawi's Polisario Front claimed independence after Spanish withdrawal in 1975, just as Morocco and Mauritania launched military bids for the region. The Mauritanians soon withdrew and Morocco occupied the bulk of the territory. They built a 1,700-mile-long, three-metre-high wall with military posts at every third mile to keep the nomadic Sahrawis out.

For the last forty years the Polisario Front have continued an Algerian-backed guerrilla insurgency, launching occasional strikes from the tiny strip of land left to them in the east. The dispute has left the area peppered with an estimated 5 million landmines. The minefields are mostly near the wall, but still I never ventured far from the safety of the road.

A village or petrol station every 250 miles allowed me to replenish supplies. Now and then I spotted military tents and got water from the soldiers policing smuggling on the bleak Atlantic coastline that I was loosely tracing.

As the days wore on and my energy faded, I fought to steer my internal monologue away from despondency. For the first time in four years I indulged in fantasies of the comforts that awaited me upon homecoming. These thoughts made me live even less in the moment and made the joyless desert cycling seem yet more pointless and painful. My mood plummeted.

One morning I approached a concrete building with weathered walls. Dogs burst aggressively from the gate but a man also appeared and waved me over. Ashraf spoke a little French and invited me into the cool building. His job was to drive a digger along a stretch of road each day and keep the sand dunes from creeping across the tarmac. He said he was relatively well-paid but it was a lonely existence. I studied his face as he spoke. A nasty knife wound ran from above his right eye to the left corner of his mouth and deep red scar tissue swelled from within it. He seemed grateful for company but noticed my heavy eyelids and set me up on a carpet with a cushion for a pillow. Glad to be out of the wind, I dropped to the floor and slept right through the day and the night. Ashraf baked bread and cooked freshly caught fish for breakfast. He reached out to shake my hand when I was about to leave; I hugged him instead. He had taken me into his hermitage and shown me kindness when I was close to breaking point and needed it most. I pedalled slowly into the wind throughout that day but didn't mind so much.

Once I left Western Sahara the towns became more frequent and the desert less barren. The wind lessened slightly too and the late-September temperature was balmy. I stopped for an hour most days at small cafés to drink cheap coffee and use the WiFi. I began to reconnect with the world, bingeing on the news and emailing friends and family. A time and date was set for my homecoming.

One morning I left the main road and spent two days winding through brown, rocky hills on dirt tracks. There were hidden valleys with simple villages of dry-stone walls. Goatherds lazed under olive trees and un-scarfed women hauled buckets of water from ancient wells. In the quaint little mosques wizened imams were always keen to chat over cups of mint tea. Each village had a shop offering fresh plums, olives, tomatoes, limes, coriander, and peppers. I ate well, washed in rivers and camped where I pleased. It was a beautiful, ramshackle, fairytale land.

The first big city, Agadir, was a shock. I wandered along the beach dumbstruck by the alarming acreage of sunburned European buttock on display. Tourists swam in clinging bikinis unaware of the covered local women frowning at them. Skinny Moroccan boys with heavily gelled quiffs peacocked back and forth, flirting with overweight western women at least twenty years their senior. I stayed less than an hour before continuing northward to camp happily on a hill and watch the sea mist roll in.

I felt the lure of Europe and the pull of home ever stronger. Casablanca kept me only a day and the capital, Rabat, flashed by with little more than a stroll through the carpet market. I entered Tangiers and didn't dismount until I reached the port's ticket office. Ten minutes later I boarded a ferry. Standing on the deck I once again listened to *The Swan*, while watching Morocco shrink.

Riding down the ramp onto Spanish tarmac was a euphoric moment. I grinned uncontrollably. After a quick supermarket stop I made a sharp hill climb and found my way to a hidden ledge. As I sat beside the tent eating a baguette crammed with chorizo and blue cheese, I looked across the water at Africa. It was still so close – only ten miles away – but in my mind I had already left it far behind. I raised a bottle of cheap rioja to my lips.

Gibraltar was an odd place; a corner of caricature Englishness at the foot of Spain. I arrived in the evening to meet my friend Jamie, who would cycle with me for two weeks. We drank tepid pints of Old Speckled Hen in a pub called The Lord Nelson. The drunk teenagers loitering outside market square pubs in ill-fitting clothes were a strangely nostalgic sight.

The road swept us into the hills. It was late October but the weather was still hot in Andalucía. The climbs were steep and exhausting but the descents were life-affirming. We slept outside every night under twisting old olive trees in groves that spread across the ruptured landscape as far as the eye could see. We sat and talked by small campfires deep into each night after huge meals washed down with sangria, beer, or whisky.

The pretty towns were all perched protectively high on steep-sided hills, a legacy of the eighth-century Umayyad conquest, when the majority of Spain fell under Muslim rule for 700 years. The narrow, cobbled streets were busy in the mornings with old women, often in shawls, walking back and forth to market. However, from lunch until 6 p.m. every town was silent and all shops shut. We looked for benches or shaded grass on which to rest and while away the warm afternoons, submitting to somnolence with the rest of the country. The capital was less sleepy but still saw a marked lull during the siesta.

Autumn arrived beyond Madrid. The days grew shorter as we probed further north. We began sleeping in the tent and had our first frost. The trees blazed with the fiery colours of decay but the crisp, cloudless skies remained.

We pushed on to Pamplona, where the rain began and accompanied us throughout the descent from the central Spanish plateau, down to the coast and into France. Jamie flew home from Biarritz. Our fortnight together had been the perfect decompression for me after a lonely and gruelling last few months in Africa. I found myself again able to relish the things I'd increasingly begun to endure rather than enjoy; I felt my jaded edges softening.

My African wardrobe of shorts, sandals and vest became insufficient, and two or three days of shivering through rain and hailstones led me to a charity shop where I bought a pair of chequered trousers, some canvas shoes, and a hat, all for €4. I looked absurd but was down to my last £80 and it was all I could find. I could no longer afford occasional cups of coffee or tea as an excuse to sit in the warmth of cafés and chase the chill from my frame. My sleeping bag was for summer but November rolled on and the cold, damp nights were wretched. I even locked myself into a heated public toilet one night in an Aquitanian market town.

I rested in Paris for a day with a Frenchman who grew up in the DRC and had been following my blog. It rained, and I rested, and the sights remained unseen. By the time I sped into Calais, excitement had been building for several days and I headed straight for the port. I'd kindly been given a complimentary ferry crossing and was welcomed aboard personally by the captain. In the Club Lounge I was treated to a champagne and eggs Benedict breakfast while approaching Dover. That night I camped atop a white cliff and lay awake deep into the night. It was nearly over. Melancholy merged with joy in my racing mind.

I had anticipated a culture shock but it never came. Everything seemed comfortably familiar as I pedalled through small southern towns: signposts, pub names, the overheard snippets of weather-related small talk, and the astringent scent of vinegar wafting from chip shops on warm soggy air. Burly men in hi-viz vests were fixing the road and skinny old men with gin-blossomed cheeks ambled slowly down streets. The schoolboys had deliberately badly tied neckties and the schoolgirls had fashionably laddered tights.

I joined the A20 to London and crossed the M25 ring road mid-morning on a crisp, sunny Thursday. I was early for my homecoming party that evening so rode around the city enjoying the last of my 1,600 days as a tourist. In Trafalgar Square I watched excited young couples from around the world take photos of themselves with selfie sticks, their fresh faces blocking the attractions they were visiting. I finished my French supermarket-branded cheese on a Hyde Park bench and then sat in a pub until after darkness fell.

As arranged, at 7 p.m. I met with some police officers on Earl's Court Road and they stopped the traffic. An escort of two outriders with blue lights flashing took me down the unusually quiet thoroughfare. I turned right. Bagpipes struck up, the flags of every country I'd visited were strung across the mews, and a chequered flag was waving. So many people I had assumed wouldn't care were there cheering me across the finish line where my parents wrapped me in a big, tearful hug.

A wonderful party ensued. I was a wreck of relief and emotion throughout. A day later I quietly began the true last leg of the journey. Under grey skies and in pensive mood I pedalled southwest. My last tented night was in a cow field on the outskirts of Basingstoke. I rode through Salisbury and marvelled at the medieval gothic cathedral with fresh eyes. It was the final echo of human history's grandeur on the long road I had ridden: a worthy peer of Persepolis and pyramids and princely Timurid madrassas. I had known the building my entire life but never truly comprehended its magnificence.

On a Sunday afternoon I rode into my parents' village, cycling the last of 43,633 miles. The villagers had been alerted and familiar figures from my childhood waved me down the lane, up the short sloping driveway and home, where the echoes ended.

EPILOGUE

*All I had to do was ask of immobility what travel
no longer brought me: peace.*
- Sylvain Tesson, *Consolations of the Forest*

A week before I reached home, Loic killed himself. I don't know how and I only have some idea as to why. He had been a warm, smiling and cheerful man but his life didn't pan out how he wanted. A friend of his in Dakar emailed me with the news a month later, while I was scrabbling around for ways to earn money and fretting about what to do with my life. Over that month, relief and satisfaction often gave way to gloom. The largest, longest, and greatest adventure of my life was over and I would likely never be so free again. Already the hardships, the fear, and the loneliness were becoming rose-tinted, while the novelties of a warm bed and good food were wearing off.

I had travelled so far. I had seen and learned so much. And yet I had to admit to myself that I had only really experienced narrow corridors of the places I visited. I had arrived home with health and family and friends. I was blessed. I had a blank slate. I could do whatever I wanted if I set my mind to it. And what I wanted was to explore more, to see more, to learn more, and to meet more of the world's overwhelmingly kind and welcoming people that so greatly outnumber the wicked. Reaching home wasn't the end at all. It wasn't the death of a journey. It was the birth of a resolution.

ACKNOWLEDGEMENTS

I'd like to thank my mother for her steadfast support and patience with the reckless and foolhardy things I've done to entertain myself over the years. You always bid me goodbye with a brave smile and welcome me home with a wonderful hug. Likewise to Emily, Harry, Amelia and Johnny.

Thanks to Denise Cowle for proofreading, and to Anthony Pelly at Rural Maps for the maps. Thank you also to Archie for vital companionship in Central Africa. I still can't believe I managed to talk you into it.

Countless people looked after me and hosted me during this journey. You are too many to mention, and most of you will never know this book exists, but I remember you all and am deeply grateful.

Last but not least, many thanks to the following whose support helped bring this edition to print:
David Brown, Kari Busman, Charlie Cottam, Morella & Robert Cottam, Lorne Cox, Robert Dabrowski, Alec Dhuse, Michael Dobbs, Ed Faulkner, Vittorio Ferrario, Hauke Holtkamp, Luna Honguet, Lee & Rowan Howe, Ah Wei Loy, Archie Montagu-Pollock, David Morris, Susan Norah, Tom Parker, Olivier Pietrantoni, Dan Polak, Nikolaus Spitzy, Richard & Lou Turnor, Richard Vassar-Smith, Chris & Ronwen Walker, Robin & Selina Walker, Rupert Walker, and Jeremy & Antoinette Watts.

What came before?

The first year and a half of the adventure is told in the prequel: *Through Sand & Snow*

'A genuinely remarkable adventure. True grit and rabid perseverance' **RANULPH FIENNES**

THROUGH
SAND & SNOW

A forty-thousand mile journey to adulthood via the ends of the earth

CHARLIE WALKER

NOTE FROM THE AUTHOR

If you've enjoyed this book, it would be really helpful and
much appreciated if you could leave a review on Amazon.

If you're a fan of audiobooks and would like to *hear* the story
as read by the author, both *Through Sand & Snow* and
On Roads That Echo are now also available on
www.audible.com

Through Sand & Snow

On Roads That Echo

To find out more about my past and upcoming adventures,
please visit www.charliewalker.org

You can also follow me on Instagram and Twitter:
@cwexplore

Printed in Great Britain
by Amazon

76707156R00215